ENEMIES OF PROMISE

ENEMIES
OF PROMISE

BY

CYRIL CONNOLLY, 1903 –

"Quando sovviemmi di contanta speme"

BOSTON

LITTLE, BROWN AND COMPANY

1939

Published April 1939

THE ATLANTIC MONTHLY PRESS BOOKS
ARE PUBLISHED BY
LITTLE, BROWN AND COMPANY
IN ASSOCIATION WITH
THE ATLANTIC MONTHLY COMPANY

PRINTED IN THE UNITED STATES OF AMERICA

To
LOGAN

CONTENTS

Part I
PREDICAMENT

Part II
THE CHARLOCK'S SHADE

vii

CONTENTS

PART III

A GEORGIAN BOYHOOD

PART I

PREDICAMENT

In vain do individuals hope for immortality, or any patent from oblivion, in preservations below the Moon.

SIR THOMAS BROWNE.

CHAPTER I

THE NEXT TEN YEARS

THIS is the time of year when wars break out, and a piece of glass betrays the woodland to the vindictive sun. Already the forest fires have accounted for a thousand hectares. They fight them by starting little manageable blazes, which burn a strip to ashes before the main conflagration has had time to arrive. These flames in turn must be extinguished and isolated by setting fire to other and still more obedient strips, till the last cinders expire in the garden where I am writing.

It is after lunch (omelette, vichy, peaches) on a sultry day. There is the plane tree with the table underneath it ; a gramophone is playing in the next room. I always try to write in the afternoon for I have enough Irish blood to be afraid of the Irish temperament. The literary form of this, known as the " Celtic twilight ", consists of an addiction to melancholy and an exaggerated use of words, and such good Irish writers as there have been exorcise this side by disciplining themselves to an alien and stricter culture. Yeats translates Greek, and Joyce and George Moore went to Paris. For myself I find Augustan Latin and Augustan English the best correctives.   But they do not work well at all times, and when I write after dark the shades of evening scatter their purple through my prose.   Then why not write in the morning ?   Unfortunately there is never very much of the morning for me, and it is curious that although I do not despise people who go to bed earlier than I, everyone is impatient with me for not getting up.   I may be reading on a wet morning and they have nothing to do but they cannot conceal their superiority and ill will.

But between the dissipated bedridden morning and the dangerous night fall the cicada hours of afternoon pregnant in their tedium, and these I now have free for the problem that is obsessing me.

THE NEXT TEN YEARS.

(1) What will have happened to the world in ten years' time ?

(2) To me ?   To my friends ?

(3) To the books they write ?

Above all to the books—for, to put it another way, I have one ambition, to write a book that will hold good for ten years afterwards.   And of how many to-day is that true ?   I make it ten years because I have written about books for ten years, and because I can say, and this is the gravest warning, that in a short time the writing of books, especially works of the imagination, which last so long, will be an extinct art.   Contemporary books do not keep.   The quality in them which makes for their success is the first to go, they turn over night.   Therefore one must look for some quality which improves with time.   The

4

short-lived success of a book may be the fault of the reader, for newspapers, libraries, book-societies, broadcasting, and the cinema, have vitiated the art of reading. But the books I am thinking about have all been read once, and have seemed good to discriminating readers. They go bad just the same.

Suppose we were describing English literature in 1928. We would mention Lawrence and Huxley and Joyce and Yeats and Virginia Woolf and Lytton Strachey. If highbrow we would add Eliot, Wyndham Lewis, Firbank, Norman Douglas, and if solid, Maugham, Bennett, Shaw, Wells, Galsworthy, Kipling. Of these Strachey, Galsworthy, Bennett, Lawrence, Firbank are dead and also out of fashion. They are as if they had never been. Suppose new books were found, a *Five Towns* by Bennett, a *Forsyte* by Galsworthy, even another novel by Lawrence, it would be a nightmare. We can discount for this prejudice as a natural reaction from the work of yesterday to that of to-day, but much of it is unnatural, because during their life-time these writers were unnaturally praised. The reputation of Shaw, Joyce, Firbank and Huxley has declined since their booms, in fact, of the eminent writers of ten years ago, only the fame of Eliot, Yeats, Maugham and Forster has increased. The young writers of ten years ago are also stringing out.

My own predicament is—how to live another ten years.

Living at first means keeping alive. The predicament is economical. How to get enough to eat. I assume however that most people who read this will have solved that to some extent, in fact I am writing for my fellow bourgeois. A writer has no greater pleasure than to reach people, nobody enjoys isolation less than an artist, least of all a difficult artist—but he must reach them by fair means—if he flatters them, if he screams at them, begs from them, lectures them or plays confidence tricks on them, he will reach only the worthless elements, and they will throw him over. Meanwhile the way I write, and the things I like to write about make no appeal to the working class, nor can I make any bridge to them till they are ready for it. I write for people who have been to schools and universities, whose interests and whose doubts I share.

The other way to keep alive is not to get killed. That question is political. The official policy by which we are not to get killed is by keeping out of war, but in order to keep out of war it is necessary to avoid the role of the good samaritan; we have to pass by on the other side.

It is a humiliating position for idealists, to have to do without their ideals, and support a cynical policy in which they do not believe. They therefore cannot be said to remain spiritually alive, and this difficulty of choosing between the danger of war and physical extermination, and the dangers of an ostrich peace and spiritual stagnation, between physical death and moral death, is another predicament.

Since our own expectation of life is at present so insecure, the only way to make certain of living another ten years is to do work which will survive

that long.   For the best work explodes with a delayed
impact, E. M. Forster, for instance, has only produced
two books since the war, yet he is alive because his
other books, which are from twenty to thirty years
old, are gaining ground among intelligent readers.
Their pollen fertilises a new generation.   There are
reasons for this.   To begin with, the novels of Forster
state the general conflict which is localised in the
political conflict of to-day.   His themes are the breaking down of barriers : between white and black,
between class and class, between man and woman,
between art and life.   " Only connect . . ." the
motto of *Howard's End*, might be the motto of all his
work.   His heroes and heroines, with their self-
discipline, their warm hearts, their horror of shams,
false emotion, of intellectual exclusiveness on the
moral plane and of property, money, authority, social
and family ties on the material one, are the precursors
of the left-wing young people of to-day, he can be
used as a take-off by them, in whatever direction they
may develop.   Thus the parable form of Forster's
novels may survive the pamphlet form of Shaw's
plays, despite their vigorous thinking, because Forster
is an artist and Shaw is not.   Much of his art consists
in the plainness of his writing, for he is certain of the
truth of his convictions and the force of his emotions.
It is the writer who is not sure what to say or what
he feels who is apt to overwrite, either to conceal
his ignorance, or to come unexpectedly on an answer.
Similarly it is the novelists who find it hard to create
character who indulge in fine writing.   This even,
unemphatic style of Forster's makes him easy to

7

re-read, for there is nothing in it except sprightliness of which one can get tired. But there is another reason why the work of Forster remains fresh. His style has not been imitated.

What kills a literary reputation is inflation. The advertising, publicity, and enthusiasm which a book receives—in a word its success—generate a reaction against it. The element of inflation in a writer's success, the extent to which it has been forced, is something that has to be written off. One can fool the public about a book but the public will store up resentment in proportion to its folly. The public can be fooled deliberately, by advertising and publicity, or it can be fooled by accident, by the writer fooling himself. If we look at the boom pages of the Sunday papers we can see the fooling of the public going on, inflation at work. A word like genius is used so many times that eventually the sentence " Jenkins has genius. *Cauliflower Ear* is immense ! " becomes true because he has as much genius, and is as immense, as are the other writers who have been praised there. It is the words that suffer, for in the inflation they have lost their meaning. The public at first suffers too, but in the end it ceases to care, and so new words have to be dragged out of retirement and made to suggest merit. Often the public is taken in by a book because, although a bad book, it is topical, up-to-dateness passes as originality, ideas seem important because they are " in the air ". *The Bridge of San Luis Rey, Dusty Answer, Decline and Fall, Brave New World, The Postman Always Rings Twice, The Fountain, Good-bye, Mr. Chips* are examples

8

of books which had a success out of proportion to their merit, and which react unfavourably on their authors, because the people who read those books have been fooled. None of the authors expected their books to become best-sellers, but they had hit upon, without knowing it, the contemporary combination of illusion with disillusion which makes books sell.

But it is also possible to write a good book, and for that book to be imitated, and for those imitations to have more success than the original, so that when the vogue they have created and surfeited is past, they drag the good book down with them. This is what has happened to Hemingway, who made certain discoveries in style which have almost led to his undoing. So much depends on style, that factor of which we are growing more and more suspicious, that although the tendency of criticism is to explain a writer either in terms of his sexual experience or his economic background, I still believe technique remains the soundest base for a diagnosis, that it should be possible to learn as much about an author's income and sex-life from one paragraph of his writing as from his cheque stubs and his love-letters, and one should also be able to learn how well he writes, and what are his influences. Critics who ignore style are liable to lump good and bad writers together in support of pre-conceived theories.

An expert should be able to tell a carpet by one skein of it ; a vintage by rinsing a spoonful round his mouth. Applied to prose there is one advantage attached to this method—a passage taken from its context is isolated from the rest of a book, and cannot depend on the goodwill which the author has established with his reader. This is important, for in all the books which become best-sellers and then flop, this goodwill is found. The author has fooled the reader, and he has done so by winning him over at the beginning, and so establishing a favourable atmosphere for putting across his inferior article—for making him accept false sentiment, writing, or situations. To write a best-seller is to set oneself a problem in seduction. A book of this kind is a confidence trick. The reader is given a cigar and a glass of brandy and asked to put his feet up and listen. The author then tells him the tale. The most favourable atmosphere is a stall at a theatre, and consequently of all things which enjoy contemporary success that which obtains it on the least merit is the average play.

A great writer creates a world of his own and his readers crowd to live in it. A lesser writer may entice them in for a moment, but soon he will watch them filing out again.

But darkness falls, frogs croak, the swallows wheel over the terrace and the slanting hours during which I can be entrusted with a pen are over.

CHAPTER II

THE MANDARIN DIALECT

BEFORE continuing it becomes necessary to have a definition of style. It is a word that is beginning to sound horrible, a thing no good writer should have. Stephen Spender can even say of Henry James :

> As always with great æstheticians there is a certain vulgarity in his work, and this vulgarity found its expression in violence. It is vulgarity of a kind that we never find in the work of coarser writers like Fielding, Smollett and Lawrence, but which we always are conscious of in writers like Flaubert, or Jane Austen, or Wilde.

The dictionary defines style as the " collective characteristics of the writing or diction or artistic expression or way of presenting things or decorative methods proper to a person or school or period or subject, manner of exhibiting these characteristics." This is confusing since the word means both the characteristics and the manner of exhibiting them, and perhaps this confusion is responsible for the distaste in which it is held. For a great number of people to-day would agree in principle with Spender, or would argue that the best writers have no style.

Style seems something artificial, a kind of ranting, or of preening. The best writing, like the best-dressed man, as Butler said, is sober, subdued, and inconspicuous.

In point of fact, there is no such thing as writing without style. Style is not a manner of writing, it is a relationship, the relation in art between form and content. Every writer has a certain capacity for thinking and feeling and this capacity is never the same as any other writer's. It is a capacity which can be appreciated, and for its measurement there exist certain terms. We talk of a writer's integrity, of his parts, or his powers, meaning the mental force at his disposal. But in drawing from these resources the writer is guided by another consideration ; his subject, or what he has to write about. Milton's prose style, for example, is different from his verse style. Not because one is prose and the other poetry ; it reveals a different set of qualities —the Milton of *Paradise Lost* is aloof, dignified, a man who makes no attempt to enter into a relationship with the reader, whose language exhibits a classical lack of detail, whose blank verse is restrained, and whose sentences, often ending in the middle of a line, suggest the voice of a man who talks to himself, trailing off into silence. The Milton of the pamphlets on the other hand is out to persuade the reader and confute the enemy, his style is forceful, repetitive, and prolix ; he bludgeons away at his opponent until he is quite certain that there is no life in him, his style is remarkable for exuberance and vitality. The same distinction can be made

12

between the prose and verse style of Marvell. The style of these writers varies with their subject and the form chosen. One can say that the style of a writer is conditioned by his idea of a reader, and varies according to whether he is writing for himself, or his friends or his teachers, or his God, an educated upper class, a wanting-to-be-educated lower class, or a hostile jury. This is less apparent in writers who live in a settled age. They very soon establish a relationship with the reader they depend on and he, usually a man of the same age, tastes, education and income, remains beside them all their life. Style then is the relation between what a writer wants to say—his subject—and himself—or what he has to say it with—between the form of his subject and the content of his parts.

Style is manifest in language. The vocabulary of a writer is his currency, but it is a paper currency and its value depends on the reserves of mind and power behind it. The perfect use of language is that in which every word carries the meaning that it is intended to, no less and no more. In this verbal exchange Fleet Street is a kind of Black Bourse which unloads words on the public for less than they are worth, and in consequence the more honest literary bankers, who try and use their words to mean what they say, who are always " good for " the expressions they use, find their currency constantly depreciating. There was a time when this was not so, a moment in the history of language when words expressed what they meant, and it was impossible to write badly. This time I think was the end of the seventeenth and the beginning of the eighteenth century, when the metaphysical conceits of the one were going out, and before the classical tyranny of the other was established. To write badly at that time involved a perversion of language, to write naturally was a certain way of writing well. Dryden, Rochester, Congreve, Swift, Gay, Defoe, belong to this period and some of its freshness is still found in the *Lives of the Poets*, and the letters of Gray and Walpole. It is a period which is ended by the work of two great Alterers, Addison and Pope.

Addison was a writer responsible for many of the evils from which English prose has since suffered. He made prose artful, and whimsical, he made it sonorous when sonority was not necessary, affected when it did not require affectation ; he enforced the essay on us, so that small boys who can hardly write are at this moment busy putting down their views on Travel, the Great Man, Courage, Gardening, Capital Punishment, and winding up with a quotation from Bacon. For though essay-writing was an occasional activity of Bacon, Walton, and Evelyn, Addison turned it into an industry. He was the first to write for the entertainment of the middle classes, the new power in the reign of Anne. He wrote as a gentleman (Sir Roger is the perfect gentleman), he emphasised his gentle irony, his gentle melancholy, his gentle inanity. He was the apologist for the New Bourgeoisie who writes playfully and apologetically about nothing, casting a smoke screen over its activities to make it seem harmless, genial, and sensitive in its non-acquisitive moments ; he anticipated Lamb and Emerson, Stevenson, Punch and the professional humorists, the delicious middles, the fourth leaders, the memoirs of cabinet ministers, the speeches of business magnates, and chiefs of police. He was the first Man of Letters. Addison had the misuse of an extensive vocabulary, and was able to invalidate a great number of words and expressions ; the quality of his mind was inferior to the language he used to express it.

> I am one, you must know, who am looked upon as a Humanist in Gardening. I have several Acres about my House, which I call my Garden, and which a skilful Gardener would not know what to call. It is a Confusion of Kitchen and Parterre, Orchard and Flower Garden, which lie so mixt and interwoven with one another, that if a Foreigner who had seen nothing of our Country should be conveyed into my Garden at his first landing, he would look upon it as a natural Wilderness, and one of the uncultivated Parts of our Country. My flowers grow up in several Parts of the Garden in the Greatest Luxuriancy and Profusion. I am so far from being fond of any particular one, by reason of its Rarity, that if I meet with any one in a Field which pleases me, I give it a place in my Garden. . . . I have always thought a Kitchen-garden a more pleasant sight than the finest Orangerie, or artificial Green-house [etc.].

It might be Beverley Nichols. Notice the presentation of the author, he is eccentric, unpractical, untidy, but glories in it, implies superiority over the foreigner, prefers home-grown vegetables to exotic fruits, and in short flatters the Little Man, and also the Soames Forsytes · of his day. The court jester with his cap and bells is now succeeded by the upper middle-class jester with his " awkward-squad " in-

15

competence, his armchair, carpet slippers, and gardening gloves.[1]

I have called this style the Mandarin style, since it is beloved by literary pundits, by those who would make the written word as unlike as possible to the spoken one. It is the style of those writers whose tendency is to make their language convey more than they mean or more than they feel, it is the style of most artists and all humbugs, and one which is always menaced by a puritan opposition. To know which party to belong to at a given moment is to know how to write with best effect, and it is to assist those who are not committed by their temperament to one party alone, the grand or the bald, the decorative or the functional, baroque or stream-lined that the following chapters are written.

Here are two more examples by Lamb and Keats of its misuse.

> My attachments are all local, purely local. I have no passion (or have had none since I was in love, and then it was the spurious engendering of poetry and books) to groves and vallies. The rooms where I was born, the furniture which has followed me about (like a faithful dog, only exceeding him in knowledge) wherever I have moved— old chairs, old tables, streets, squares, where I have sunned myself, my old school—these are my mistresses.

> I had an idea that a man might pass a very pleasant life in this manner. Let him on a certain day read a

---

[1] " For these reasons there are not more useful Members in a Commonwealth than Merchants. They knit Mankind together in a mutual Intercourse of good Offices, distribute the gifts of Nature, find Work for the Poor, add Wealth to the Rich, and Magnificence to the great." Compare Addison's attitude to the Merchants with Congreve's, a decade earlier.

certain page of full Poesy or distilled Prose, and let him wander with it, and muse upon it, and reflect from it, and bring home to it, and prophesy upon it, and dream upon it, until it becomes stale—but when will it do so ? Never ! When Man has arrived at a certain ripeness in intellect any one grand and spiritual passage serves him as a starting-post towards all the two and thirty Palaces. How happy is such a voyage of conception, what delicious diligent indolence ! A doze upon a sofa does not hinder it, and a nap upon Clover engenders ethereal finger-pointing. The prattle of a child gives it wings . . . [etc., etc.].

Notice how untrue these sentiments are. Lamb's old school is not his mistress, nor is his old book-case. The book-case has to be packed up and put on a van when it moves ; to compare it to a faithful dog is to suggest that Lamb is beloved even by his furniture. Beverley Nichols probably believes it, for Essayists must be lovable, it is part of their role.

" Until it becomes stale—but when will it do so ? Never ! " Now, Keats is lying. " I am often hard put to it not to think that a Man never fares so far abroad as when he is anchored to his own Armchair ! " One could turn this out almost fast enough to keep up with the anthologies. " The Man," " your Man," always occurs in these essayists. (Addison : " There is nothing in the World that pleases a Man in Love so much as your Nightingale.")

Here are two modern examples also from the *Oxford Book of English Prose*. The authors are Compton Mackenzie and Rupert Brooke.

Some four and twenty miles from Curtain Wells on the Great West Road is a tangle of briers among whose blossoms

17

an old damask rose is sometimes visible. If the curious traveller should pause and examine this fragrant wilderness, he will plainly perceive the remains of an ancient garden, and if he be of an imaginative character of mind will readily recall the legend of the Sleeping Beauty in her mouldering palace ; for some enchantment still enthralls the spot, so that he who bravely dares the thorns is well rewarded with pensive dreams, and, as he lingers a while gathering the flowers or watching their petals flutter to the green shadows beneath, will haply see elusive Beauty hurry past. *The Basket of Roses* was the fairest dearest inn down all that billowy London Road . . .

Heigh ho ! Georgian prose ! Notice the words, especially the adverbs which do not aid but weaken the description, only serving to preserve the architecture of the sentence. They are Addison's legacy. A catalogue of flowers follows. I will begin at flower thirty-five.

There was Venus' Looking-glass and Flower of Bristol, and Apple of Love and Blue Helmets and Herb Paris and Campion and Love in a Mist and Ladies' Laces and Sweet Sultans or Turkey Cornflowers, Gillyflower Carnations (Ruffling Rob of Westminster amongst them) with Dittany and Sops in Wine and Floramer, Widow Wail and Bergamot, True Thyme and Gilded Thyme, Good Night at Noon and Flower de Luce, Golden Mouse-Ear, Prince's Feathers, Pinks and deep red Damask Roses.
It was a very wonderful garden indeed.

He was immensely surprised to perceive that the actual earth of England held for him a quality which he found in A—— and in a friend's honour, and scarcely anywhere else, a quality which, if he'd ever been sentimental enough to use the word, he'd have called " holiness ". His astonishment grew as the full flood of " England " swept him on from thought to thought. He felt the triumphant helplessness of a lover. Grey, uneven, little fields, and

18

small, ancient hedges rushed before him, wild flowers, elms, and beeches. Gentleness, sedate houses of red brick, proudly unassuming, a countryside of rambling hills and friendly copses. He seemed to be raised high, looking down on a landscape compounded of the western view from the Cotswolds, and the Weald, and the high land in Wiltshire, and the Midlands seen from the hills above Princes Risborough. And all this to the accompaniment of tunes heard long ago, an intolerable number of them being hymns.

" England has declared war," he says to himself, " what had Rupert Brooke better feel about it ? " His equipment is not equal to the strain and his language betrays the fact by what might be described as the " Worthington touch". " If he'd ever been senti- mental he'd have called it ' holiness '," i.e. he calls it holiness. " Triumphant helplessness of a lover " has no meaning. It is a try-on. " Little, small, grey, uneven, ancient, sedate, red, rambling, friendly, un- assuming "—true escapist Georgian adjectives. They might all be applied to the womb.

Pope as an Alterer is a very different case. He is one of the great poets of all time and the injury he did to English Verse consisted in setting a standard to which it could not live up. He drove out lyricism except from isolated artists like Burns and Blake, and set his successors the task of continuing in a form which he had already perfected, and for which they had neither the invention nor the ear. Consequently by the time of the Romantics poetry had become barren and pompous, once again the content of the poetical mind was unequal to the form. The first Romantics, Wordsworth, Southey and Coleridge,

19

therefore, set themselves to write simply, to get poetry away from the notion of the Grand Style and the Proper Subject ; their language was monosyllabic, plebeian, their subjects personal, or everyday. They wore their own hair.

CHAPTER III

THE CHALLENGE TO THE MANDARINS

THE quality of mind of a writer may be improved the more he feels or thinks or, without effort, the more he reads, and as he grows surer of this quality so he is the better able to make experiments in technique or towards simplification, towards its apparent abandonment and the expression of strong emotion or deep thought in ordinary language. The great speeches in *Lear* and *Samson Agonistes* do not seem revolutionary to us because we do not recognise them as superb and daring manipulations of the obvious. Any poet of talent could write : " The multitudinous seas incarnadine" or "Bid Amaranthus all his beauty shed ", but only a master could get away with " I pray you undo this button ", or Lear's five " Nevers ".

Style is a relation between form and content. Where the content is less than the form, where the author pretends to emotion which he does not feel, the language will seem flamboyant. The more ignorant a writer feels, the more artificial becomes his style. A writer who thinks himself cleverer than his readers writes simply, one who is afraid they are

cleverer than he, will make use of mystification :
good style is arrived at when the language chosen
represents what the author requires of it without
shyness.

At its best the Mandarin style is the richest and
most complex expression of the English language. It
is the diction of Donne, Browne, Addison, Johnson,
Gibbon, De Quincey, Landor, Carlyle and Ruskin
as opposed to that of Bunyan, Dryden, Locke, Defoe,
Cowper, Cobbett, Hazlitt, Southey, and Newman. It
is characterised by long sentences with many dependent
clauses, by the use of the subjunctive and conditional,
by exclamations and interjections, quotations, allusions, metaphors, long images, Latin terminology,
subtlety and conceits. Its cardinal assumption is
that neither the writer nor the reader is in a hurry,
but both possessors of a classical education and a
private income. It is Ciceronian English.

The last great exponents of the Mandarin style
were Pater and Henry James, who, although they
wrote sentences which were able to express the subt-
lest inflexions of sensibility and meaning, at the
worst were the prisoners of their style, and evolved
a long euphonious way of saying nothing. Such
writers, the devotees of the long sentence, end
by having to put everything into its framework,
because habit has made it impossible for them to
express themselves in anything else. They are like
those birds who weave intricate nests and are as
happy trying to hatch out a pebble in them as an
egg. But the case of Henry James is sadder still,
for his best writing, that found in his later books,

charged with all the wisdom and feeling of his long life, went unappreciated. As he reminded Gosse, he remained " insurmountably unsaleable ", and of his collected edition of 1908 he could say, like Ozymandias, " Look on my *works* ye mortals and despair ".

The reason for this failure of James to reach an audience lay in the change that had come over the reading public, a change to which he could not adapt himself. The early books of James appeared as three-volume novels which sold at thirty-one and sixpence. They reached a small leisured collection of people for whom reading a book—usually aloud— was one of the few diversions of our northern winters. The longer a book could be spun out the better, and it was the duty of the author to spin it. But books got cheaper, and reading them ceased to be a luxury, the reading public multiplied and demanded less exacting entertainment, the struggle between litera- ture and journalism began. Literature is the art of writing something that will be read twice ; journ- alism what will be read once, and they demand different techniques. There can be no delayed impact in journalism, no subtlety, no embellishment, no assumption of a luxury reader, and since the pace of journalism is faster than that of literature, literature found itself in a predicament. It could react against journalism and become an esoteric art depending on the sympathy of a few, or learn from journalism, and compete with it. Poetry, which could not learn from journalism, ran away, and we get, from the nineties to the war, desolate stretches, with no poets able to make a living and few receiving any attention from the public. The stage is held by journalist-poets like Kipling and Masefield, while Yeats, Bridges, de la Mare, Munro, and a few others blossom in neglect.

Prose, with the exception of Conrad, who tried to pep up the grand style, began to imitate journalism, and the result was the " modern movement " ; a reformist, but not a revolutionary attack on the Mandarin style, which was to give us the idiom of our age. Shaw, Butler, and Wells attacked it from the journalistic side—George Moore, Gissing, and Somerset Maugham, admirers of French realism, of the Goncourts, Zola, Maupassant, from the æsthetic.

Only Wilde belonged to the other camp, and the style he created was his own variation of the introspective essayist :

> On that little hill by the city of Florence, where the lovers of Giorgione are lying, it is always the solstice of noon, of noon made so languorous by summer suns that hardly can the slim naked girl dip into the marble tank the round bubble of clear glass, and the long fingers of the lute-players rest idly upon the chords. It is twilight also for the dancing nymphs whom Corot set free among the silver poplars of France. In eternal twilight they move, those frail diaphanous figures, whose tremulous white feet seem not to touch the dew-drenched grass they tread on.

Notice the amount of " romantic " words, now well-known hacks, " solstice, languorous, eternal, frail, diaphanous, tremulous ", which help to date the passage while Shaw, who was the same age, was writing :

> This is the true joy in life, the being used for a purpose recognised by yourself as a mighty one ; the being

24

thoroughly worn out before you are thrown on the scrap-heap ; the being a force of Nature instead of a feverish selfish little clod of ailments and grievances complaining that the world will not devote itself to making you happy. And also the only real tragedy in life is the being used by personally minded men for purposes which you recognise to be base. All the rest is at worst mere misfortune or mortality ; this alone is misery, slavery, hell on earth ; and the revolt against it is the only force that offers a man's work to the poor artist, whom our personally minded rich people would so willingly employ as pander, buffoon, beauty monger, sentimentaliser, and the like.

This sentence might have been written to-day. It is not a question of subject. The beauty of the Giorgione picture is just as alive as a sense of social injustice. Giorgione is not Sir Alma Tadema. But the first passage is dead, constructed of false sentiment and faulty linguistic material, the second is in the idiom of our time. For the idiom of our time is journalistic and the secret of journalism is to write the way people talk. The best journalism is the conversation of a great talker. It need not consist of what people say but must include nothing that cannot be said. The Shaw passage could be talked ; the Wilde passage could not even be recited.

Moore also was not to remain a realist for long—but Moore, after his *Esther Waters* period, carried on his warfare against the Mandarin style from another position. In his *Ave, Salve, Vale* books he describes the Irish rebellion against the official literary language.

Alas, the efforts of the uneducated to teach the educated would be made in vain ; for the English language is perishing and it is natural that it should perish with the race ; race and grammatical sense go together. The English have striven and done a great deal in the world; the English are a tired race and their weariness betrays itself in the language, and the most decadent of all are the educated classes.

He saw, however, the gathering unreality of Anglo-Irish, of Yeats and Synge filling their notebooks with scraps of tinker's dialogue which could only be used in plays, and only in plays about tinkers, and moulded instead for himself a simplified prose in which he could describe pictures and books and people and places, complex sensations—yet always maintain an unassuming unsophisticated equality with the reader.

> The artist should keep himself free from all creed, from all dogma, from all opinion. As he accepts the opinions of others he loses his talent, all his feelings and ideas must be his own.

> .   .   .   .

> I never knew a writer yet who took the smallest pains with his style and was at the same time readable. Plato's having had seventy shies at one sentence is quite enough to explain to me why I dislike him.
> Men like Newman and R. L. Stevenson seem to have taken pains to acquire what they called a style as a pre-liminary measure—as something that they had to form before their writings could be of any value. I should like to put it on record that I never took the smallest pains with my style, have never thought about it, and do not know or want to know whether it is a style at all, or whether it is not, as I believe and hope, just common, simple straightforwardness. I cannot conceive how any man can take thought for his style without loss to himself and his readers.

Here is Samuel Butler attacking the Mandarin style in 1897 in colloquial English. The musing introspective attitude of Pater, Wilde's essays, etc., is replaced by a social, argumentative one.[1] This *arguing* style as opposed to the soliloquy is typical of the new relationship with the reader which is to sweep over the twentieth century and dominate journalism and advertising. It may be described as you-writing from the fact that there is a constant tendency to harangue the reader in the second person. It is a buttonholing approach. The Addison manner on the other hand, has degenerated into whimsical we-writing. " We have the best goods. We're funny that way. We like quality," is one sort of advertising. " You realise the inconveniences of inadequate plumb. ing. Then why not of inadequate underclothing ? " is the other.

Meanwhile, Wells, also, was not inactive (though it was not till 1915 that he attacked Henry James in *Boon*, a bogus autobiography). Henry James, in two magnificent letters (Vol. II, pp. 503–8, of his letters) answers Wells's criticism.

Wells wrote :

> To you literature, like painting, is an end, to us litera-ture, is a means, it has a use. Your view was, I felt, altogether too prominent in the world of criticism and I assailed it in lines of harsh antagonism. I had rather be called a journalist than an artist, that is the essence of it, and there was no antagonist possible than yourself.

James replied that his view can hardly be so

---

[1] " Mr. Walter Pater's style is, to me, like the face of some old woman who has been to Madam Rachel and had herself enamelled. The bloom is nothing but powder and paint and the odour is cherry blossom. Mr. Matthew Arnold's odour is as the faint sickliness of hawthorn."—Butler.

prominent or it would be reflected in the circulation of his books.

But I have no view of life and literature, I maintain, other than that our form of the latter (the novel) in especial is admirable exactly by its range and variety, its plasticity and liberality, its fairly living on the sincere and shifting experience of the individual practitioner . . . Of course for myself I live, live intensely and am fed by life, and my value, whatever it be, is in my own kind of expression of that . . . Meanwhile I absolutely dissent from the claim that there are any differences whatever in the amenability to art of forms of literature æsthetically determined, and hold your distinction between a form that is (like) painting and a form that is (like) architecture for wholly null and void. There is no sense in which architecture is æsthetically " for use " that doesn't leave any other art whatever exactly as much so ; and so far from that of literature being irrelevant to the literary report upon life, and to its being made as interesting as possible, I regard it as relevant in a degree that leaves everything else behind. It is art that *makes* life, makes interest, makes importance, for our consideration and application of these things, and I know of no substitute whatever for the force and beauty of its process. If I were Boon I should say that any pretence of such a substitute is helpless and hopeless humbug ; but I wouldn't be Boon for the world, and am only yours faithfully, Henry James.

The justification for Wells's attack must lie in the defence it provoked, for these two majestic letters from the dying giant form a creed which he might not otherwise have left us. One is reminded of a small boy teasing an elephant which gets up with a noble bewilderment, gives him one look, and ambles away.

We are not concerned with the people who prefer to be journalists rather than artists, but with those who tried to make journalism into an art, and already it is possible to grade the opponents of the Man-

darin style, those who tried to break it up into something simpler, and terser, destroying its ornamen-
tation, attacking its rhythms and giving us instead
the idiom of to-day. Thus Moore's new language is
somewhat lyrical, his standards are æsthetic. Norman
Douglas is intellectual, with a strong imaginative side.
Maugham is also imaginative, though play-writing
interferes with his literary development, but Butler,
Shaw, Wells, Bennett, write as plainly as they can.
If Henry James could have given up the hope of being
read, abandoned novels, and written only a few magnificent pages about ideas that stirred him, he might
have been happier, and had greater influence. But he
was obsessed with the novel, to the neglect even of his
long short stories; he still considered the novel the
supreme art form, as it had been for Turgenev, Balzac
and Flaubert. So he continued to write novels, which
came into competition with the journalistic novels of
Wells and Bennett, or the speeded-up Jamesian of
Conrad, when he might have taken refuge in the
stronghold of the leisurely style—memoirs, autobiography, or books of criticism, or else ventured out
into the experimental forms of the short story. The
younger writers whom he patronised—Rupert Brooke,
Compton Mackenzie, and Hugh Walpole [1]—were
more remarkable for talent, personal charm and
conventionality, than for the " beginning late and
long choosing " of genius, the crabwise approach to
perfection.

[1] It is interesting to speculate on the effect Henry James might
have had on, say, E. M. Forster, Virginia Woolf and Lytton
Strachey had he bestowed on them the criticism he lavished on
the others.

CHAPTER IV

THE MODERN MOVEMENT

MEANWHILE Butler's dictum " A man's style in any art should be like his dress—it should attract as little attention as possible," reigned supreme, though only since Brummel had this strangle-hold of convention been applied to dress.

> Here, on these remote uplands, I prefer to turn my back on the green undulations of Massa and Sorrento, on Vesuvius and Naples, Ischia and Phlegræan fields : all these regions are trite and familiar. I prefer to gaze towards the mysterious south, the mountains of Basilicata, and the fabled headland Licosa, where Leucosia, sister-siren of Parthenope, lies buried. At this height the sea's horizon soars into the firmament smooth as a sheet of sapphire, and the eye never wearies of watching those pearly lines and spirals that crawl upon its surface, the paths of silver-footed Thetis—a restful prospect, with dim suggestions of love and affinity for this encircling element that reach back, for aught we know, to primeval days of Ascidian-life. There is a note of impotence in the sea's wintry storms, for it can but rage against its prison bars or drown a few sailormen, an ignoble business : true grandeur is only in its luminous calm.

This is a good example of reformed Mandarin. It is leisurely, but not too leisurely, the syntax is easy, the thought is simple, the vocabulary humdrum. The use of classical names implies a reader who will accept their currency. The intellectual attitude is evident in the genial mastery of the author over Nature, and his calm analysis. It is readable, good-mannered, and seems to-day a little flat, for the names mean less to us, and is redeemed by the lovely image of the patterns one sees on the sea from a height—if we know who Thetis is. It comes from Douglas's *Siren Land* (1911).

The poor little wife coloured at this, and, drawing her handkerchief from her pocket, shed a few tears. No one noticed her. Evie was scowling like an angry boy. The two men were gradually assuming the manner of the committee room. They were both at their best when serving on committees. They did not make the mistake of handling human affairs in the bulk, but disposed of them item by item, sharply. Calligraphy was the item before them now, and on it they turned their well-trained brains. Charles, after a little demur, accepted the writing as genuine, and they passed on to the next point. It is the best, perhaps the only way, of dodging emotion. They were the average human article, and had they considered the note as a whole it would have driven them miserable, or mad. Considered item by item, the emotional content was minimised, and all went forward smoothly. The clock ticked, the coals blazed higher, and contended with the white radiance that poured in through the windows. Unnoticed, the sun occupied his sky, and the shadows of the tree stems, extraordinarily solid, fell like trenches of purple across the frosted lawn. It was a glorious winter morning. Evie's fox terrier, who had passed for white, was only a dirty grey dog now, so intense was the purity that surrounded him. He was discredited, but the black-birds that he was chasing glowed with Arabian darkness, for all the conventional colouring of life had been altered. Inside, the clock struck ten with a rich and confident note. Other clocks confirmed it, and the discussion moved towards its close.

To follow it is unnecessary. It is rather a moment when

the commentator should step forward. Ought the Wilcox's to have offered their home to Margaret? I think not. The appeal was too flimsy.

This is a passage from E. M. Forster's *Howard's End* (1910) and shows a great departure from the writing of the nineteenth century. Extreme simplicity, the absence of relative and conjunctive clauses, an everyday choice of words (Arabian darkness is the only romanticism, for darkness in Arabia can be no different from anywhere else) show a more revolutionary break from the Mandarin style than any we have quoted. Twenty-two short sentences follow. How remote it is from James, Meredith, Conrad, Walter Pater, whom one cannot imagine interpolating themselves into a novel to ask a question, and answer " I think not " ! From a passage like this derives much of the diction, handling of emotional situations, and attitude to the reader of such writers as Virginia Woolf, Katherine Mansfield, David Garnett, Elizabeth Bowen.

The hardest task in modern criticism is to find out who were the innovators, who really started something. I think it is clear that Forster did, that novels like *The Longest Journey* and *Howard's End* established a point of view, a technique, and an attitude to the reader that were to be followed by psychological novelists for another thirty years. Intellectual rebels against the grand style, such as Norman Douglas, still wrote for Oxford and Cambridge graduates, for educated men, and so only modified it. Forster wrote for men and women, chiefly women, of a larger though still cultured world, and evolved a more simplified, disintegrated, and readable, that is to say colloquial, form of art.

Now we are getting on to the tracks of the writers of 1927–8. They are going to be judged by the contents of their mind and the form of their books and what they make of them. From their failures and their successes we shall endeavour to learn how to avoid further failure, and create that great book which will last a round ten years. This list is the next stage in their pursuit.

Some Books in the Modern Movement—1900–22

1900. Dreiser, *Sister Carrie.*
1901. Gissing, *By the Ionian Sea.*
1902. James, *The Wings of a Dove*; Yeats, *The Celtic Twilight*; Maugham, *Mrs. Craddock*; Belloc, *The Path to Rome.*
1903. Butler, *Way of all Flesh*; Gissing, *Private Papers of Henry Rycroft*; James, *The Ambassadors.*
1904. Baron Corvo, *Hadrian VII.*
1905. Wilde, *De Profundis*; Forster, *Where Angels Fear to Tread*; Firbank, *Odette D'Antrevernes*; James, *The Golden Bowl*; H. G. Wells, *Kipps.*
1906. Galsworthy, *The Man of Property.*
1907. Forster, *The Longest Journey*; Beardsley, *Venus and Tannhäuser*; Gosse, *Father and Son*; James, *The American Scene*; Joyce, *Chamber Music.*
1908. Conrad, *A Set of Six*; Forster, *A Room with a View.*
1909. Stein, *Three Lives*; Beerbohm, *And Even Now.*
1910. Forster, *Howard's End*; Bennett, *Old Wives' Tale*; Wedgwood, *Shadow of a Titan*; Saki's Stories; Wells, *Mr. Polly*; Shaw, *Plays Pleasant and Unpleasant.*
1911. Beerbohm, *Zuleika Dobson*; Douglas, *Siren Land*; Lawrence, *The White Peacock*; Moore, *Ave*; Lytton Strachey, *Landmarks in French Literature*; Lowes Dickinson, *A Modern Symposium.*

33

1912. Douglas, *Fountains in the Sand*; Samuel Butler, *Notebooks*; Beerbohm, *Christmas Garland*; Moore, *Salve*; Forster, *Celestial Omnibus*; Stephens, *Crock of Gold*; *Georgian Poetry* (to *1918*).

1913. Conrad, *Chance*; Lawrence, *Sons and Lovers*; Mansfield, *In a German Pension*.

1914. Wyndham Lewis, *Blast*; Moore, *Vale*; Imagists' *Anthology* (Aldington, H. D., Pound, etc.); Monro, *Children of Love*; James Joyce, *Dubliners*; Compton Mackenzie, *Sinister Street*.

1915. Douglas, *Old Calabria*; Firbank, *Vain Glory*; Somerset Maugham, *Of Human Bondage*; *Catholic Anthology* (includes Eliot's *Prufrock*); Virginia Woolf, *The Voyage Out*; Brooke, *1914*, etc.; D. H. Lawrence, *The Rainbow*.

1916. Moore, *The Brook Kerith*; Firbank, *Inclinations*; Joyce, *The Portrait of the Artist*; *Ulysses* starts in the *Little Review*.

1917. Douglas, *South Wind*; Eliot, *Prufrock*; *Wheels* (includes Sitwells); Firbank, *Caprice*.

1918. Strachey, *Eminent Victorians*; Lewis, *Tarr*; Pearsall-Smith, *Trivia*; Bridges, *The Poems of Gerald Manley Hopkins* and *The Spirit of Man*; Waley, *170 Chinese Poems*.

1919. Walpole, *Fortitude*; Cabell, *Jurgen*; Firbank, *Valmouth*; Maugham, *The Moon and Sixpence*; Daisy Ashford, *The Young Visiters*; Barbellion, *Diary of a Disappointed Man*; Anderson, *Winesburg-Ohio*; Beerbohm, *Seven Men*.

1920. Huxley, *Limbo* and *Leda*; Eliot, *The Sacred Wood*; Wilfrid Owen, *Poems*; Henry James, *Letters*.

1921. Huxley, *Crome Yellow*; Strachey, *Queen Victoria*; Virginia Woolf, *Monday or Tuesday*, *Oxford Book of English Verse*, *Poems of To-day*.

1922. Housman, *Last Poems*; Mansfield, *The Garden Party*; Garnett, *Lady Into Fox*; Strachey, *Books and Characters*; Beerbohm, *Rossetti and His Circle*; Yeats, *Later Poems*; Gerhardi, *Futility*; Galsworthy, *Forsyte Saga*; James Joyce, *Ulysses*; Virginia Woolf, *Jacob's Room*.

Not all of these books are important, but they show how early most of our well-known writers began, how many had started before the armistice. There are several new names to talk about on our way to 1928.

I do not group writers under movements, for the reason that it is hard to discover any between the nineties and the present day. I recognise a complicating trend or inflation in the nineties, a simplifying one or deflation (realism, Georgian poetry) that followed. Then a further complicating process (Bloomsbury) and a further deflation (Hemingway), and I find the simplest guide the words used by writers, and the purposes for which they are used. One thing unite the writers discussed, with the exception of Shaw and Wells; whether realists, intellectuals, or imaginative writers, from Pater to Joyce, they believed in the importance of their art, in the sanctity of the artist, and his sense of vocation. They were inmates of the Ivory Tower.

An ivory tower is a vague image and those who adopted it were permitted to differ from each other. The image was taken by Flaubert from Alfred de Vigny, and all who accept it are to some extent pupils of his; if they do not admire *Bouvard*, they admit *Bovary*; if they reject *Bovary* they will recognise the *Letters*, *Salambo*, the *Tentation*, or the *Education Sentimentale*.

We write in the language of Dryden and Addison, Milton and Shakespeare, but the intellectual world we live in is the world of Flaubert and Baudelaire; it is through them, and not through their English contemporaries that we know the meaning of modern life. The artist who accepts the religion of the Ivory Tower, that is to say of an art whose reward is perfection, and whose perfection can only be attained by a separation of his standards from those of the non-artist is led to adopt one of four roles : the High Priest (Mallarmé, Joyce, Yeats), the Dandy (Firbank, Beerbohm, Moore), The Incorruptible Observer (Maugham, Maupassant), or the Detached Philosopher (Strachey, France). What he will not be is a Fighter or a Helper.

The tradition of dandyism is purer in France. Baudelaire was obsessed with " l'éternel superiorité, du Dandy," as were Nerval, Laforgue, D'Aurevilly. When the wit and lyricism are shallow the resulting dandyism will have a popular success—and we get Noel Coward and Paul Morand—when deep, the most delicate achievements of conscious art. Meanwhile there are one or two more contributions to the idiom of our time to be considered.

The period 1900–14 was that of the Dublin School— Yeats, Moore, Joyce, Synge and Stephens. The sentiment of these writers was anti-English ; they found the Mandarin style the language of their oppressors, for they were sufficiently interested in the National Movement to consider themselves oppressed. For them England was the Philistine, and since they could not use Gaelic, their aim was to discover what blend of Anglo-Irish and French would give them an explosive that would knock the pundits of London off their chairs. All had lived in Paris, and all had absorbed French culture. Moore kept strictly to it, using his Irish background as an excuse for spiteful criticism and ponderous ancestor-worship, but always choosing simple and racy expressions and unforced sentences as the basis of his style. Yeats was engrossed in mysticism, and Gaelic legends; the French influence is more apparent in his verse-forms, and his cryptic utterances, sanctioned by Mallarmé. Synge went on from Villon to pick up peasant talk on the Aran islands and twine it into plays.

> It isn't that I haven't prayed for you, Bartley, to the Almighty God. It isn't that I haven't said prayers in the dark till you wouldn't know what I'd be saying, but it's a great rest I'll have now, and it's time surely. It's a great rest I'll have now, and great sleeping in the long nights after Samhain, if it's only a bit of wet flour we do have to eat, and maybe a fish that would be stinking.

There could be no clearer example than this of the extent of the provincial rebellion which was the Celtic movement, against the prose of the capital.

James Stephens's *The Crock of Gold* was an attempt to reconcile Classical mythology with Celtic. It proved that the Irish could beat the English at their own game and produce a rival to the *Wind in the Willows* and *Peter Pan*.

Of greater importance is *Dubliners* and *The Portrait of the Artist*. These books are written in a reformed Mandarin, influenced by French Realism. The style is not as unconventional as Yeats's or Synge's, or even as Moore's, and fits in more with the English of Maugham (*Of Human Bondage*) and the Lawrence of *Sons and Lovers*. The favourite adjective of all these writers at that time was " grey ".

(*a*) The park trees were heavy with rain and rain fell still and even in the lake, lying grey like a shield. A game of swans flew there and the water and the shore beneath were fouled with their green-white slime. They embraced softly impelled by the grey rainy light, the shield-like witnessing lake, the swans.—Joyce.

(*b*) The day broke grey and dull. The clouds hung heavily, and there was a rawness in the air that suggested snow. A woman servant came into the room in which a child was sleeping, and drew the curtains.—*Of Human Bondage*, opening paragraph.

(*c*) I stood watching the shadowy fish slide through the gloom of the mill-pond. They were grey, descendants of the silvery things that had darted away from the monks in the young days when the valley was lusty. The whole place was gathered in the musing of old age. The thick-piled trees on the far shore were too dark and sober to dally with the sun ; the weeds stood crowded and motionless.—Lawrence, *White Peacock*.

Nineteen fourteen-fifteen were important years in the Modern Movement. Besides *Dubliners*, Joyce's first prose book, we have, *Of Human Bondage*, the first poems of Eliot, Firbank's *Vainglory*, Lawrence's *Rainbow*, Douglas's *Old Calabria* and Virginia Woolf's *Voyage Out*. Wyndham Lewis edits *Blast*. The most serious artists among them continue to produce throughout the war. Joyce wrote *The Portrait of the Artist* and *Ulysses*, Firbank a novel a year from his rooms in Oxford. Lytton Strachey, a conscientious objector, was able to launch *Eminent Victorians* on a war-weary world in 1918. Moore produced *The Brook Kerith* and Douglas *South Wind*, Huxley appears in two slim volumes of poetry, Eliot in *Prufrock* and the Sitwells emerge in *Wheels* ; Lewis writes *Tarr*, and Pearsall-Smith publishes *Trivia* in unashamed

Mandarinese. Nineteen-fourteen was also the year of an important bad book, *Sinister Street*. It is a work of inflation, important because it is the first of a long line of bad books, the novels of adolescence, auto-biographical, romantic, which squandered the vocabulary of love and literary appreciation, and played into the hands of the Levellers and Literary Puritans.

In condemning such books it must be remembered that the language of a bad book depreciates that of a good one, as weak stocks drag down gilt-edged. *Sinister Street*, for instance, has had a bad effect on the *Portrait of the Artist*. It popularised schoolboy friendships, incense, Oxford and the English countryside, literature as the pool of Narcissus into which one gazes, the romance of prostitution, of priests and murderers, and the ugliness of London and first love. It is a pastiche of the Pater of *Marius the Epicurean* and the Wilde of *Dorian Grey* brought up to date and expanded, it is prose Rupert Brooke in the fashionable pseudo-intellectual reformed Mandarin of the day. Always the ' municipal ampelopsis ', the clever adjective with the classy noun.

South Wind came three years afterwards, a book which although one now recognises in it reiterations and longueurs, remains a flower of the intellectual school, a book that was to reform for a while Compton Mackenzie, and which stated for the first time the predicament (when anxious to be successful in love or at making a living) of the Petrouchka of the Twenties, the Clever Young Man. The case of Dedalus, in revolt against the Jesuits, is too particular ; Michael Fane is a born success ; it is Denis of *South Wind* pursuing the Italian chambermaid, cut out by the rough young scientist, who is the hero of *South Wind* and the years that follow, the Oxford Boy, the miserable young man on the flying trapeze.

CHAPTER V

ANATOMY OF DANDYISM

THE dandies in literature have often begun by making fun of the Mandarin style, for it is the enemy of their qualities of wit and lyricism, though in the end they come round to it. Dandyism is capitalist, for the Dandy surrounds himself with beautiful things and decorative people, and is deaf to the call of social justice. As a wit he makes fun of seriousness, as a lyricist he exists to celebrate things as they are, not to change them. Moore's *Confessions of a Young Man* is a typical dandy book, but one finds much dandyism in Wilde, and some in Saki, who, however, adulterated his Wilde to suit the *Morning Post* and procure the immediate impact of journalism. The reactionary implication of dandyism is very clear in his work.

Of the young men of these years (1914–18) Firbank, Eliot, and Huxley, the three most prominent, were dandies. Firbank followed Beardsley and Apollinaire, Eliot followed Laforgue, Huxley Eliot and Firbank. They were intellectuals, but Firbank took pains to conceal the fact in his writing and so can best be taken as an example of the type. He harked back to the dandyism of the seventeenth century ; his play

The Princess Zoubaroff is based on Congreve, and among his few allusions are one to the Memoirs of Grammont and another to the acting of Betterton. He was an impressionist; his sentences are hit or miss attempts to suggest a kind of character or conversation, or to paint in a landscape in a few brush strokes. When something bored him, he left it out, a device which might have improved the quality of innumerable novelists. Firbank is not epigrammatic, he is not easily quotable, his object was to cast a sheen of wit over his writing. Like all dandies, like Horace, Tibullus, Rochester, Congreve, Horace Walpole, and the youthful Beckford, like Watteau and Guardi, he was obsessed with the beauty of the moment, and not only the beauty, but the problem of recording that beauty, for with one false touch the description becomes ponderous and over-loaded, and takes on that unreal but sickly quality often found in modern paganism. Firbank, like Dégas, was aware of this and, like Dégas, he used pastel.

What is his contribution to modern literature ? To what extent can we profit from him if we wish to write well ourselves ?

One thing which we recognise not to have kept is an element of sexuality. Firbank was homosexual, which is not a factor of importance in the assessment of a writer's style, but he was the kind with a permanent giggle, and the result is a naughtiness in his books, a sniggering about priests and choirboys, nuns and flagellation, highbrows and grooms which shocks us because it does not come off. It is meant to be a joke, but it actually betrays the author, his inhibitions and his longings, and it is his capacity for not betraying himself that is the secret of his art. It is this element which looks back to the nineties, to Beardsley and Corvo, when so much more looks forward. For the " queen " being usually a parasite on society, a person with an inherited income and no occupation, can only criticise that society at a moment when it is well disposed. When goaded by wars and slumps it will become unfriendly, and any criticism, however frivolous, will seem impertinent. Firbank, like most dandies, disliked the borgeoisie, idealised the aristocracy, and treated the lower classes as a brothel.

It is customary to assume that Firbank was frivolous because frivolity was his only medium of self-expression. In fact he was no less serious than Congreve, or Horace Walpole, but he recognised frivolity as the most insolent refinement of satire. The things Firbank hated were the moral vices of the bourgeoisie, stupidity, hypocrisy, pretentiousness, greed, and the eye on the main chance. What distinguishes the characters he writes about is their unworldliness, and he believed that the most unworldly people were those who were born with everything. It was complete vagueness about money, a warm erratic unjudging heart, a muddled goodness, an instinctive elegant disorder that he liked. The quality common to his characters is their impulsiveness, their virtue is in their unawareness of evil. Where they are ambitious, their ambitions are preposterous. To be perpetuated by a stained-glass window, to shine in the highest circles of Cuna-Cuna, to go to Athens, to be a great

43

tragic actress, and yet to remain unconscious of the difficulty of attaining these ends, was what appealed to him. Whom he disliked were the schemers, the Bovarys, the Babbitts. Here is Mrs. Sixsmith, thinking of her dead friend, Sally.

> Those fine palatial houses, she reflected, must be full of wealth . . . old Caroline plate and gorgeous green Limoges : Sally indeed had proved it ! The day she had opened her heart in the Café Royal she had spoken of a massive tureen *too heavy even to hold*.
> Mrs. Sixsmith's eyes grew big.

Or :

> And now a brief lull, as a brake containing various delegates and " representatives of English Culture " rolled by at a stately trot—Lady Alexander, E. V. Lucas, Robert Hichens, Clutton Brock, etc.—the ensemble, the very apotheosis of the worn-out *cliché*.

For what he hated was vulgarity and vulgarity of writing as much as vulgarity of the heart. Indeed, the writers with the most exquisite choice of words, those who take pains to avoid the outworn and the obvious, to achieve distinction of phrasing, are equally susceptible to the fine points of the human heart. The world to Congreve is a sink out of which a few young people manage to drag themselves, to Horace Walpole an arena which friendship alone makes tolerable. They are strongly conscious of good and evil. " To write simply ", explains Maugham, " is as difficult as to be good." Perhaps one requires the other. For Dandies are perfectionists and Perfectionism involves disappointment, and from the disappointments is built up the idea of an elect, of a few human beings gifted with distinction of mind and heart heaving themselves up from the general mud-bath. Some are kept out for a few years by their beauty, breeding, or charm, but all those without moral qualities and a courageous intelligence are bound to flop back.

" Now that the ache of life with its fevers, passions, doubts, its routine, vulgarity and boredom was over, his serene unclouded face was a marvelment to behold. Very great distinction and sweetness was visible there together with much nobility and love, all magnified and commingled," writes Firbank of the death-mask of Cardinal Pirelli, and it was the last sentence but two he ever wrote ; his most serious, though not his most successful, for he is nervous of his own seriousness and suddenly produces a word, " marvelment " out of his old 1890 past to reassure him. But it is the sentence of an ascetic, as all those who are dandies in the fullest sense must be.

The lesson one can learn from Firbank is that of inconsequence. That is the vein which he tapped and which has not yet been fully exploited.

His method was to write in dialogue, and omit what would not fit in. Narrative prose, as opposed to dialogue is used only for vignettes of places, or descriptions of characters when they first appear. It is the most brisk and readable form of writing, making demands on the reader's intelligence but none on his eye or ear, and it is to Firbank that we owe the conception of dialogue—not as a setpiece in the texture of the novel, as are the conversations of Wilde and Meredith—but as the fabric itself. A book by Firbank is in the nature of a play where the descriptive prose passages correspond to the stage directions.

As a prose writer Firbank did not have a large or interesting vocabulary, and his work is full of spelling mistakes, but he wrote with a horror of the cliché and a regard for the words he used, achieving the freshness he needed by grammatical inversions, and by experiments in order. He also applied impressionism with startling results.

> The mists had fallen from the hills, revealing old woods wrapped in the blue doom of Summer.

> Boats with crimson spouts, to wit, steamers, dotted the skyline far away, and barques with sails like the wings of butterflies, borne by an idle breeze, were winging more than one ineligible young mariner back to the prose of the shore.

> It was the Feast night. In the grey spleen of evening through the dusty lanes towards Mediavilla, country-society flocked.

Do they come off? On the whole yes, better than his overloaded passages in *Cardinal Pirelli* and *Santal*, for it is one of the weaknesses of the dandy's position that the seriousness on which it is based must be concealed. The preoccupation of the dandy is with the moment.

> Every moment some form grows perfect in hand or face; some tone on the hills or the sea is choicer than the rest; some mood or passion or insight or intellectual excitement is irresistibly real and attractive for us—for that moment only. Not the fruit of experience, but experience itself, is the end. A counted number of pulses only is given to us of a variegated dramatic life. How may we see in them all that is to be seen in them by the finest senses? How shall we pass most swiftly from point to point, and be

46

present always at the focus where the greatest number of vital forces unite in their purest energy ? To burn always with this hard gemlike flame, to maintain this ecstasy is success in life. . . . Not to discriminate every moment some passionate attitude in those about us, and in the brilliancy of their gifts some tragic dividing of forces on their ways, is, on this short day of frost and sun, to sleep before evening.

So wrote Pater, calling an art-for-art's-sake muezzin to the faithful from the topmost turret of the ivory tower. If one leaves out the affected " any stirring of the senses, strange dyes, strange colours, and curious odours, or work of the artist's hands, or the face of one's friend " it is one of the great passages of Mandarin writing, and, as a text, it concentrates as much on the moment in personal relations, on the ethical moment, as on the sensual one. Henry James spent his life in " discriminating passionate attitudes and tragic divisions in those about him " as thoroughly as Wilde investigated his own moods or Moore and Yeats and Joyce waited for " some tone on the hills or the sea ". Pater, when he realised its implications, suppressed the passage which is only the philosophy of the refractory pupil of Socrates, Aristippus of Cyrene, who believed happiness to be the sum of particular pleasures and golden moments, not, like Epicurus, a prolonged intermediate state between ecstasy and pain.

The artistic fault of Cyrenaic philosophy is a tendency to fake these golden moments, which is inevitable when they are regarded as the only things worth living for ; the artist becomes like the medium who has to produce a psychic experience to earn her money,

47

and the result is that he leans too heavily on the moment, producing that effect of satiety which runs, for instance, through the translations of Mackail. In the same way, if we examine the kind of poetry we read and appreciate when we are unhappy, it will be found that it is not really the best kind, or if the best, that we appreciate it for the wrong reasons, we over-emphasise it and make it support a weight which it was not intended to bear. The perfectionists, the art-for-art's-sakers, finding or believing life to be intolerable, except for art's perfection, by the very violence of their homage, render art imperfect. This was the danger of Firbank's growing seriousness, it is a danger which besets all lyric poets, dandies, and ephemerids, although it is a danger which by emotional awareness and technical discipline can be avoided.

At the moment Dandyism, in its extreme form, Perfectionism, is on the increase, for Perfectionists, like the hermits of the Thebaid, take refuge from the world in private salvation. I have known many perfectionists all of whom are remarkable for the intense stripping process they are carrying out. Their lives are balloons from which more and more ballast has to be cast, they never have more than one suitcase, wear no pyjamas or underclothes, travel constantly and are the mystics of our time " pressé de trouver le lieu et la formule ". An element of guilt and expiation in their activity awakens distrust in the complacent herd and certainly perfection has a bleaching deathwishful quality. But it is seldom attained, and a little respect for it would do no harm to its detractors.

48

It will be seen then that dandyism, despite its roots in the *status quo*, and its tendency to pessimism, is a tenable position—since any position which can be shown to produce good writing is tenable—for as long as the writer can count on a natural constitutional gaiety to inform his lyricism. When that disappears, as in Housman, the wit becomes bitter, the lyricism morbid. It is therefore suitable to young writers or those with plenty of money. They have their roots in manure, but the orchid blooms the richer for it, until ultimately, the bloom dies down, and only the manure is left. Tibullus, Rochester, Watteau and Leopardi—the greatest perfectionist of them all— died before this could happen. Congreve retired ; Walpole and Beckford became ancestor-worshipping, and reactionary antiquarians, only Horace and Dégas, obedient always to the discipline of their art, and intellectually agile, arrogant, and tough, remained perfectionists to the end. Firbank would not have written worse had he lived, he would have written differently.

CHAPTER VI

A BEAST IN VIEW

I HAVE taken Firbank as the type of the dandy writer but what has been said of him is also true of the early Eliot and the early Huxley. Eliot is the purest of the three, for a lyric poet works in a more distilled medium than narrative prose.

> Let us go then, you and I,
> When the evening is spread out against the sky,
> Let us go, through certain half-deserted streets . . .

I have often wondered what it must have felt like to discover these opening lines of *Prufrock* in *Blast* or the *Catholic Anthology* in 1914–15 with the Rupert Brooke poems, Kitchener's Army, and *Business as Usual* everywhere. Would one have recognised that new, sane, melancholy, light-hearted and fastidious voice ?

> There will be time, there will be time
> To prepare a face to meet the faces that you meet ;
> There will be time to murder and create.

Surely one would have noticed it, would have " lingered in the chambers of the sea ", and experienced that exquisite sensation, the apprehension of the first sure masterful flights of a great contemporary writer. But few people did.

What can one learn from Eliot? Not to be ashamed of borrowing, and to assimilate what we borrow. Yet his influence on young writers is disconcerting; Auden, I think, is the only young poet to survive it. The reason I believe is that Eliot, the purest artist and most austere critic in England to-day, is yet a writer whose background is unfamiliar—the most unlike anyone else's. He is an American expatriate who is escaping from a far more refined and cultivated, though perfectly barren society, than any he can find here—in other words, he is not running away from a rough America to a cultured England, but from an overpolite and civilised humanism to the bellyworld of post-war London. Consequently his poetry is a struggle to break down inhibitions in himself by which the coarser Englishman is not troubled, and his solution, the Anglo-Catholic church, one that makes small appeal to his imitators.

Yet in spite of this he is a master; he has created for us a world of his own. There are places where I miss Firbank, in Knightsbridge or Rome, going over some Balkan palace, or in an autumnal cathedral city; there are remarks one overhears, or scenes between simple, fatuous, complacent people when one realises that the artist who could best have done them justice is no more. But there exists a mood whose expression we owe to Eliot, the mood of dissatisfaction and despondency, of barrenness and futility—the noonday devil, the afternoon impotence, which are curiously unpoetical and which no one else has been able so adequately to render into verse.

The idea of futility is an important concept in the

twenties and dominates the poetry of Eliot (up to
Ash Wednesday), the novels of Huxley (to *Point
Counter Point*) and much of the work of Lawrence,
Hemingway, and Joyce. It is an extension of the
ivory tower attitude, which arises from a disbelief
in action, and in the putting of moral slogans into
action, engendered by the Great War. Thus Henry
James and the authors who were killed in the war
had no experience of it, it was left to those who survived beyond 1917 to make the discovery.

> Behold, behold, the goal in sight
> Spread thy fans and wing thy flight

sings Janus, in Dryden's *Secular Masque*, and Venus
adds :

> Calms appear when storms are past
> Love will have his hour at last,

but the chorus is not taken in :

> All, all of a piece throughout :
> Thy chase had a beast in view ;
> Thy wars brought nothing about ;
> Thy lovers were all untrue.
> 'Tis well an old age is out,
> And time to begin a new.

And that might have been the device of the writers
of the early twenties.

I have said that futilitarianism is an extension of
the philosophy of the Ivory Tower, because no writer
of that group pretended that art was futile ; it is
the men of action who do that. Behind the concept of futility is a passionate belief in art, coupled
with a contempt for the things which art is made
about. This puts too great a strain on technique,

for even Flaubert, in *Bouvard and Pecuchet*, that bible of futility, has not been able to avoid boring the reader unintentionally. But the novelists of the 1920's were not Flaubert's equal in construction. They knew that they had been " had " and they were in a hurry to tell the world about it. Those who had been fooled most were the young men who had fought in the war, and who had survived, and in consequence the literature of that time is predominantly masculine, revolving round a theme which may be called " The Clever Young Man and the Dirty Deal ". When I search for the most representative work of that time, I am inclined to choose *Petrouchka*, for the ballet expresses the situation with the greatest clarity. The people at the fair are the audience whom Petrouchka, the introspective young masochist, wishes to win over, the Magician who controls him is Fate, that cruel deity of the Housman poems, or the Vile Old Man, the general, the father too old to fight, gleefully sacrificing his son. Petrouchka's problem is how to keep alive, and have a successful love affair, and his rival, the Moor, is the hated man of action, the accomplished womaniser who has not been to Balliol, and has nothing of Hamlet in him, but in whom vulgarity triumphs. This situation or relationship has a way of turning up in many books.

The father chorus in these books is not malignant, rather is it wistful and friendly, in some books of the period he is a Priest. The chief thing we can learn from this school is the danger of allowing more literary vices, cleverness and self-pity, to come up

Characteristics of the Clever Young Men and their Dirty Deals

Author	Man	Place of Education	Nature of Predicament	Solution
Douglas	Denis, *South Wind*	Oxford	Inability to seduce a woman. Rival, young scientist. Father, Keith	Acquires virility and self-respect by assisting drunken pseudo-father to sober up.
Huxley	Denis, *Crome Yellow*	Oxford	Inability to seduce a woman. Rivals, painter and rich young peer. Father, Scogan	Flight to London (" and what on earth was he going to do in London when he got there ? ")
Huxley	Chelifer, Gumbril, Quarles	Oxford	Inability to seduce a woman. Rivals, all his friends. Father, Cardan, etc.	Expatriation (Mantua) the picture gallery and the reading-room
Eliot	Alfred Prufrock	?	General indecision and fear of experience. Rival, Sweeney. Runs away from women.	Polite resignation
Joyce	Stephen Dedalus	Clongowes	Superiority to vulgar surroundings, yet at mercy of them. Rival, Buck Mulligan. Father, Bloom	" Silence, exile and cunning." Expatriation, discovery of pseudo-father (Bloom)
Hemingway	Jake *The Sun also rises.*	?	War wound, hence inability to seduce a woman, economic inability to get enough to drink. Rivals, boxer, bull-fighter, etc.	Trout-fishing, drink, the Catholic Church

for air.   It was, however, the clever young men who
were the first to see the vanity of the war, and the
greater vanity of the peace.   They could not settle
down to boring jobs and unprofitable careers with
pre-war patience, and cleverness seemed a liability
rather than an asset.   Besides women did not like it.
Nor were they yet sure if they liked women, for they
were still romantic enough to be appalled by the distinction between love and lust, and to find the inevitable transition degrading.

> He is afraid seeing her lie so still,
> So utterly his own ; afraid lest she
> Should open wide her eyes and let him see
> The passionate conquest of her virgin will
> Shine there in triumph, starry bright with tears.
> He thrusts her from him : face and hair and breast,
> Hands he had touched, lips that his lips had pressed,
> Seem things deadly to be desired.   He fears
> Lest she should body forth in palpable shame
> Those dreams and longings that his blood, aflame
> Through the hot dark of summer nights, had dreamed
> And longed.   Must all his love, then, turn to this ?
> Was lust the end of what so pure had seemed ?
> He must escape, ah God ! her touch, her kiss.

> Guy drew her towards him and began kissing the soft,
> warm mouth.   He touched the bare arm that encircled
> his neck ; the flesh was resilient under his fingers ; he felt
> a desire to pinch it and tear it.
> It had been just like this with that little slut Winnie,
> just the same—all horrible lust.   He remembered a curious
> physiological fact out of Havelock Ellis.   He shuddered as
> though he had touched something disgusting, and pushed
> her away.

These quotations, from Huxley's *Defeat of Youth*
(1917) and *Happily Ever After* (*Limbo*, 1920) show
that he suffered from a belief in sacred and profane

love, from having read Dante and Plato. Such a state of war between intellect and the senses, unless a genuine truce is made between them, can only end unhappily. Either the senses conquer the mind, and we get the erudite sensualist, the Keith of *South Wind*, the Cardan of *Those Barren Leaves*, with their consciousness of wasted opportunities, or the mind is triumphant, and we have, what Huxley became, a moralist and a puritan. I have considered him in his early works as a dandy, for it is only in them that he is an artist, and in them that the irony and lyricism is unadulterated. *Leda*, *Limbo*, *Crome Yellow*, and the stories of *Little Mexican* belong to this period, *Antic Hay* begins another.

I quote him often because he is the most typical of a generation, typical in his promise, his erudition, his cynicism, and in his peculiar brand of prolific sterility.

CHAPTER VII

THE NEW MANDARINS

IT is as difficult to foretell the weather in a language as in the skies, and as vital. The problem in our case is to find out what sort of writing, at this moment at the end of the thirties, is likely to last. We have seen that there are two styles, which it is convenient to describe as the realist, or vernacular, the style of rebels, journalists, common sense-addicts and unromantic observers of human destiny, and the Mandarin, the artificial style of men of letters, and those in authority who make letters their spare-time occupation.

The lyrical or dandy style merges into the Mandarin.

There is an interaction between these two styles ; as in party government, one will seem in or out of office at a given moment ; when one style is in abeyance it will receive new blood and be thrust forward, when the other is at the height of its success, it will wither away. The panjandrums of the nineteenth century, Ruskin, Arnold, Pater, Meredith, Henry James, Swinburne, Conrad, give way to the realists, Gissing, Butler, Moore, Maugham, Bennett, Wells, and Shaw. It was now their turn to be driven from the temple. It was in 1906, I think, that the disheartened Conservative party, after being trounced in the general election, were elated by an attack made on their victors by young F. E. Smith. In the same year, in the pages of a dull review, another gifted young man, also a dark horse, was attacking the successful literary doctrine of the day, and the day's most eminent critic.

The study of Sir Thomas Browne, Mr. Gosse says, " encouraged Johnson, and with him a whole school of rhetorical writers in the eighteenth century, to avoid circumlocution by the invention of superfluous words, learned but pedantic, in which darkness was concentrated without being dispelled ". Such is Mr. Gosse's account of the influence of Browne and Johnson upon the later eighteenth century writers of prose. But to dismiss Johnson's influence as something altogether deplorable, is surely to misunderstand the whole drift of the great revolution which he brought about in English letters. The characteristics of the pre-Johnsonian prose style—the style which Dryden first established and Swift brought to perfection—are obvious enough. Its advantages are those of clarity and force ; but its faults, which, of course, are unimportant in the work of a great master, become glaring in that of the second-rate practitioner. The prose of Locke, for instance, or of Bishop Butler, suffers, in spite of its clarity and vigour, from grave defects. It is very flat and very loose ; it has no formal beauty, no elegance, no balance, no trace of the deliberation of art. Johnson, there can be no doubt, determined to remedy these evils by giving a new mould to the texture of English prose ; and he went back for a model to Sir Thomas Browne. . . . With the *Christian Morals* to guide him, Dr. Johnson set about the transformation of the prose of his time. He decorated, he pruned, he balanced ; he hung garlands ; he draped robes ; and he ended by converting the Doric order of Swift into

58

the Corinthian order of Gibbon. . . . Attacks of this kind—attacks upon the elaboration and classicism of Browne's style are difficult to reply to, because they must seem, to anyone who holds a contrary opinion, to betray such a total lack of sympathy with the subject as to make argument almost impossible. . . . The truth is that there is a great gulf fixed between those who naturally dislike the ornate, and those who naturally love it. There is no remedy ; and to attempt to ignore this fact only emphasises it the more. . . . Browne's " brushwork " is certainly unequalled in English literature, except by the very greatest masters of sophisticated art, such as Pope and Shakespeare ; it is the inspiration of sheer technique.

It was not till 1918, however, that the author, Lytton Strachey, became well known with *Eminent Victorians*.

Eminent Victorians is a revolutionary book. Through what at first sight seemed only biographical essays—on Arnold, Florence Nightingale, General Gordon and Cardinal Manning, dead for half a century—the author contrived to attack and undermine all that was most cherished in the morality of to-day. The public-school system, public service, philanthropy, the army, the empire, the Church, all were questioned in these sleek periods, and behind them, authority itself, the nature of the will, the hypocrisy by which good men climb and cling to power was examined and exposed. *Eminent Victorians* is the work of a great anarch, a revolutionary text-book on bourgeois society, written in the language through which the bourgeois ear could be lulled and beguiled, the Mandarin style. And the bourgeois responded with fascination to the music, like seals to the Eriskay love-lilt. At first the suave tones brought nothing but pleasure : this was the civilisation they had been fighting to save : these were the humanities again, the accent of the " studious cloisters of Trinity " : too late they realised that four Victorian idols had been knocked off their pedestals in such a way that they have never been replaced, or deemed in any degree replaceable. And after they had dismissed the book as " clever, but unsound ", worse was to follow, a questioning of the values the Victorians stood for, and, reflected from the eyes of their demobilised and disillusioned children, of themselves.

The trial of Oscar Wilde was responsible for a flight from æstheticism which lasted twenty years. He had himself done much to discredit it by the vulgar and insincere element which he had intro- duced, his conviction was the climax. From that moment the philistine triumphed, and although there were still poets and critics who loved beauty, who were in fact romantic, their romanticism had to be hearty. Hence the cult of beer and Sussex, of walk- ing and simplicity, which ended with Masefield, Brooke, Squire, and Gould ; hence the leanest years in the history of English verse and the manly criticism of Quiller-Couch and Walter Raleigh. It was left to Lytton Strachey to lay the ghost of Reading Gaol, to proclaim " un peu de faiblesse pour ce qui est beau—voilà mon défaut," and make noncon- formity permissible again.

With the success which his first two books gained him, Strachey's bitterness disappeared, he became a lion, and settled down to a quiet life of private pleasure. His gifts appear as with all fine critics, when he is able to love and to admire, and for this reason he is at his best when writing about the eighteenth century. As a critic he is admirable, as a biographer he is slightly vulgar. In *Queen Victoria*, his second book, his insurrectionary movement expired, he could not dislike Melbourne or Disraeli, or such a human bundle as his subject. By *Elizabeth and Essex* his style has become an elaborate experiment in cliché, which rises to fine passages, but contains not a little of the sniggering which has been commented on in Firbank. It is his first book (*Eminent Victorians*) admirably argued, and admirably constructed, original, polished, and daring, to which we can profitably return, with his criticism and essays. There is much to be learnt from his gifts, his intellectual pride, his forceful phrasing, his love of beauty and gesture, his grasp of character; " he is not dead but sleepeth ", and one day these gifts will be rescued from the neglect into which, by his noisy success, they were precipitated.

Another Mandarin to emerge from his retreat in 1918 was Pearsall-Smith, whose *Trivia* was the preliminary bombardment in a long attack, which is not yet exhausted, against puritanism in English letters. His anthology of English prose (1919), which omits Dryden and devotes only twelve pages to the eighteenth century, from Addison to Lamb, concentrating entirely on fine writing and the purple patch, continued the onslaught. He is with Professor Mackail the last of the old Mandarins, the men of the eighties, and the most intransigent.

Meanwhile a new Mandarin was taking over the

novel. In 1915 Virginia Woolf published *The Voyage Out*. This was followed by *Night and Day, Monday or Tuesday* (1921), *Jacob's Room* (1922), *Mrs. Dalloway* (1925), *To The Lighthouse* (1927) and *Orlando* (1928), one of the books in which, like *Elizabeth and Essex* or *Point Counter Point*, the new Mandarin movement of the twenties culminates.

Virginia Woolf seemed to have the worst defect of the Mandarin style, the ability to spin cocoons of language out of nothing. The history of her literary style has been that of a form at first simple, growing more and more elaborate, the content lagging far behind, then catching up, till, after the falseness of *Orlando*, she produced a masterpiece in *The Waves*.

Her early novels were not written in an elaborate style. Her most significant early book is *Monday or Tuesday* (1921) and demonstrates the rule that Mandarin prose is the product of those who in their youth were poets. That is to say, it is romantic prose. Not all poets were romantic prose writers (e.g. Dryden) but most romantic prose writers have attempted poetry.

The development of Virginia Woolf is the development of this lyrical feeling away from E. M. Forster, with his artlessness, and simple, poetical, colloquial style, into patterns of her own. The reveries of a central character came more and more to dominate her books. In *The Waves* she abandoned the convention of the central figure and described a group of friends, as children, as young people, and finally in late middle age. In a series of tableaux are contrasted the mystery of childhood, the promise of youth, the brilliance of maturity, and the complex, unmarketable richness of age. If *The Years* seems an impressionist gallery with many canvases, landscapes, portraits, and conversation pieces, then *The Waves* is a group of five or six huge panels, which celebrate the dignity of human life and the passage of time. It is one of the books which comes nearest to stating the mystery of life, and so, in a sense, nearest to solving it.

In *Mr. Bennett and Mrs. Brown*, Virginia Woolf attacked Bennett, Wells, and Galsworthy for their materialism, for the doctrine of realism which they had made all powerful in the 1900's.

For Mandarin prose is romantic prose and realism is the doctrine of the vernacular opposed to it. Thus among the new Mandarins of the twenties were several who began as poets; besides Virginia Woolf and Lytton Strachey, it includes the work of the Sitwells, with their flowery periods and predilection for highly coloured and sophisticated settings.

But the greatest Mandarin was Proust, who has become so familiar as almost to rank as an English writer. He exhibits, beyond all others, the defect of the Mandarin style; the failure of the writer's intellectual or emotional content to fill the elaborate frame which his talent plans for it. The honeycombs continue to develop, but only a few pollen-bags are emptied into them. There are many great passages where the complexity is worthy of the emotion expended on it, where very subtle and difficult truths are presented in language that could only express them if difficult and subtle.

Notwithstanding, now that the element of novelty and snobbery has worn off, much of Proust, like much of his master Ruskin, must stand condemned. He is often repetitive and feeble, the emotions of envy, jealousy, lust, and snobbishness around which his book is built, though they generate an enormous impetus, are incapable of sustaining it through twenty or thirty volumes; Swann's jealousy of Odette is enough without Proust's jealousy of Albertine, Saint-Loup's of Rachel, and Charlus's of Morel, and if the emotions repeat themselves, so also do the stories, the situations, the comments, parentheses, and clichés. Proust will remain a great writer, but his titles to fame will have to be reconsidered. His hatred and contempt for the life of action suited the war-weary and disillusioned generation he wrote for, his snobbery offered them both a philosophy and a remunerative career, he believed also in art for art's sake. He was in no sense a new writer, although it was the illusion of novelty which contributed so much to his success. His models are pre-war, his artists are taken from the *haute bourgeoisie,* like his politicians and men of science, they are members of the terrifying class which ruled in France, and which corresponded to the Forsytes in England; his nobility are of the same period, so are his operas, his dinner-parties; it is the world of the Dreyfus Case, the Victorian world. He was modern enough to attack the values of this world, but he had nothing to put in their place, for their values were his own, those of the narrator of the book who spends his life in going to parties and watching snobs behave, but is never a snob himself.

Thus Proust does not contemplate a revolution of feeling by which a Princesse de Guermantes ceases to be the centre of attraction at a party, or is not asked to parties, or even no longer exists, only an alteration by which the new Princesse de Guermantes is no longer of royal German birth, but the pushing hostess Madame Verdurin, who has married the Prince and consequently goes to those parties in the role which her title exacts.

And with Proust's artistic world it is the same; he is unable to contemplate a *monde* in which the painting of Elstir, the writing of Bergotte, the music of Vinteuil is out of fashion, or unappreciated. The lions of his own Dreyfusard youth, Anatole France, Saint-Saens, César Franck, Debussy, Monet, remain lions for ever, always difficult, always original, always the geniuses who, in spite of fifty years of parties, can only be appreciated by the initiated.

In short, although he is preoccupied with time, his world is static, because in al' the movements of his book, there is no movement of ideas. "Everything changes", he seems to say, "and I am the historian of that change", but what he really says is that nothing changes except the small social set which he admired in his youth, and which fell to pieces. How did they change? They grew older and went out less, or got mixed up in anti-social love affairs, or lost their money or died—but nothing else changed for him. There was a new face with an old title in a box at the opera—but the title and the box are always there, coveted and prized by the ruling class of six or seven countries; there are no new ideas, no revolution

65

in wisdom, no reversals of taste, nobody to declare that they never want to see an opera again.

Proust was a reactionary writer so steeped in the lore of the high society which he envied in the nineties, and with such a nostalgia for the emotions of his own childhood, he was so much the introspective masochist, that he admitted no change in his world, except the inescapable evidences of old age that confronted him. The aim of his book was how to revive his past, and he discovered that by remembering everything that had happened, and relying on intuitive visions produced by familiar smells and noises, such revival was possible. And where he failed to revive it, his style, that blend of unselective curiosity with interminable qualification, would carry on, like a lumbering, overcrowded, escaped tram that nobody can stop.

What Proust lives by are his extrovert satirical scenes, his balls and dinner-parties, the great ironical spectacle of the vanity of human wishes displayed by the Baron de Charlus and the Duchesse de Guermantes, and the delightful pictures which he provides of the countryside and his neighbours, the plain of Chartres, the coast, the quiet streets which Swann climbed in the Faubourg St. Germain. Where his egocentric masturbatory self-analysis begins to function, and his anxiety neurosis about his grandmother or Albertine, love or jealousy, comes into play, then all is tedious and unreal, like that asthma which his psychiatrist said he was unwilling to cure since something more unpleasant would be bound to take its place.

There are two more of these new Mandarins worth

examining. We have seen that Aldous Huxley is a writer particularly accessible to the spirit of his time and by the middle twenties his period of dandyism was over. The influence of Mallarmé and Prufrock waned, and he set himself to moralise on the flux around him. Witty, serious, observant, well-read, sensitive and intelligent, there can have been few young writers as gifted as Huxley—as can be seen from his early stories, *Happily Ever-After*, *Richard Greenow*, *Little Mexican*, *Young Archimedes* or *The Gioconda Smile*.

Yet he had the misfortune to suffer from what he considered, quoting Buddha, to be the deadliest of mortal sins, unawareness, for he was both unaware of his own nature as a writer, and unaware of the temptations into which he was falling. His nature was a very English one, that of the divided man, the lover of beauty and pleasure dominated by the puritan conscience. At first his dichotomy is apparent in his treatment of love. Love means everything to him but sex, and sex, although he is obsessed by it, is disgusting. The conflict is extended to become a warfare between the senses on one side, and the intellect, generously moralising in the moment of victory, on the other, until Huxley the intellectual pulls the lower self along like a man pulling a dog by a leash ; there are glimpses of other dogs, lamp-posts, green grass, trousers, and tree-trunks ; then comes a jerk, " eyes look your last," and a scientific platitude.

It is a question whether anyone so at war with himself can be a novelist, for to the novelist a complete integration is necessary ; the proper medium for the split-man is the *Journal Intime*, or the Dialogue. *Ends and Means* owes its success to being a complete break with the novel, for as a novelist, apart from being at war with himself, Huxley was hampered by his inability to create character or see a character except in an intellectual way.

The greatness of a novelist like Tolstoy is that he creates characters who, being real creations, are able to think and behave unlike themselves, to be false to type. Proust also had some of this greatness, and in English, Thackeray. But weaker novelists can only sling a few traits on to the characters they are depicting and hold them there. " You can't miss So-and-so ", they explain, " he stammers, and now look, here he comes—' What's your name ? ' ' S-s-s-so-and-s-s-s-s-so.' There you see, what did I tell you ! " Nearly all English novels are written to this prescription. Huxley suffers from the intellectual's difficulty of communicating with the people around him, except through the intellect. In consequence the only people he can write about at length are those with whom he can carry on an intellectual discussion.

But the consequences of Huxley's *artistic* unawareness are more serious. He is a defaulting financier of the written word, and nobody since Chesterton has so squandered their gifts. A contract to produce two books a year forced him to vitiate that keen sense of words with which he started, and as he had less to say, so, by a process which we have noticed, he took longer in which to say it. For such a writer who had to turn out 200,000 words a year, the Mandarin style was indispensable.

PREDICAMENT

By dinner-time it was already a Story—*the latest addition* to Mary Amberley's *repertory*. The *latest*, and as good, it seemed to Antony's *critically attentive ear* as the *finest classics of the collection*. Ever since *he received her invitation*, he now realized, *his curiosity had been tinged* with a *certain vindictive hope* that she would have *altered for the worse, either relatively in his own* knowledgeable *eyes, or else absolutely* by reason of the *passage of these twelve long years*; would have degenerated from what she was, or what he had imagined her to be, at the time when he had loved her. Discreditably enough, *as he now admitted to himself, it was with a touch of disappointment* that he had found her *hardly changed from the Mary Amberley of his memories*. She was forty-three. *But her body was almost as slim as ever, and she moved with all the old swift agility.* With *something more than the old agility indeed*; for he had noticed that she was now agile on purpose, that she acted the part of one who is *carried away by a youthful impulse* to break into quick and violent motion—acted it, moreover, in circumstances where the impulse could not, if natural, possibly have been felt.

.   .   .   .

After a lonely dinner—for Helen was keeping her room on *the plea of a headache*—Gerry went up to sit with Mrs. Amberley. He was *particularly charming that evening*, and so *affectionately solicitous that Mary forgot* all her *accumulated grounds* of complaint and *fell in love* with him *all over again*, and for *another set of reasons*—not because he was so *handsome, so easily and insolently dominating*, such a ruthless and *accomplished lover*, but because he was *kind, thoughtful, and affectionate*, was everything, *in a word*, she had previously known he wasn't.

I quote these as examples of Huxley's writing, of the muse's revenge, but they also show the influence of Proust in all its flatulence. Thus, although the clichés I have italicised are examples of the lack of distinction in Huxley's writing, like the use of unnecessary adverbs or the dogged repetition, the

69

determination to hit the nail on the head and then hit it on the head and then hit it on the head, that vulgarity with which we are familiar, there is also here the Proustian note : " . . . either relatively . . . or else absolutely . . . what she was, or what he had imagined her to be, etc." It is fake analysis and fatigued introspection, a combination in Mandarinism at its worst.

The last and strangest arrival among these new Mandarins was Joyce. *Work in Progress* is a Mandarin book, which demands, and demands in vain, complete leisure, the widest education, and devoted patience from the reader who wishes to understand it. It could not be more remote from colloquial English, from the spoken word. But on his way there Joyce had experimented with both styles. Thus *Dubliners* and *The Portrait of the Artist* are in reformed or anti-Mandarin, belonging to the early years of Joyce's Irish rebellion against the academic pundits and the literature of the ruling class, while the value of *Ulysses* and its importance to this analysis of the trends in English prose lies in the mixture of styles to be found there. In *Ulysses*, Joyce, a sensitive stylist, is trying to make up his mind which side he will take in the battle of the books. Thus we have in the passages where Stephen Dedalus holds the stage the Anglo-Irish lyrical mixture that we find in the *Portrait of the Artist*. But whenever Bloom is on the scene the language becomes the demotic journalese current where people like Bloom exist, and corresponding to the French of Celine, who in *Voyage au Bout de la Nuit* creates a Bloom-like character. In the two reveries, that of Mrs. Bloom and the Nameless One, the style is petty bourgeois, almost proletarian.

The quality common to the Mandarins was inflation, either of language or imagination, or of both, and it was this inflation which made inevitable a reaction against them. For their success was enormous. In the history of literature there can have been few books more talked and written about; few names more mentioned than those of Proust, Joyce, Lytton Strachey, Virginia Woolf, the Sitwells, and Paul Valéry. Their moment was propitious. After the post-war disillusion they offered a religion of beauty, a cult of words, of meanings only understood by the initiated, at a time when people were craving such initiations.

The world had lived too long under martial law to desire a socialised form of art, for human beings in the mass had proved but a union of slaughterers. There was more hope and interest in extreme individuality. This romantic restatement of the individual was of value to the younger generation, since it enabled them to inflate their own lives, and to give to them a depth and importance which they otherwise lacked. Soon the universities were flooded with emotional dud cheques, stumers on the bank of experience forged in the name of Swann or Dedalus, Monsieur Teste or Mrs. Dalloway. Proustians developed a wool-winding technique in friendship, an indefatigable egotism in affairs of the heart, combined with a lively social ambition. Valérians made it clear that everything was a little more difficult than it seemed, and then more difficult again. The Dedalus young men were defeatist, proud and twisted, their rudeness was justified by the impact of some ancestral curse; the Waste Landers were more miserable still, while the young Huxleys found relief in epigrams and bawdy erudition.

> "Oh yes, decidedly
> Having a sense of humour and a past
> One will amuse oneself, decidedly . . ."

The Gidian immoralists were perverse and moody, the Stracheyites wore fringes and spoke with a dying pejorative fall, the Virginians were impulsive, the Mansfieldians very simple and " back-to-childhood ", the Sitwellians went to the ballet in white ties and began their sentences with lingering sibilance : " I must say I do definitely think . . ." It was the golden age of Bloomsbury, under the last long shadow of the Ivory Tower, a romantic, affected, and defeatist epoch ; action was discredited, it had caused the war ; " And as for goodness—listen to Freud. Truth ? but what about Einstein ? History ? Have you read the *Decline of the West?* Nothing remains but beauty. Have you read Waley's *170 Chinese Poems* ? Beauty—and, of course, one's intellectual integrity and personal relations."

I have not dealt at length with these writers because I am assuming that the reader for whom this book is written, the artist in his search for a relative immortality, will know the most important book about them, Edmund Wilson's *Axel's Castle* (Scribner's, 1931), which includes essays on Yeats, Valéry, Eliot, Proust, Joyce, and Gertrude Stein. His summing up is against them, in so far as it is against their cult of the individual, which he feels they have carried to such lengths as to exhaust it for a long time to come, but it is a summing up which also states everything that can be said in their favour, when allowance for what I have termed "inflation" has been made. Here is the last paragraph:

> The writers with whom I have here been concerned have not only, then, given us works of literature which, for intensity, brilliance, and boldness as well as for an architectural genius, an intellectual mastery of their materials, rare among their Romantic predecessors, are probably comparable to the work of any time. Though it is true that they have tended to overemphasise the importance of the individual, that they have been preoccupied with introspection sometimes almost to the point of insanity, that they have endeavoured to discourage their readers, not only with politics, but with action of any kind—they have yet succeeded in effecting in literature a revolution analogous to that which has taken place in science and philosophy : they have broken out of the old mechanistic routine, they have disintegrated the old materialism, and they have revealed to the imagination a new flexibility and freedom. And though we are aware in them of things that are dying— the whole belle-lettreistic tradition of Renaissance culture perhaps, compelled to specialise more and more, more and more driven in on itself, as industrialism and democratic education have come to press it closer and closer—they none the less break down the walls of the present and wake us to the hope and exaltation of the untried, unsuspected possibilities of human thought and art.

On this verdict we will leave them.

CHAPTER VIII

THE NEW VERNACULAR

THE mass attack on the new Mandarins was launched in the late twenties. By that time they had squandered their cultural inheritance, for their inflation period coincided with the Boom, and their adversaries were to come into their own with the Slump. In spite of their apparent success, and publicity, the three Mandarin books of 1928, *Orlando*, *Elizabeth and Essex*, *Point Counter Point*, were disappointing ; they were not, except in America, popular successes and met also with considerable highbrow opposition.

This opposition may be said to have come from three quarters. One quarter was that of the old realists, the remainder of those young men who had rejected Pater, Swinburne, Meredith, and James. Of these Moore was too ill-read to be a good critic, Bennett too successful, for he was anxious to conceal by his indiscriminate welcome to novelty the poverty of his exhausted impulse ; the opinion of Galsworthy, Shaw, Wells, Kipling was not of value in matters of art. It remained for Somerset Maugham, after his long excursion as a playwright, to return as the champion of " lucidity, euphony, simplicity, and the story with a beginning, a middle and an end ", the doctrines of his French masters.

The second quarter was Paris, which held in the attack on the new Mandarins, the line taken by Dublin against their predecessors thirty years before. It was here that conspirators met in Sylvia Beach's bookshop where *Ulysses* lay stacked like dynamite in a revolutionary cellar, and scattered down the Rue de l'Odéon on the missions assigned to them. Here Gertrude Stein had launched her attacks on English culture, by rinsing the English vocabulary, by a process of constant repetition, of all accretions of meaning and association. The prose style of Ezra Pound was hardly academic, and Joyce also, till he became the mandarin of *Work in Progress*, remained a king over the water for those who were discontented with the court of Bloomsbury. James Joyce and Gertrude Stein were the exiled royalties, round whom centred the plots against Virginia Woolf and Lytton Strachey.

Any estimate of Miss Stein must largely depend on the pleasure derivable from her creations, but she applied to the writing of English as early as 1909 (*Three Lives*) a method which was to have far-reaching results. It was a simplification, an attack on order and meaning in favour of sound, but of sound which in itself generated a new precision. Two young men were to be influenced by it, Sherwood Anderson and Ernest Hemingway, who took Gertrude Stein's method and added to it his own quality of readability. The paper *Transition* was the court circular of these kings in exile.

The third quarter from which opposition to the Mandarins came was from their contemporaries, Lawrence and Lewis. Lawrence, as the early lyricism of his pre-war books evaporated, became a master of the colloquial style. Though his work is marred by carelessness, repetition, and want of ear, and a tendency to preach and rant which ill-health accentuated, it is always vigorous, thoughtful, and alive, the enemy of elaboration and artifice, of moral hypocrisy and verbal falseness. The poems in *Pansies* and *Nettles* are examples of the vernacular style at its best, as is the satire in his later books and stories, such as *Lady Chatterley*. Around Lawrence centred Middleton Murry and his wife, Katharine Mansfield, who said in her diary that the greatest pleasure she had received from her stories was that they had given pleasure to the printer who set them up, and several younger writers, of whom Richard Aldington, who also had one foot in Paris, and Robert Graves were the most important. A friend of Lawrence, though more influenced by George Moore, was David Garnett, whose *Lady Into Fox* and *Sailor's Return* were excellent anti-Mandarin books, combining something of the dandyism of Eliot and Firbank with a rustic basis, a fantasy logically worked out in language as simple as Defoe's.

The most dangerous enemy of the new Mandarins was Wyndham Lewis, who after his realistic novel *Tarr* (1918) was preparing his onslaught on the citadels of literary culture; on the one hand Stein's simplicity and Joyce's complexity were to be attacked, with Hemingway, Faulkner, and all other derivatives, while in England, Bloomsbury was to tremble, Lawrence to be chastised for his worship of the black sun of the solar plexus, and the Sitwells to be exterminated by an assassination five hundred pages long. Roy Campbell, in *The Georgiad*, brought up the rear. Being a painter turned writer, the style of Lewis is difficult of analysis, as it is strongly marked by the visual quality of his imagination. His early books are full of fine onsets and satires and descriptions written in a technique of his own, while his later ones are more colloquial, or what he would call informal.

To estimate his work is not easy. *The Art of Being Ruled, Time and Western Man, The Childermass, The Enemy*, and *The Apes of God* contain some of the most vigorous satire, original description, and profound criticism produced by the twentieth century ; Lewis was unique in being a philosophical critic, who, attacking the modern conception of " time ", was able to illustrate the workings of that conception by ranging up and down the whole of contemporary literature, from the best poetry to the best sellers, the best seller to the lowest kind of journalism or jazz.

As a constructive critic however he has little to offer, a belief in reason as opposed to metaphysical or sexual mysticism, a belief in western civilisation, in the physical world, in the comic aspect of love, in the external approach to things (describing people via their personal appearance) and in the value of humour and satire. All this is not negligible, but it is not on a scale with the world he has set out to destroy or with his machinery of destruction.

What Lewis believes in most is himself, the measure he applies to his contemporaries is how far they differ from that yardstick and how far they stand in his way. His criticism also suffers from a lack of proportion. He will attack a writer on philosophical, or moral grounds and then as violently, for the most superficial and frivolous of errors, or he will turn from rending an important writer to maul an obscure and inconsiderable hack. He is like a maddened elephant which, careering through a village, sometimes leans against a house and carelessly demolishes the most compact masonry, trumpeting defiance to the inhabitants within, sometimes pursues a dog or a chicken, or stops to uproot a shrub or bang a piece of corrugated iron. His writing can be redundant and slovenly, his dialogue is often dull, his novels begin with scenes worthy of a great master and gradually lose themselves in unplanned verbosity. His last volume of criticism, *Men Without Art*, while containing brilliant glimpses of his mind, is unexpectedly trivial and often bullying and unfair. His later books are ragged and his style has become somewhat unbuttoned. From an article of his in the Fascist quarterly, *British Union*, one gets the impression that it is because he is writing now for a new class of reader, the petty bourgeois, the philistine small tradesman, the Fascist underdog.

What is necessary for Lewis is that some of his admirers, or he himself, should make an omnibus Lewis, an anthology of his best thought and finest passages, applying to his work the selection and compression which in the spate of his original creation have been wanting.

To go further it is necessary to bring the production chart up to date, and I have added after some of the books the letters (M) or (V) according as to whether they are written in the Mandarin, or Vernacular or Colloquial style.

1923. Mansfield, *The Dove's Nest* (V); Huxley, *Antic Hay* (M); Firbank, *The Flower beneath the Foot* (Dandy); Hemingway, *In our Time* (V); Willa Cather, *A Lost Lady*; Elizabeth Bowen, *Encounters*; Eliot, *The Waste Land*.

1924. Mansfield, *Something Childish* (V); Huxley, *Little Mexican*; Firbank, *Prancing Nigger*; Forster, *Passage to India*; Garnett, *Man in the Zoo* (V); Edith Sitwell, *The Sleeping Beauty* (M); Osbert Sitwell, *Triple Fugue* (M).

1925. Huxley, *Those Barren Leaves* (M); Dreiser, *American Tragedy* (V); Eliot, *Poems* (M); Compton-Burnett, *Pastors and Masters*; Garnett, *Sailor's Return* (V); Fitzgerald, *The Great Gatsby*; Loos, *Gentlemen Prefer Blondes* (V); Woolf, *Mrs. Dalloway* (M); Day Lewis, *Beechen Vigil*; Noel Coward, *The Vortex* (V); Geoffrey Scott, *Portrait of Zelide* (M).

1926. Huxley, *Two or Three Graces* (M); Hemingway, *Torrents of Spring* (V); Quennell, *Poems* (M); Lawrence, *Plumed Serpent*; Baring, *Daphne Adeane* (V); Cather, *My Mortal Enemy* (V); Fowler, *Modern English Usage*; V. Woolf, *To the Lighthouse* (M); Maugham, *The Casuarina Tree* (V).

1927. Bowen, *The Hotel* (M); Lehmann, *Dusty Answer* (M); Hemingway, *The Sun Also Rises* (V), *Men Without Women* (V); Lewis, *The Wild Body, Time and Western Man, The Lion and the Fox*; Mackenzie, *Vestal Fires*; Wilder, *Bridge of San Luis Rey* (M); Westcott, *The Grandmothers* (M).

1928. Sassoon, *Memoirs of a Fox-hunting Man*; Woolf, *Orlando* (M); Lawrence, *Lady Chatterley's Lover* (V);

Nicolson, *Some People* ; Edwards, *Winter Sonata*
(V) ; Waugh, *Decline and Fall* (V) ; Isherwood,
All the Conspirators (V) ; Lewis, *The Childermass* ;
Mackenzie, *Extraordinary Women* ; Strachey, *Elizabeth and Essex* (M) ; Huxley, *Point Counter Point*
(M) ; E. Sackville-West, *Mandrake Over the Water-Carrier* (M).

1929. Compton-Burnett, *Brothers and Sisters* ; H. Green,
Living (V) ; W. Faulkner, *The Sound and the Fury* (M) ; Hemingway, *Farewell to Arms* (V) ;
Lawrence, *Pansies* (V) ; Joyce, *Fragments of Work in Progress* (M) ; Quennell, *Baudelaire and the Symbolists* (M) ; Graves, *Goodbye to All That* (V) ;
Aldington, *Death of a Hero* (V).

1930. Kafka, *The Castle* ; Dashiel Hammett, *Maltese Falcon*
(V) ; O. Sitwell, *Dumb Animal* (M) ; Maugham,
Cakes and Ale (V), *The Gentleman in the Parlour* ;
W. H. Auden, *Poems* ; T. S. Eliot, *Ash Wednesday*
(M) ; Evelyn Waugh, *Vile Bodies* (V) ; Spender,
Twenty Poems ; Lewis, *The Apes of God*.

1931. V. Woolf, *The Waves* (M) ; Roy Campbell, *The Georgiad* (V) ; A. Powell, *Afternoon Men* (V) ;
Edmund Wilson, *Axel's Castle*.

1932. W. H. Auden, *The Orators*.

There are, we know, many kinds of vernacular ; the
colloquial language of Hemingway is different from
the colloquial language of Maurice Baring, yet each
believes in informality and simplicity, they never
use a word that they would not in conversation—
words like ' nay ', ' notwithstanding ', ' pullulating ',
' mephitic ', ' sublunary ', ' Babylon ', ' lest ', ' corpulent ', ' futurity ', ' ecstasy ', etc.

The outstanding writer of the new vernacular is
Hemingway, and he was aided by the talkies as were
realists a generation before by journalism. The talking picture popularised the vocabulary with which

Hemingway wrote and enabled him to use slang words in the knowledge that they were getting every day less obscure, he surf-rode into fame on the wave of American popular culture. Here, taken from *Death in the Afternoon*, is a spat between him and a Mandarin which is in itself a defence of the new style :

Mr. Aldous Huxley writing in an essay entitled *Foreheads Villainous Low* commences : " In [naming a book by this writer] Mr. H. ventures, once, to name an Old Master. There is a phrase, quite admirably expressive " [here Mr. Huxley inserts a compliment], " a single phrase, no more, about ' the bitter nail-holes ' of Mantegna's Christ ; then quickly, quickly, appalled by his own temerity, the author passes on (as Mrs. Gaskell might hastily have passed on, if she had somehow been betrayed into mentioning a water-closet) passes on, shamefacedly, to speak once more of Lower Things."

" There was a time, not so long ago, when the stupid and uneducated aspired to be thought intelligent and cultured. The current of aspiration has changed its direction. It is not at all uncommon now to find intelligent and cultured people doing their best to feign stupidity and to conceal the fact that they have received an education " —and more ; more in Mr. Huxley's best educated vein which is a highly educated vein indeed.

What about that, you say ? Mr. Huxley scores there, all right, all right. What have you to say to that ? Let me answer truly. On reading that in Mr. Huxley's book I obtained a copy of the volume he refers to and looked through it and could not find the quotation he mentions. It may be there, but I did not have the patience nor the interest to find it, since the book was finished, and nothing to be done. It sounds very much like the sort of thing one tries to remove in going over the manuscript. I believe it is more than a question of the simulation or avoidance of the appearance of culture. When writing a novel a writer should create living people ; people, not

81

characters. A *character* is a caricature. If a writer can make people live there may be no great characters in his book, but it is possible that his book will remain as a whole ; as an entity ; as a novel. If the people the writer is making talk of old masters ; of music ; of modern painting ; of letters ; or of science ; then they should talk of those subjects in the novel. If they do not talk of those subjects and the writer makes them talk of them he is a faker, and if he talks about them himself to show how much he knows, then he is showing off. No matter how good a phrase or a simile he may have, if he puts it in where it is not absolutely necessary and irreplaceable, he is spoiling his work for egotism. Prose is architecture, not interior decoration, and the Baroque is over. For a writer to put his own intellectual musings, which he might sell for a low price as essays, into the mouths of artificially con-structed characters, which are more remunerative when issued as people in a novel, is good economics, perhaps, but does not make literature. People in a novel, not skilfully constructed *characters*, must be projected from the writer's assimilated experience, from his knowledge, from his head, from his heart, and from all there is of him. If he ever has luck as well as seriousness and gets them out entire they will have more than one dimension and they will last a long time. A good writer should know as near every-thing as possible. Naturally he will not. A great enough writer seems to be born with knowledge. But he really is not ; he has only been born with a quicker ratio to the passage of time than other men and without conscious application, and with an intelligence to accept or reject what is already presented as knowledge. There are some things which cannot be learned quickly, and time, which is all we have, must be paid heavily for their acquiring. They are the very simplest things and because it takes a man's life to know them the little new that each man gets from life is very costly and the only heritage he has to leave. Every novel which is truly written contributes to the total of knowledge which is there at the disposal of the next writer who comes, but the next writer must pay, always, a certain nominal percentage in experience to be

82

able to understand and assimilate what is available as his birthright and what he must, in turn, take his departure from. If a writer of prose knows enough about what he is writing about he may omit things that he knows and the reader, if the writer is writing truly enough, will have a feeling of those things as strongly as though the writer had stated them. The dignity of movement of an iceberg is due to only one-eighth of it being above water. A writer who omits things because he does not know them only makes hollow places in his writing. A writer who appreciates the seriousness of writing so little that he is anxious to make people see he is formally educated, cultured or well-bred, is merely a popinjay. And this too, remember : a serious writer is not to be confounded with a solemn writer. A serious writer may be a hawk or a buzzard or even a popinjay, but a solemn writer is always a bloody owl.

The passage is an excellent example of Hemingway's style, notice the clumsy, facetious get-away, the admirable relation between the language used and the thought to be conveyed of the central passage, the polemical anti-climax at the end, and notice also the slovenliness of such a phrase as " if the writer of prose knows enough about what he is writing about he may omit things that he knows ". Like most writers of the thirties Hemingway seems terrified to blot a line.

Hemingway's difficulties as a writer arise from the limitations of realism. His style, derived from Huck Finn, Stein, Anderson, with perhaps a dash of Firbank, is the antithesis of fine writing. It is a style in which the body talks rather than the mind, one admirable for rendering emotions ; love, fear, joy of battle, despair, sexual appetite, but impoverished for intellectual purposes. Hemingway is fortunate in possessing a physique which is at home in the world of boxing, bull-fighting, and big game shooting, fields closed to most writers, and especially to Mandarins ; he is supreme in the domain of violence and his opportunity will be to write the great book, and there have been no signs of one so far, about the Spanish war. Hemingway's tragedy as an artist is that he has not had the versatility to run away fast enough from his imitators. The talkies that facilitated his success brought on a flood of talkie-novels, the trick of being tough, the knack of writing entirely in dialogue interrupted only by a few sentimental landscapes caught on, and with each bad copy the prestige of the original was affected. A Picasso would have done something different ; Hemingway could only indulge in invective against his critics—and do it again. His colleagues in American realism, Dos Passos, O'Hara, Caldwell, have found the same difficulties, and the Hemingway style is now confined to sporting journalists on the daily papers, advertising men with literary ambitions, cinema critics, and the writers of thrillers. The first you-man sentence of the *Portrait of the Artist*, " when you wet the bed first it is warm, then it gets cold ", a sentence intended to represent the simple body-conscious needs of early childhood, after dominating fiction for years, would seem to have had its day.

Lewis has attacked Hemingway for being a " dumb ox ", for choosing stupid inarticulate heroes who are the passive victims of circumstance rather than active and intelligent masters of their fate. Yet at the moment at which Hemingway wrote his best books it was necessary to be a dumb ox. It was the only way to escape from Chelsea's Apes of God, and from Bloomsbury's Sacred Geese.

The most resolute and coherent of the opponents of fine writing has been Somerset Maugham, although his hostility arises, he tells us, from his incapacity.

> I discovered my limitations and it seemed to me that the only sensible thing was to aim at what excellence I could within them. I knew that I had no lyrical quality, I had a small vocabulary and no efforts that I could make to enlarge it much, availed me. I had little gift of metaphors ; the original and striking simile seldom occurred to me. Poetic flights and the great imaginative sweep were beyond my powers. . . . I knew that I should never write as well as I could wish, but I thought with pains I could arrive at writing as well as my natural defects allowed. On taking thought it seemed to me that I must aim at lucidity, simplicity and euphony. I have put these three qualities in the order of the importance I assigned to them.

Maugham (I am quoting from *The Summing Up*, though some of the arguments there are to be found in earlier books) then goes on to criticise Ruskin and Sir Thomas Browne with justice, and to attack the influence of King James's Bible on English prose.

> Ever since, English prose has had to struggle against the tendency to luxuriance. When from time to time the spirit of the language has reasserted itself, as it did with Dryden and the writers of Queen Anne, it was only to be submerged once more by the pomposities of Gibbon and Dr. Johnson. When English prose recovered simplicity with Hazlitt, the Shelley of the letters, and Charles Lamb at his best, it lost it again with de Quincey, Carlyle, Meredith, and Walter Pater. . . .

For to write good prose is an affair of good manners. It is, unlike verse, a civil art. . . . Poetry is baroque. I cannot but feel that the prose writers of the baroque period, the authors of King James' bible, Sir Thomas Browne, Glanville, were poets who had lost their way. Prose is a rococo art. It needs taste rather than power, decorum rather than inspiration and vigour rather than grandeur. . . . It is not an accident that the best prose was written when rococo, with its elegance and moderation, attained its greatest excellence. For rococo was evolved when baroque had become declamatory, and the world, tired of the stupendous, asked for restraint. It was the natural expression of persons who valued a civilised life. Humour, tolerance, and horse-sense made the great tragic issues that had preoccupied the first half of the seventeenth century seem excessive. The world was a more comfortable place to live in and perhaps for the first time in centuries the cultivated classes could sit back and enjoy their leisure. It has been said that good prose should resemble the conversation of a well-bred man. Conversation is only possible when men's minds are free from pressing anxieties. Their lives must be reasonably secure and they must have no grave concern about their souls. They must attach importance to the refinements of civilisation. They must value courtesy ; they must pay attention to their persons (and have we not also been told that good prose should be like the clothes of a well-dressed man, appropriate but unobtrusive ?). They must fear to bore, they must be neither flippant, nor solemn, but always apt ; and they must look upon " enthusiasm " with a critical glance. This is a soil very suitable for prose. It is not to be wondered at that it gave a fitting opportunity for the appearance of the best writer of prose that our modern world has seen, Voltaire. . . . The writers of English, perhaps owing to the poetic nature of the language, have seldom reached the excellence that seems to have come so naturally to him. . . . If you could write lucidly, simply, euphoniously and yet with liveliness you would write perfectly ; you would write like Voltaire.

I have quoted this passage because it is a typical

defence of vernacular prose, as also of much literary wish-fulfilment. Maugham thinks with pleasure of the civilised and wealthy society of the eighteenth century, he has made his own life wealthy and civilised and therefore would like to believe that the prose of the eighteenth century is the best. But supposing a new age of " great tragic issues " is now in being, then a prose of humour, tolerance, and horse-sense will seem frivolous and archaic ! And what writer could have been more lucid and simple, more admired by Maugham than Swift, who living in the heart of that courteous and cultivated age contrived to go mad in it ? Nor is the prose of Blake so negligible. Incidentally the defects of the colloquial style are well illustrated in this passage. The vocabulary is flat. " Sit back and enjoy ", " pressing anxieties ", " reasonably secure ", " grave concern ", " critical glance ", " fitting opportunity ", " it is not to be wondered at ", while not yet officially clichés, are phrases so tarnished as to be on the way to them. They come from the vocabulary of political journalism, from the atmosphere where words deteriorate faster than in any other, and the defect of the colloquial style, the breathlessness, the agitated dullness of the sentence which is too short for both eye and ear, becomes apparent. The phrases rattle like peas being shelled into a tin, the full stops bring the reader up short, the effect, owing to the absence of any relative clauses, is of reading a list of aphorisms, and the best aphorists, even La Rochefoucauld, can only be read for a few pages. Again, the language of the Bible is more plain than complicated; its bad influence on English style has been in the direction of archaistic simplicity and is apparent in a writer like Kipling. It is no accident, as Maugham would say, that he goes on to praise American literature, ignorant, he claims, of the Authorised Version, and to flatter American writers, galvanised by their journalism.

This concludes the case for the vernacular style. There remains one other argument often heard in its favour. 'If culture is to survive it must survive through the masses; if it cannot be made acceptable to them there is no one else who will be prepared to guarantee it, since the liberal capitalist society who protected it, will not be in a position to do so after another slump and a war. Much that is subtle in literature and life will have to be sacrificed if they are to survive at all; consequently it is necessary for literature to approach its future custodians in a language they will understand.'

The old world is a sinking ship, to get a place in the boats that are pushing off from it not money nor leisure, the essayist's elegance, nor the pedant's erudition will avail, the sailors are not impressed by courtesy or attention to one's person, nor even by good clothes and the conversation of a well-bred man; we cannot take our armchair with us. Nothing will admit us but realism and sincerity, an honest appeal in downright English. As far back as 1847 Tennyson said that the two great social questions impending in England were the " housing and education of the poor man before making him our master, and the higher education of women ", and as the time for making him our master grows nearer, so his education becomes more and more vital, since on it depend the cultural values which he will choose to preserve.

For this reason left-wing writers have tended to write in the colloquial style while the Mandarins, the wizards, and prose charmers remain as supporters of the existing dispensation. In England the ablest exponents of the colloquial style among the younger writers are Christopher Isherwood and George Orwell, both left-wing and both, at the present level of current English, superlatively readable. Here is an experiment :

The first sound in the mornings was the clumping of the mill-girls' clogs down the cobbled street. Earlier than that, I suppose, there were factory whistles which I was never awake to hear. There were generally four of us in the bedroom, and a beastly place it was, with that defiled impermanent look of rooms that are not serving their rightful purpose. One afternoon, early in October, I was invited to black coffee at Fritz Wendel's flat. Fritz always invited you to " black coffee " with emphasis on the black. He was very proud of his coffee. People used to say it was the strongest in Berlin. Fritz himself was dressed in his usual coffee-party costume—a thick white yachting sweater and very light blue yachting trousers. You know how it is there early in Havana, with the bums still asleep against the walls of the buildings ; before even the ice waggons come by with ice for the bars ? Well we came across the square from the dock to the Pearl of San Francisco to get coffee. My bed was in the right-hand corner on the side nearest the door. There was another bed across the foot of it and jammed hard against it (it had to be in that position to allow the door to open), so that I had to sleep with my legs doubled up ; if I straightened them out I kicked the occupant of the other bed in the small of the back. He was an elderly man named

Mr. Reilly. He greeted me with his full-lipped luscious smile.

" 'Lo, Chris ! "

" Hullo, Fritz. How are you ? "

" Fine." He bent over the coffee-machine, his sleek black hair unplastering itself from the scalp and falling in richly scented locks over his eyes. " This darn thing doesn't go," he added.

We sat down and one of them came over.

" Well," he said.

" I can't do it," I told him. " I'd like to do it as a favour. But I told you last night I couldn't."

" You can name your own price."

" It isn't that. I can't do it. That's all. How's business ? " I asked.

" Lousy and terrible." Fritz grinned richly.

Luckily he had to go to work at five in the morning so I could uncoil my legs and have a couple of hours proper sleep after he was gone.

This passage is formed by adding to the first three sentences of Orwell's *Road to Wigan Pier* the first five sentences of Isherwood's *Sally Bowles* and then the first two sentences of Hemingway's *To Have and Have Not*. I have woven the beginning of the three stories a little further. Next three sentences by Orwell, then dialogue by Isherwood to " added ", by Hemingway to " That's all ", by Isherwood to " richly " and last sentence by Orwell again. The reader can now go on with whichever book he likes best, Orwell and his bed, Fritz and his coffee, or Harry Morgan and Havana. As Pearsall-Smith says of modern writers : " The diction, the run of phrase of each of them seems quite undistinguishable from that of the others, each of whose pages might have been written by any one of his fellows."

This, then, is the penalty of writing for the masses. As the writer goes out to meet them half-way he is joined by other writers going out to meet them half-way, and they merge into the same creature—the talkie journalist, the advertising, lecturing, popular novelist.

The process is complicated by the fact that the masses, whom a cultured writer may generously write for, are at the moment overlapped by the middle-class best-seller-making public, and so a venal element is introduced.

According to Gide, a good writer should navigate against the current ; the practitioners in the new vernacular are swimming with it ; the familiarities of the advertisements in the morning paper, the matey leaders in the *Daily Express*, the blather of the film critics, the wisecracks of newsreel commentators, the know-all autobiographies of political reporters, the thrillers and 'teccies, the personal confessions, the *I was a so-and-so*, and *Storm over such-and-such*, the gossip-writers who play Jesus at twenty-five pounds a week, the straight-from-the-shoulder men, the middlebrow novelists of the shove-halfpenny school, are all swimming with it too. For a moment the canoe of an Orwell, or an Isherwood, bobs up, then it is hustled away by floating rubbish, and a spate of newspaper pulp.

It is interesting to notice the conflict between the two ways of writing in Auden. In the ballads he has lately been writing, excellent of their kind, he has attempted to reduce poetry to a record of simple and universal experience expressed in colloquial language.

91

O plunge your hands in water
Plunge them in up to the wrist
Stare, stare in the basin
And wonder what you've missed.

The glacier knocks in the cupboard
The desert sighs in the bed,
And the crack in the tea-cup opens
A lane to the land of the dead.

At the same time the bulk of his poetry has always remained private and esoteric.

CHAPTER IX

THE COOL ELEMENT OF PROSE

IT now seems time to express an opinion on the
battle between the styles. I do not say that
one is better than the other ; there is much to admire
in both ; what I have claimed is a relationship
between them, a perpetual action and reaction ; the
realists had it their way in the years before the war ;
the new Mandarins ruled supreme from 1918 to 1928,
the period of Joyce, Proust, Valéry, Strachey, Woolf,
the Sitwells, and Aldous Huxley. From 1928 to
1938 the new realists have predominated. The defla-
tionary activities of the Cambridge critics (Richards,
Leavis) have replaced the inflationism of Bloomsbury. But we have had ten years of this new realism
also ; ten years in which it has grown more popular,
and more tyrannical. Its vocabulary, never rich, has
been worn away by the attrition of success ; its
exponents have been wearied by the enormity of
their imitators.

It is possible to bring forward other causes for the
silence or the deterioration of a writer than the weaknesses of his literary school, and the other causes are
as likely to be correct. All we can say of the realists

of the last ten years, is that nothing in their creed seems to have propped them up against the disastrously short term of the writer's life. Realism, simplicity, the colloquial style, they seem to have triumphed everywhere at the moment—yet where are their triumphant professors ? With the exception of Isherwood among the young, and Maugham among the old, they are not there to enjoy it. The movement has passed out of their hands, has sunk to a wider and more anonymous strata, to the offices, studios, and novelist's week-end cottages where is produced the great bulk of the commercial writing of to-day.

I have talked about this with Isherwood, whom I regard as a hope of English fiction, and I have suggested how dangerous might become that fatal readability of his. The first person singular of the German stories, Herr Christoph, or Herr Issyvoo, is the most persuasive of literary salesmen, one moment's reading with him and one is tobogganing through the book, another moment and one has bought it—but he is persuasive because he is so completely bland and anonymous, nothing rouses him, nothing shocks him. While secretly despising us he could not at the same time be more tolerant ; his manners are charming, and he is somehow on our side against the characters, confidential, as, when playing with children, one child older or less animal than the rest, will suddenly attach itself to the grown-ups, and discuss its former playmates.

Now a price has to be paid for this ; Herr Issyvoo is not a dumb ox, for he is not condemned to the solidarity with his characters and their background which Hemingway's conception of his art enforces, but he is much less subtle, intelligent and articulate than he might be. In the little knitted skein from the three books it will be remembered that not only was the language almost identical and the pace the same, but the three " I's " of Isherwood, Orwell, and Hemingway were also interchangeable ; three colourless reporters.

In Isherwood's earlier *The Memorial*, on the other hand, there is no first person. The hero is a character who is more favoured than the others, and in the Berlin diary (*New Writing*, No. 3) the first person singular, unhampered by the conventions of fiction, at once postulates a higher level of culture and intelligence, and possesses a richer vocabulary. In the conversation, Isherwood, while admitting the limitations of the style he had adopted, expressed his belief in construction as the way out of the difficulty. The writer must conform to the language which is understood by the greatest number of people, to the vernacular, but his greatness as a novelist will appear in the exactness of his observation, the justice of his situations, and in the construction of his book. It is an interesting theory, for construction has for long been the weak point in modern novels. It is the construction that makes *The Memorial, Passage to India, Cakes and Ale*, remarkable books.

But will the construction, however rigid and faultless, of future books, if written in what will be by then an even more impoverished realist vocabulary be enough to set those books apart from the copies made by the ever-growing school of imitators ? At present it is impossible to tell ; the path is beset by dangers ; it is fortunate that Isherwood, who possesses the mastery of form, the imaginative content of a true novelist, is able to see them.

The most convincing attack on the realism of the thirties is that made by Pearsall-Smith in his pamphlet on *Fine Writing* (reprinted in *Reperusals*, 1936). A Mandarin of the generation of the eighties, an admirer of Pater and Jowett, a friend of Henry James, he represents not a reaction against realism, but the old Adam, the original sinner that many of them rebelled against. He, in return, attacks their austerity :

> May it be accounted for by the fact that the spirit of Puritanism, having been banished from the province of moral conduct, has found a refuge among the arts ? Do these critics of the art of writing, like certain critics of other arts, occupy themselves with the craft of literary composition because they think it wrong ? . . . I shall make to our modern critics, especially of the Cambridge school, a few suggestions which are not amiable, and are perhaps unfair. The disconcerting fact may first be pointed out that if you write badly about good writing, however profound may be your convictions or emphatic your expression of them, your style has a tiresome trick of whispering, " Don't listen," in your reader's ears. And it is possible also to suggest that the promulgation of new-fangled æsthetic dogmas in unwieldy sentences may be accounted for—not perhaps unspitefully—by a certain deficiency in æsthetic sensibility ; as being due to a lack of that delicate, unreasoned, prompt delight in all the varied and subtle manifestations in which beauty may enchant us.

96

He goes on to suggest that economic causes are also responsible :

> Are not the authors who earn their livings by their pens, and those who, by what some regard as a social injustice, have been more or less freed from this necessity— are not these two classes of authors in a sort of natural opposition to each other ? He who writes at his leisure, with the desire to master his difficult art, can hardly help envying the profits of the money-making authors, since his own work at least till years, and often many years, have passed, has no appreciable market value. Unsale-ability seems to be the hall-mark, in modern times, of quality in writing.

Puritanism, in other people we admire as austerity in ourselves, yet there is much truth in Pearsall-Smith's accusation. Writing is a more impure art than music or painting. It is an art, but it is also the medium in which many millions of inartistic people express themselves, describe their work, sell their goods, justify their conduct, propagate their ideas. It is the vehicle of business and propaganda. Since it is harder to paint or compose without a certain affection for painting or music, the commercial element, advertisers, illustrators, are recognisable, and in a minority, nor do music and painting appeal to the scientific temperament.

But writing does. It is an art in which the few who practise it for its own sake are being always resented, and jostled through its many galleries, by the majority who do not. And the deadliest of these are the scientific investigators, clever young men who have themselves failed as artists, and who bring only a passionate sterility and a dark, wide-focusing resent-

ment to their examination of creative art. The aim
of much of this destructive criticism, though not as
yet publicly avowed, is entirely to eliminate the
individual style, to banish imaginative beauty and
formal art from writing. Prose will not only be as
unassuming as good clothes, but as uniform as bad
clothes. For there is no use in Maugham arguing
that a writer, to be distinct from others, must heighten
his colloquial modern style by reading Newman and
Hazlitt ; he is by now, if he is like any other modern
writer, moving too fast, and such authors will seem
to him, if he has the patience to read them, so occupied
with unreal problems and so infected with a leisurely
attitude to life, as to be hardly less archaic than their
stylistic rivals, Lamb, Ruskin, Pater, Matthew Arnold.
The remedy is proposed too late.

The only way by which a cure can be undertaken
is to persuade such writers to re-read their own books
or the contemporary books which, up to a year ago,
they most admired. Then, however jauntily they
may protest—" Well, it was what the public wanted
at the time—it was in me and it had to come out ;
it means no more to me now than my old toe-nails—
and, hell, who wants to read the same book twice,
anyway," a doubt will have arisen.

On the other hand Maugham expresses a truth when
he says that much writing of the kind he dislikes is
the work of " Poets who have lost their way ". The
defect of Mandarin writing is not that it is poetical or
imaginative prose, but that much of it is not prose, but
bad poetry. It is a fact of importance that the prose of
true poets is firm and muscular. Landor, Coleridge,

Shelley, Donne, Shakespeare, Milton, Dryden, Blake, Hopkins, Yeats, Eliot, Gray, Cowper, to name but a few, can write admirable prose—for poetry is a more precise art than prose, and to write it implies qualities which prove valuable in the " other harmony ".

Yet the poetry of prose writers is unworthy of them and very often they will have become prose writers only after the failure of a slim volume of verse. Since the decay of the Romantic Movement poetry has gone through a bad patch, and severe discipline has been necessary to those who write it, consequently others who start out with only facility, sensibility, and a lyrical outlook, rather than undergo the hardships of the training, have allowed their poetical feeling to relax in prose. The result has been to inflate and romanticise prose, in its turn, and thus to bring about a philistine, puritan and pedestrian reaction. The Tough Guy, of whom we are now growing tired, is the necessary offspring of the androgynous Orlando. There is no reason why prose should not be poetical, provided that the poetry in it is assimilated to the medium, that its rhythms follow the structure of prose and not of verse—it is the undisciplined, undigested, unassimilated poetry often written in unconscious blank verse and bearing no relation to the construction, if any, of the book, that has discredited " fine writing ".

At the moment the vernacular is triumphant. Damon Runyon sweeps the land. The You-men are everywhere victorious. I open a number of the *New Statesman* at the review of a book called, *You Make Your Own Life.*

99

I am less afraid of overpraising Mr. Pritchett's new volume of short stories than of failing to convey their really remarkable quality. He is one of the happy authors who can establish in a few lines of dialogue both the social sphere and the individual tang of their characters. The first story in his book, *Sense of Humour*, deserved the salvo of applause which greeted it when it appeared in a volume of *New Writing* : fresh, original, complete, and true, it sticks in your memory long after you have finished it. A commercial traveller gets to know the girl behind the cash-desk of a provincial hotel, an Irish girl with a sense of humour. The author catches the tune of their preliminary banter with the precision of Cecil Sharp collecting a folk song :

" Lord, I'm fed up with this line," she said.

" What line ? " I said. " The hotel line ? "

" Yes," she said. " I'm fed right up to the back teeth with it."

" And you've got good teeth," I said.

" There's not the class of person there used to be in it," she said. " All our family have good teeth."

" Not the class ? "

" I've been in it five years and there's not the same class at all. You never meet any fellows."

The inconsequential zig-zag of talk has been noted before, but hardly so economically as that, so surely, so truthfully. While they gossip, and without a word of description, a whole background has sprung up behind them : houses, people, garages.

Such criticism is a symptom of the condition of contemporary writing, " failing to convey their really remarkable quality " is the language of advertisement. —" You can't overpraise these Kensitas, Bolitho." " No, Sir Edward, I was only afraid I had failed to convey their really remarkable quality." " *He is one of the happy authors who can establish in a few lines of dialogue both the social sphere and the individual tang of their characters*." But what else is dialogue for if it is not used to convey facts about the people who talk it ? He is, in fact, one of the happy authors who has taken up authorship—and been greeted with a salvo of applause, for writing a short story so good that " it sticks in your memory long after you have finished it ". This last expression reveals more than any, the barrenness and poverty of contemporary appreciation. One imagines how it would sound applied to *Lycidas* or *Hamlet*. Yet for a piece of writing to-day to " stick in your memory long after you have finished it " is a fact worth recording.

Then follows the dialogue, the zig-zag of talk, which, we are told, " has never been noted so economically as that, so surely or so truthfully before ". " Not even by me ? " exclaim perhaps from the shades, Flaubert, Dickens, Jane Austen, Chekov, Firbank, and George Moore ; and solemnly the answer reverberates, " not even by you." Meanwhile such is the power of this dialogue that " without a word of description, a whole background has sprung up behind them, houses, people, garages."—By using only the plain words, " She ", " I ", " You ", " Class of person ", " all our family ", " good teeth ", and " fellows ", the novelist has evoked by the magic of his art, a background of people, " people with houses ! " That he has also suggested " garages " to the reviewer is a masterstroke of implication.

I have also before me another document, a pamphlet published by *Left Review*, " *Authors take sides on the Spanish War* ". In this one hundred and fifty writers answer the question : " Are you for or against the legal government and the people of Republican Spain ? Are you for or against Franco and Fascism ? "

A hundred and fifty answers to a question that is not elastic must of necessity exhibit a certain sameness, but anybody reading through them must have been struck less by the uniformity than by the poverty of the diction, the clichés, the absence of distinction, or of any phrases which could be used as slogans, despite the sincerity of the contributors. I quote three examples, one of moth-eaten Mandarin (note the air of self-conscious loftiness which sets the author above the Spanish people, and the English reader), one of typical modern journalism, (the clichés are underlined), and one of the You-man He-man type in the new vernacular.

(1) In Politics, I care chiefly that a man's thought be not regimented or his art censored, and that he may live as long as he pleases so long as, within a rule of law he has shared in making, he offer no violence to the health and integrity of others. Neither contestant in Spain aims at this, and between them I will not choose, thinking it better to preserve the surviving liberties of England and France within the peace of Europe than to persecute in the false belief that the only alternative to a tyranny of the Right is a tyranny of the Left. (Charles Morgan.)

(2) As one who has *no political axe to grind*, is *attached to no political party* and detests all tyrannical government *whether it be of the Right or the Left*, I believe that the subjugation of the people of Republican Spain by Franco and his *foreign confederates will, if it is effected, mark the end of freedom and civilisation in Europe.* Fascism—which in practice is *merely gangsterism on a national scale*—involves the enslavement of peoples, *the destruction of culture*, and the persecution of *all real religion.* *And it depends for its*

102

continued existence on the perpetual fomentation of new wars. *In the light of recent history*, and of history *now in the making*, I am astonished that *any man or woman of good will* can *remain blind to these plain facts.* (Gerald Bullett.)

(3) Don't be a lot of saps. If X and Y want to cut one another's throats over Z, why on earth must people who do not believe in the ideas propounded by either X, Y or Z have to " choose between them " ? If you want to know, I do think Fascism is lousy. So is your Communism, only more so. But there are other ideas in the world besides either of them—thank God (whom neither of you believe in).

For the love of Mike cut loose from this fixation that the artist can no longer have the guts to be what every artist worth his salt has always been—*an individualist.* . . . (May I say how much I like your postal address ?) Yours contemptuously, Sean O'Faolain.

· · · · · · ·

That is the situation. Is there any hope ? Is there a possibility of a new kind of prose developing out of a synthesis of Orlando and the Tough Guy ? Will the strong writers of the colloquial school heighten the form of their work or the Formalists deepen their content ? We must look to the poets for a lead, for there are signs that from them is coming a revival of imaginative prose. I like to detect a foreshadowing of it in Landor's description of the lioness with her young, which appears, like an oasis, in Richard's *Principles of Literary Criticism.*

On perceiving the countryman, she drew up her feet gently, and squared her mouth, and rounded her eyes, slumberous with content, and they looked, he said, like sea-grottoes, obscurely green, interminably deep, at once awakening fear and stilling and suppressing it.

103

Such a phrase belongs to the real texture of prose, a texture now rarely seen, where syntax and a rich vocabulary are woven in a pattern to match the thought of the maker.

> I know that I am I, living in a small way in a temperate zone, blaming father, jealous of son, confined to a few acts often repeated, easily attracted to a limited class of physique, yet envying the simple life of the gut, desiring the certainty of the breast or prison, happiest sawing wood, only knowledge of the real disturbances in the general law of the dream ; the quick blood fretting against the slowness of the hope ; a unit of life, needing water and salt, that looks for a sign.
>
> .   .   .   .   .   .
>
> From the immense bat-shadow of home ; from the removal of land-marks, from appeals for love and from the comfortable words of the devil, from all opinions and personal ties ; from pity and shame ; and from the wish to instruct . . . in the moment of vision ; in the hour of applause ; in the place of defeat ; and in the hour of desertion, O Holmes, Deliver us.
>
> .   .   .   .   .   .

These two quotations from *The Orators* (W. H. Auden ; Faber, 1932) show imaginative prose coming to life again by way of a young poet imitating Rimbaud and the Prayer Book. And when the language comes to life, it ceases to be an imitation. The prose of Spender is also unusual, and in his critical book, *The Destructive Element*, he makes a study of that great Mandarin, Henry James, which must affect the values of any contemporary who reads it, for he has restated to his generation the relationship between writing and ethics. The revival of the poetical drama and the Group Theatre gives writers

104

like Eliot, Auden, Isherwood, and MacNeice opportunities for declamatory and non-commercial prose.

Other glimpses of a revival in imaginative writing may be found in George Barker's *Janus* (Faber, 1935) Hugh Sykes-Davies *Petron* (Dent), Davy Jones' *In Parenthesis* (Faber), Djuna Barnes' *Night wood* (Faber), Henry Miller's *Tropic of Cancer* (Obelisk Press), and Henry Green's remarkable novel *Living* (Dent).[1]

One further question is raised by Maugham. " I have never had much patience ", he states, " with the writers who claim from the reader an effort to understand their meaning." This is an abject surrender, for it is part of the tragedy of modern literature that the author, anxious to avoid mystifying the reader, is afraid to demand of him any exertions. " Don't be afraid of me," he exclaims, " I write exactly as I talk—no, better than that—exactly as you talk." Imagine painters painting or Beethoven composing ' exactly as he talked ' ! The only way to write is to consider the reader to be the author's equal ; to treat him otherwise is to set a value on illiteracy and all that results from Maugham's condescension to a reader from whom he expects no effort, is a latent hostility to him, as of some great chef waiting on a hungry Australian. As Richards says of the poet : " It is hard and, in fact, impossible, to deny him his natural and necessary resources on the ground

[1] Readers who find the lioness quotation to stir them, like the memory of something of which they have been long deprived, may amuse themselves in searching for this quality in modern prose, this combination of imagination and accuracy into magic, and they will be fortunate if they can discover a single example.

that a majority of his readers will not understand. This is not his fault but the fault of the social structure."

For a book to be written at the present time with any hope of lasting half a generation, of outliving a dog, or a car, of surviving the lease of a house or the life of a bottle of champagne, it must be written against the current, in a prose which both makes demands on the resources of our language and the intelligence of the reader. From the Mandarins it must borrow art and patience, the striving for perfection, the horror of clichés, the creative delight in the material, in the possibilities of the long sentence, the splendour and subtlety of the composed phrase.

From the Mandarins, on the other hand, the new writer will learn not to capitalise indolence and egotism nor to burden a sober and delicate language with exhibitionism. There will be no false hesitation and woolly profundities, no mystifying, no Proustian onanism. He will distrust the armchair clowns, the easy philosophers, the prose charmers. He will not show off his small defects, his preferences or his belongings, his cat and pipe and carpet slippers, bad memory, clumsiness with machinery, absent-mindedness, capacity for losing things, ignorance of business, of everything which might make the reader think he wrote for money. There will be no whimsy, allusiveness, archaism, pedantic usages, wrong colloquialisms, or sham lyrical outbursts ; there will be no " verily " and " verity ", no " when all is said and done ", no " to my way of thinking ", " hardly of my own choosing ", " I may be very stupid but ",

106

and no " If it be a sin to be half in love with the old days then I must aver ", there will be no false relationship between art and experience, none of those dodges by which the sedentary man of letters is enabled to write about women, fighting, dancing, drink, by substituting a prepared set of literary equivalents, called Venus, Mars, Bacchus, and Terpsichore. References to infinity, the remoteness of the stars and planets, the littleness of man, the charm of dead civilisations, to Babylon and Troy, " on whose mouldering citadel lies the lizard like a thing of green bronze " will be suspect. The adventurers " among their books ", the explorer who never leaves his desk, will be required to live within their imagination's income.

From the realists, the puritans, the colloquial writers and talkie-novelists there is also much that he will take and much that he will leave. The cursive style, the agreeable manners, the precise and poetical impact of Forster's diction, the lucidity of Maugham, last of the great professional writers, the timing of Hemingway, the smooth cutting edge of Isherwood, the indignation of Lawrence, the honesty of Orwell, these will be necessary, and the touch of those writers of English who give to every word in their limited vocabulary its current topical value. But most it is construction that can be learnt from the realists, that discipline in the conception and execution of a book, that planning which gives simply-written things the power to endure, the pruning without which the imagination reverts to the wilderness.

107

But he will not borrow from realists, or from their imitators, the flatness of style, the homogeneity of outlook, the fear of eccentricity, the reporter's horror of distinction, the distrust of beauty, the cult of a violence and starkness that is masochistic. Nor will he adopt the victory mentality of those left-wing writers who imagine themselves already to be the idols of a conquering proletariat, and who give their laws in simple matter-of-fact hard-hitting English to a non-existent congregation. That time is not yet ; the artist to-day is in the position of a patient Mahomet to whom the great art-hating mountain of the British public must eventually come.

This would seem the state of our literature. The battle between the schools I think has been proved to exist, but as with all civil wars, there are places where and moments when the fight rages with greater violence than at others. I have concentrated on writers at the forefront in that battle, and any criticism I have made of them is intended only to relate them to that battle. Thus to call Proust a bad influence is not to deny that he is a great writer, but to consider his work in terms of what can be learnt from it to-day. It is the privilege of living in the twentieth century that one can take both sides in controversies.

What I claim is that there is action and reaction between these styles, and that necessary as it was, and victorious though it seems, the colloquial style of the last few years is doomed and dying. Style, as I have tried to show, is a relationship between a writer's mastery of form and his intellectual or emotional content.   Mastery of form has lately been held, with reason, to conceal a poverty of content, but this is not inevitable, and for too long writers have had to prove their sincerity by going before the public in sackcloth and ashes, or, rather, a fifty-shilling suit and a celluloid collar.   Now the moment has come when the penance is complete, and they may return to their old habit.   It is not a question of taking sides about one way of writing or another, but a question of timing, for the you-man writing of he-men authors is going out, and the form must be enriched again.   Our language is a sulky and inconstant beauty, and it is important to know at any given moment what liberties she will permit.   Now all seems favourable.   Experiment and adventure is indicated, the boom of the twenties has been paid for by the slump of the thirties ; let us try and break the vicious circle by returning to a controlled expenditure, a balanced literary budget, a reasoned extravagance.

PART II

THE CHARLOCK'S SHADE

The Strongest Poison ever known
Came from Cæsar's Laurel Crown.

BLAKE.

CHAPTER X

THE BLIGHTED RYE

WE have seen to what extent the style of a book may effect its expectation of life, passing through a charnel house where we have observed the death and decomposition of many works, confident, ten years ago, of longevity, hailed as masterpieces of their period, and now equal in decay. A few, only, present an air of health, and claim some immunity from the venom of time. It is necessary now to analyse the conditions which govern the high rate of mortality among contemporary writers, to enter a region, " where the thin harvest waves its wither'd ears . . ." a sombre, but, to those for whom it is not too late, a bracing territory.

There thistles stretch their prickly arms afar,
And to the ragged infant threaten war ;
There Poppies nodding, mock the hope of toil,
There the blue Bugloss paints the sterile soil ;
Hardy and high, above the slender sheaf,
The slimy Mallow waves her silky leaf ;
O'er the young shoot the Charlock throws a shade,
And clasping Tares cling round the sickly blade ;
With mingled tints the rocky coasts abound,
And a sad splendour vainly shines around.

Let the " thin harvest " be the achievement of young authors, the " wither'd ears " their books, then the " militant thistles " represent politics, the " nodding poppies " day-dreams, conversation, drink and other narcotics, the " blue Bugloss " is the clarion call of journalism, the " slimy mallow " that of worldly success, the " charlock " is sex with its obsessions, and the " clasping tares " are the ties of duty and domesticity. The " mingled tints " are the varieties of talent which appear ; the " sad splendour " is that of their vanished promise. These enemies of literature, these parasites on genius we must examine in detail ; they are blights from which no writer is immune.

Before making further use of Crabbe's description of the heath, with it's convenient symbols, the question must be answered which is put by certain literary die-hards, old cats who sit purring over the mouse-holes of talent waiting for what comes out. " Is this age ", they pretend to ask," more unfavourable for writers than any other ? Have not writers always had great difficulty in surviving ? Indeed, their path to-day seems much easier than it was, to give an example, for myself ! " The answer, if they wanted an answer, is yes. Yes, because a writer needs money more than in the ivory tower decade, since he can no longer live in a cottage in the country meditating a blank verse historical drama and get the best out of himself. Yes, because he is more tempted to-day than at any other time by remunerative substitutes for good writing, journalism, reviewing advertising, the cinema, but most of all because a writer to-day can have no confidence in posterity and therefore is inclined to lack the strongest inducement to good work, the desire for survival prominent even in the philistine Butler.

For it is clear that " posterity " to Butler, writing in the last century, meant the reading public of the next few hundred years, while the uncertainties of fame have so increased since then that Maugham confines it to two generations. A writer to-day must grow used to the idea that culture as we know it may disappear and remain lost for ever, or till it is excavated, a thousand years hence, from a new Herculaneum. Horace's boast of immortality, his " *non omnis moriar* ", did not anticipate the hostility of the church nor the ignorance of the Dark Ages. Of his two thousand years of posthumous life, a thousand went by in a coma. One has only to consider the dearth of writers in Italy and Germany, the extinction of the cultural activity of the Weimar republic, or the war waged by those countries against the intelligentsia of Spain, to realise how ephemeral are to-day the securest literary reputations, the most flourishing movements. At any moment the schools of Athens may be closed, the libraries burnt, the teachers exterminated, the language suppressed. Any posthumous fame, the existence of any posterity capable of appreciating the arts we care for, can be guaranteed only by fighting for it, and for many who fight, there will be no stake in the future but a name on a warmemorial.

Often the love of posthumous fame is a psychological substitute for the love of perfection, even as the love of perfection may prove a projection into the world of art of our sense of guilt. Thus Astrologers find this love of perfection to go with being born under the sign of Virgo ; it is to the artist what virginity is to the nun, and they declare this love of purification confined to those born between the end of August and the end of September. To-day a writer should be less conscious of such abstractions as perfection and posterity, " the cackle of the unborn about the grave ", he should be above a flirtation with time, determined only to restore to the world in a form worthy of his powers something of what he has taken from it. He must be a helping writer, telling us what he sees through his periscope, or there will be no writers and no readers left.

Otherwise Butler has stated the problem clearly. What ruins young writers is over-production. The need for money is what causes over-production ; therefore writers must have private incomes. " No gold, no holy ghost." Genius is independent of money, but the world will destroy it if it can. A writer, then, to avoid over-production, unless he acquires a private income, must either learn to make more money from his books, or to earn money in other ways congenial to the writing of them.

To make more money from a book it is necessary either to potboil, to give way to the taste of the reading public at the expense of the judgment of the author, or to find technical ways of improving sales. The other ways of earning money and still finding time to write, consist of journalism, teaching, advertising, the civil service, and the family business. Journalism will be discussed separately. Of the other remedies, teaching provides long holidays, and the work is not such as to make inroads on the creative imagination, but not many people can teach or enjoy teaching, and in spite of the long holidays, the work seems to make any enlargement of the writer's experience awkward and unwelcome. Of the dons at Oxford and Cambridge remarkably few attain literary eminence, and the best known among them are the writers who have mixed in the world outside the universities. This is more true of schoolmasters. Nor is the Civil Service the Parnassus which it was in the nineties ; its talent seems to have run dry with Humbert Wolfe. Since being a civil servant is a static, arid, and parasitic occupation, it is not likely that anyone who is content with it will possess the imagination which creates, or the talent which will mature and ripen.

Most unsatisfactory is advertising, for there is something about copy-writing which so resembles the composition of lyric poetry as to replace its process. When a writer, in order to satisfy a corset manufacturer in search of a slogan, has to think of the rousing or the lapidary phrase, the assonance of vowels and consonants, the condensation of thought, the inflections of delicate meaning at his disposal, he will be in no mood to write anything else. The family business, if we have such a family and if it does no business, is the best way out.

An outside job is harmful to a writer in proportion as it approximates to his vocation. Thus reviewing poetry is the worst profession for a poet, while even advertising, journalism or lecturing pluck feathers from the phœnix of inspiration and cast them on the wind. Living at home, on the other hand, confines the writer's experience to the family circle ; rich marriages do not usually go with congenial tastes or a mutual love of the literary life, and patrons are capricious and hard to come by ; besides, a relationship with one in these days is open to imputation.

It is curious that while the brief-flowering and quick extinction of modern talent is everywhere so apparent, yet little should have been written on the subject. Our two sages, Pearsall-Smith and Maugham, croak their warnings, but there is no sign that they are regarded.

As soon as any glimmering of talent, any freshness or originality, makes its appearance, it is immediately noted and exploited [Pearsall-Smith, *Prospects of Literature* (Hogarth Press, 1927)]. Editors of the weekly and even of the daily papers seize upon it ; they have acquired, one may almost say of them, the habits of cannibals or ogres ; they suck the brains of young writers, and then replace them by a new bevy of adolescent talent. Publishers also compete nowadays with editors in killing the goose whose golden eggs they live on. As soon as a young author makes a success his publisher urges him to repeat it at once ; other publishers are eager to win his patronage, and he is not infrequently offered a fixed income on the condition that he shall regularly provide one or two volumes a year. It would be invidious to mention names, but in following the careers of the more recent writers whose first books have charmed me, I almost invariably find that their earliest publications, or at least their earliest successes, are their best achievements ; their promise ripens to no fulfilment ; each subsequent work tends to be a feeble replica and fainter echo of the first.

Maugham is more inclined to blame the talent that

118

is so easily exhausted, and which he calls " the natural creativity of youth ".

> One of the tragedies of the arts is the spectacle of the vast numbers of persons who have been misled by this passing fertility to devote their lives to the effort of creation. Their invention deserts them as they grow older, and they are faced with the long years before them in which, unfitted by now for a more humdrum calling, they harass their wearied brain to beat out material it is incapable of giving them. They are lucky when, with what bitterness we know, they can make a living in ways, like journalism or teaching, that are allied to the arts.

The causes are interlocking. The trouble is that authors are not paid enough. If three hundred pounds were the normal advance on a book instead of fifty, a writer could take his time over it and refuse other work ; that it is not is due to the intermediate profits and expenses of book production, and to the indifference of the reading public, which is growing more impatient with books as it becomes more dependent on magazines. " The Reader's Digest " and its fellows will soon read the books for him.

The torpor of the reading public conditions the publisher; parsimonious to authors who fail to dispel that torpor, he is exacting and impatient with those who have succeeded. When publishers vacillate (and as repressed sadists are supposed to become policemen or butchers, so those with an irrational fear of life become publishers), the second villain, the editor, steps in— even Tennyson complained of him. " All the magazines and daily newspapers, which pounce upon everything they can get hold of, demoralise literature. This age gives an author no time to mature his work."

CHAPTER XI

THE BLUE BUGLOSS

LET us now tackle the problem of journalism—deadliest of the weeds on Crabbe's Heath—in its relation to literature. We have seen that the difference between them is that journalism must obtain its full impact on the first reading, while literature can achieve its effects on a second, being intended for an interested and not an indifferent public. Consequently the main difference between them is one of texture. Journalism is loose, intimate, simple, and striking ; literature formal and compact, not simple, and not immediately striking in its effects. Carelessness is not fatal to journalism, nor are clichés, for the eye rests lightly on them. But what is intended to be read once can seldom be read more than once ; a journalist has to accept the fact that his work, by its very to-dayness, is excluded from any share in to-morrow. Nothing dates like a sense of actuality, than which nothing in journalism is more valuable. A writer who takes up journalism abandons the slow tempo of literature for a faster one, and the change will do him harm. By degrees the flippancy of journalism will become a habit and the pleasure of being paid on the nail, and especially of being praised on the nail, grow indispensable. And yet, of the admirable journalism that has appeared in the literary weeklies, how little bears reprinting, how little even has been reprinted! The monthly and quarterly papers approximate more to literature and permit subjects to be treated at greater length, but there are few of them! For length is all-important; it is the two-thousand word look which betrays journalism, which makes the reader hurry on when he opens a volume of criticism, and finds it to consist of jerky and disjointed essays, " The Prose of Keats ", " Beddoes Revisited ", " The English Hexameter ", " Hazlitt's Aunt ", " After Expressionism What ? ", " Miss Austen's Nephew ", all with the fatal asterisk directing the reader to the title of the book reviewed.

There are certain people who benefit from journalism. They are easily recognised and fall into two classes. The first are amateur writers who through lack of a public, or through not having to consider a public, are verbose and obscure, who have acquired so many mannerisms, or private meanings for the words they use, or who employ such leisurely constructions that only an editor, since they will not listen to their friends, can cure them. The other class who benefit are the well-stored minds who suffer from psychological sloth, and can only reveal their treasures in short articles for quick returns. But this class includes few young writers, and they would soon succumb to the atmosphere that is breathed with impunity by a Hazlitt or a wise old literary editor.

There is one other fortunate class : those who are masters of a literary style which so resembles journalism that they can make the transition from one tempo to the other without effort. Readers of *Abinger Harvest* by E. M. Forster will have found that there is about those essays nothing ephemeral since they are in the language of E. M. Forster the novelist. His literary style is cursive and no concession has to be made. The styles overlap ; the tempos coincide. This is also true of Lytton Strachey, who imposed his literary style on his editors. To-day there are several writers in the same position as Forster. The danger for them is that, if their journalism is literature, their literature is journalism, and Hemingway, for example, appears unable to distinguish between them, which accounts for the unevenness of such books as *Green Hills of Africa* or *Death in the Afternoon.*

Maugham detects another evil in journalism besides the vulgarisation of a writer's style.

> There is an impersonality in a newspaper that insensibly affects the writer. People who write much for the press seem to lose the faculty of seeing things for themselves ; they see them from a generalised standpoint, vividly often, sometimes with hectic brightness, yet never with that idiosyncracy which may give only a partial picture of the facts, but is suffused by the personality of the observer. The press, in fact, kills the individuality of those who write for it.

Journalism for most writers means reviewing.

Let Walter Savage Shelleyblake be a young author. Let his book be called *Vernal Aires.* Soon will come the delicious summons from the literary editor of *The Blue Bugloss.* " Dear Shelleyblake, I was so interested to meet you the other night, and have the chance to tell

you what I think of *Vernal Aires.* I have been
wondering if you would like to try your hand at a
little reviewing for us. We are looking for someone to
do the Nonsuch *Boswell,* and your name cropped
up."

The Nonsuch *Boswell* alone is worth four guineas,
and soon a signed review, " Expatriate from Auch-
inleck ", by Walter Savage Shelleyblake, appears in
the literary supplement of the *Blue Bugloss.* It is
full of ideas, and Mr. Vampire, the editor, bestows
on it his praise. The next book which Shelleyblake
reviews, on Erasmus Darwin, is not so good, but his
article, " Swansong at Lichfield ", is considered " extremely bright ". Suddenly his name appears under
a pile of tomes of travel ; the secrets of Maya jungles,
Kenya game-wardens, and ricochetting American
ladies are probed, by him. In a year's time he will
have qualified as a maid-of-all-work and be promoted
to reviewing novels. It is promotion because the
novel review is a regular feature, because more people
read them, and because publishers " care ". If he is
complimentary and quotable he will be immortalized
on the dust wrapper, and find his name in print on
the advertisements. And eight or ten novels a fortnight, sold as review copies, add to his wage.

Certain facts must now be made clear. However
much Mr. Vampire admired *Vernal Aires* and however
fond he is of Walter Shelleyblake, he is, before anything else, an editor. He is concerned with *The Blue
Bugloss* and whether each number is bright enough
to paint the sterile soil. In so far as he is developing
in Walter latent gifts, competence, a turn for satire,

lucidity, polish, his interests coincide ; but they can never be the same, and how Walter employs those gifts, is not his own concern but Mr. Vampire's. The competition for the best books, the Nonsuch *Boswells*, is fierce, Mr. Vampire is often lucky to get one of them himself, and so if Shellyblake is anxious to write several thousand words on the influence of Horace on English poetry, or the psychological reasons for the retirement of Congreve, he will have to go on being anxious, and hurry up with his copy on *Backstairs and Petticoats* (a chronicle of famous Royal Mistresses), or six autobiographies, headed by *Fifty Years Down Under*.

Myself a lazy, irresolute person, overvain and over-modest, unsure in my judgments, and unable to finish what I have begun, I have profited from journalism, owing to the admirable manipulation of my manager and trainer. Yet even so I would say to Shelleyblake, who clearly does not belong to the Hazlitt group, that any other way of making money would be better, that reviewing is a whole-time job with a half-time salary, a job in which the best in him is generally expended on the mediocre in others. A good review is only remembered for a fortnight ; a reviewer has always to make his reputation afresh, nor will he find time for private reading or writing, for he is too busy reading other people's books, and this will disincline him to read when he is not working. The sight of his friends' books accumulating depresses him, and he knows that, besides losing the time to write books of his own, he is also losing the energy and the application, frittering it away on trash, and discovering that it is his flashiest efforts which receive most praise.

There are only four or five posts in reviewing that carry with them money, freedom and dignity, whose holders can inherit the mantle of Arnold and Sainte-Beuve, so that the most Shelleyblake can expect is that, by reading two books a day and writing for three papers, he may make about four hundred a year. During this time he will incur the hostility of authors, the envy of other reviewers, and the distrust of his friends, against whose books he will seem invariably prejudiced ; the public will view him with indifference or accept him as an eccentric on whom they will launch their views and their manuscripts, while old friends will greet him with, " Are you writing anything now ? "—" apart of course from your articles," they will add. " I read you—but I don't say I agree with you," will be another approach, to which, " I know you, but I don't say I like you," is the correct answer.

No, if Walter Shelleyblake must be a journalist, there is only one chance for him. He must declare war on his employers, and so manœuvre them that he never reviews a bad book, never reviews more than one at a time, and never writes a review that cannot be reprinted, that is not of some length, and on a subject of permanent value. He will know that the bad books he reads are like hours on a sundial, *vulnerant omnes, ultima necat,* all wound, the last one is fatal, nor will he spend himself on cheap subjects, nor put down his whole view of life in a footnote, for he will write only about what interests him. But whatever happens to him (and there are no pensions for literary hacks), he must realise that he is not indispensable.

> Brightness falls from the air,
> Queens have died young and fair . . .

but not *The Blue Bugloss*, and Mr. Vampire and his new young men are perfectly able to get on without him.

CHAPTER XII

THE THISTLES

AT the moment politics, the thistles

> . . . that stretch their prickly arms afar,
> And to the ragged infant threaten war

are more dangerous to young writers than journalism. They are dangerous because writers to-day feel that politics are necessary to them, but have not yet learnt how best to be political.

Indifference to politics among artists has always gone with a feeling of impotence. Thus the great non-politicals, the ivory-tower dwellers, flourished helpless, under the second Empire, or in the Paris of 1870, after defeat in the Franco-Prussian war. English writers, in the late Victorian age, were equally helpless ; only Kipling, who celebrated the jingoism and imperialism of the ruling class, and the materialism of the time, and Shaw who attacked them, obtained a political foothold. The " nineties " were a reaction of artists against a political world they abhorred and could not alter. Only William Morris, of the Victorian writers, combined poetry with socialism, and Tennyson's conception of the role of the poet as the supreme Endorser of new achievement in material progress, was so forbidding as to deter younger writers from taking any interest in such subjects. This widespread indifference to politics crystallised into a theory that politics were harmful, that they were not artistic material of the first order, that an artist could not be a politician. Politics belonged to that realm of action which Proust and Strachey had discredited. A belief in action indicated a belief in progress, a belief in progress was Victorian and ridiculous.

Yet if we look at writers through the ages we see that they have always been political. Greek poets were political, they championed democracy or defended oligarchs and tyrants according to their sentiment. Pindar was political, so were Aeschylus and Euripides, Plato and Aristotle, Catullus and Cicero, Virgil and Horace. Dante was engrossed in politics as were most of the artists of the Renaissance. Nobody told Byron he would be a better writer if he did not attempt *The Vision of Judgment*, or Wordsworth not to bother with *Toussaint l'Ouverture* ; Swift was not considered to have cheapened himself by *The Drapier Letters* or *The Conduct of the Allies*, nor Dryden to have let down poetry by *Absalom and Achitophel*. To deny politics to a writer is to deny him part of his humanity. But even from a list of political writers we can deduce that there are periods in the history of a country when writers are more political, or more writers are political, than at others. They are not the periods of greatest political tension, they are the periods in which the writers can do most, can be listened to, can be important, influence people, and get their way. Thus Roman writers ceased to

128

be political after the Empire because they were powerless. A writer during the age of Augustus could not play the part of Cicero. Writers flourish in a state of political flux, on the eve of the crisis, rather than in the crisis itself; it is before a war or a revolution that they are listened to, and come into their own, and it was because they were disillusioned at their impotence during the war that so many became indifferent to political issues after the peace.

It is clear that we are living now in a transition period as suited to political writing as were the days of Ship Money or the reign of Queen Anne. To-day writers can still change history by their pleading, and one who is not political neglects the vital intellectual issues of his time, and disdains his material. He is not powerless, like the Symbolists of 1870, the æsthetes of the eighties and nineties, the beer-and-chivalry addicts of the nineteen hundreds or the demobilised Georgian poet on his chicken farm. He is not a victim of his time but a person who can alter it, though if he does not, he may well be victimised. He has to be political to realise himself, and he must go on being political to protect himself. To-day the forces of life and progress are ranging on one side, those of reaction and death on the other. We are having to choose between democracy and fascism, and fascism is the enemy of art. It is not a question of relative freedom, there are no artists in Fascist countries. We are not dealing with an Augustus who will discover his Horace and his Virgil, but with Attila, or Hulaku, destroyers of European culture, whose poets can contribute only battle-cries and sentimental drinking songs. Capitalism in decline, as in our own country, is not much better as a patron than fascism. Stagnation, fear, violence and opportunism the characteristics of capitalism preparing for the fray, are no background for a writer, and there is a seediness, an ebb of life, a philosophy of taking rather than giving, a bitterness and brutality about right-wing writers now which was absent in those of other days, in seventeenth-century Churchmen or eighteenth-century Tories. There is no longer a Prince Rupert, a Doctor Johnson, a Wellington, Disraeli, or Newman, on the reactionary side.

We have seen that writers are politically-minded when they are able to accomplish something ; that these periods are those of change, on the eve of revolutions and civil wars, and before the resort to arms takes matters out of their control, and we have seen that we are in such a period now, and that unless writers do what they can it will be too late, war will break out, and the moment be past when the eloquence of the artist can influence the destiny of humanity.

If political writing is simply the exercise of the instinct of self-preservation, there can be no reason for classing " politics " among the weeds ,that stifle writers. But there are dangers about being political which writers are unaware of, and seldom avoid. Thus being political is apt to become a whole time job ;

> To-day the expending of powers
> On the flat ephemeral pamphlet and the boring meeting,

writes Auden, though copies of his pamphlets are

excessively rare. For sensitive writers, canvassing, making speeches, and pamphleteering are not the best medium. They involve much time and can be better done by someone else. To command a listening senate, however, is a secret ambition of many writers, and it is easy to justify it to be " thankful that my words can be any comfort to these poor men ", etc. The truth is that oratory is a coarser art than writing, and to become addicted to it, is to substitute the ruses of the platform for the integrity of the pen. Neither is a writer improved by sitting on committees, and cultivating the chairmanities.

Another effect of being too political is that such activity leads to disillusion. Thus writers become disheartened by the vulgarity of politicians. They find it hard to realise that the militants and executives of a movement may be narrow-minded, envious, ambitious and ungrateful, yet the cause remain fundamentally just and right. Their political judgment is often unsound, for they refuse to allow for the slow motion of public opinion; they are disheartened by personal rebuffs, and bored by drudgery. Defeatism is their occupational disease.

Politicians, on their side, can be unappreciative. The arts they prefer are those which are enjoyed in relaxation, light music or Mickey Mouse, the Oxford Book of English Verse, Edgar Wallace, Wodehouse, Webb. They do not want art to be exacting and difficult ; they may envy the artists who collaborate with them because they can not understand their success, but they seem to them, with their idealism and their tender consciences, priggish and patronising.

131

The enmities of highbrow and lowbrow, man of action and man of thought, classical side and modern side, are not yet buried, and they reappear, over the ephemeral pamphlet or at the boring meeting, in unexpected forms.

In what way then should a writer be political ? How can he make best use of his weapons ?

Firstly, by satire. This is a satirical age, and among the vast reading public the power of an artist to awaken ridicule has never been so great. To make the enemies of freedom look silly, to write like Low's cartoons, or like

> I met murder on the way,
> He wore the mask of Castlereagh,

is the duty of any writer who can.

Then, if he is intelligent, he can analyse situations, draw attention to tendencies, expose contradictions and help his more active colleagues by cultivating lucidity, profundity, and detachment. And lastly, he can contribute the idealism without which any movement fails. He must, in his serious writing, avoid propaganda, and by propaganda I mean the presence in his work of lumps of unassimilated political material.[1] His role is to digest, like the termites who

---

[1] It is objectionable because it introduces into the form a lower level of workmanship, that of the pamphlet or the tract, and an imperfect fusion with the creative process. Propaganda is betrayed by an air of naïveté, as in, " To-morrow he would canvas as he had never canvassed before," and " I had met the insidious power of Ann and defeated it, and now there was a splendid synthesis forming inside me," or " He was an admirable man and I felt warmed and happy when I looked at him. At Oxford he got up and stretched. I think he had read every word

chew up the food for the fighters, the experience they bring him. For this reason the poets are the best political writers, for they have the best digestions, and can absorb their material. A poem like *Locksley Hall*, which has been so distilled, remains an alive and contemporary piece of thought.

Men, my brothers, men the workers, ever reaping something new :
That which they have done but earnest of the things that they
    shall do.
For I dipt into the future, far as human eye could see,
Saw the vision of the world, and all the wonder that would be ;
Saw the heavens fill with commerce, argosies of magic sails,
Pilots of the purple twilight, dropping down with costly bales ;
Heard the heavens fill with shouting, and there rain'd a ghastly
    dew
From the nation's airy navies grappling in the central blue.

The " ghastly dew " must have seemed an absurd conceit a hundred years ago. Another passage is, even more up-to-date.

I must mix myself with action lest I wither in despair
What is that which I should turn to, lighting upon days like these ?
Every door is barred with gold, and opens but to golden keys,
Every gate is thronged with suitors, all the markets overflow
I have but an angry fancy : what is that which I should do ?

---

of the *Daily Worker* in the eighty minutes since we had left Paddington." Those are from a very young author. Here is an example from Upward :
    " ' There will be a time of harshness and bitter struggle, but out of it will come flowers ; splendour and joy will come back to the world. And life will be better than it has ever been in the world's history.'
    " ' How soon can I join the worker's movement ? '
    " ' . . . You can join some time within the next few days.'
    " ' I don't want to wait.' "
This passage in a thoughtful novel brings a whiff of the Salvation Army. Right-wing propaganda, however, can be detected by an appeal to the reader to be " realistic."

Similarly the best modern political writing is in such a book as Spender's *Trial of a Judge*, or a poem like Day Lewis's,

Yet living here,
As one between two massing powers I live,
Whom neutrality cannot save
Nor occupation cheer.

The novelists who feel their responsibilities are also searching for something deeper and more universal than superficial realism, and are finding it in the allegory. A story of Isherwood like *The Novaks*, shows how political reality can inform and deepen, can be informed and deepened, by private experiences ; and Spender's *Cousins* and his *Burning Cactus* are also excellent illustrations. To strike deep and keep general should be the maxim of the writer, and he should avoid describing any experience that he has not first integrated, and made part of him. He must take pains with his vocabulary, for political writing is honeycombed with clichés ; having been deadened to their meaning by oratory politicians have no feeling for words ; a phrase which seems healthy at night will be on the sick list by morning. There is a tendency for left-wing journalists to criticise left-wing poets for being obscure, which is dangerous and stupid. The public are not expected to understand the formulas from which are evolved a new explosive or a geodetic aeroplane. The poet is a chemist, and there is more pure revolutionary propaganda in a line of Blake than in all *The Rights of Man*.

But if he wishes to be respected and let alone

by politicians, to be treated as an ally to whom a certain eccentricity is permitted, a writer must let them alone and refrain from taking sides in political quarrels. There is a general left-wing position which has not been defined but which permits a working agreement with the parties, as they now stand, and which is well suited to a writer. To abandon this general position is safe for a militant journalist; for an artist, it may lead to a damaging retreat. There is so much side-choosing, heresy-hunting, witch-burning, and shadow cabinet-making among the parties of the left, so much victory mentality among people for whom victory is still uncertain, that caution in a writer should be welcome. It is no time to quarrel with one's own side.

I will conclude this excursion among the Thistles by quoting two points of view of left-wing writers, both communists, Upward and Stephen Spender. Upward, I find, is too logical for the times, his pronouncement on the only possible way for a writer to live is reminiscent of Tolstoy's socialist analysis of art which proved that Hugo's *Les Miserables* and Harriet Stowe's *Uncle Tom's Cabin* were the only two great books of the nineteenth century. Spender lacks the narrowness and aridity of Marxist critics.

A writer to-day who wishes to produce the best work that he is capable of producing, must first of all become a socialist in his practical life, must go over to the progressive side of the class conflict. . . . He must be told frankly that joining the workers' movement does mean giving less time to imaginative writing, but that unless he joins it his writing will become increasingly false, worthless as literature. Going over to socialism may prevent him,

135

but failing to go over *must* prevent him from writing a good book (*The Mind in Chains*).

What is meant by " going over " ?   Upward thinks it must mean the abandonment of the bourgeois life and immersion in the work of the socialist parties. I do not think so.   I think a writer " goes over " when he has a moment of conviction that his future is bound up with that of the working classes.   Once he has felt this his behaviour will inevitably alter. Often it will only be recognised by external symptoms, a disinclination to wear a hat or a stiff collar, an inability to be rude to waiters or taxi-drivers, or to be polite to young men his own age with rolled umbrellas, bowlers and " Mayfair men " moustaches, or to tolerate the repressive measures of his class. He is like a caterpillar whose skin dulls and whose appetite leaves it before becoming a chrysalis. Often a writer is unable to go over.   He approaches the barrier, shies, and runs away.   Such writers will externalise their feelings and satirise those who have made the transition, who have jumped off the slowly-moving train, for the one which they believe leads towards life and the future.   The angriest are the most frightened.   But these fears can be surmounted by a moment of vision.   It may be practical, a glimpse of the power of the writer in the socialist state, or of his impotence in a capitalist one, going in perhaps, like Turgeniev, sixty-first, at a fashionable dinner, or it may be a mystical feeling of release and emancipation.   It is too early yet to say whether writers have done anything for Spain, but it is clear that Spain has done a great deal for writers, since many have had that experience there, and have come back with their fear changed to love, isolation to union, and indifference to action.

> This is a time then when anyone who is anxious to avert a protracted world war will have to work very hard to undermine the whole system of armed alliances. If we hope to go on existing, if we want a dog's chance of the right to breathe, to go on being able to write, it seems that we have got to make some choice outside the private entanglements of our personal life. We have got to try somehow to understand that objective life moving down on us like a glacier, but which, after all, is essentially not a glacier is an historic process, the life of people like ourselves, and therefore our " proper study ".

> Ultimately, however interested the writer may be as a person, as an artist he has got to be indifferent to all but what is objectively true. The road the future will tread may be the road of Communism, but the road of the artist will always be some way infinitely more difficult than one which is laid down in front of him.

These two quotations are from Stephen Spender's *Destructive Element*, and express a point of view that is sometimes forgotten. Political writing is dangerous writing, it deals not in words, but in words that affect lives, and is a weapon that should only be entrusted to those qualified to use it. Thus a burst of felicitous militancy with the pen may send three young men to be killed in Spain, for whose deaths the author is responsible. If human beings have any right they have the right to know what they are dying for. " Better live an hour as a lion than a lifetime as a lamb " is stencilled all over Italy—but supposing one is a lamb ?

137

There is one final warning that must be given. In Blake's words, "The eagle never lost so much time as when it submitted to learn from the crow" —if one looks back at the political activities of artists, however necessary and satisfying they may have been at the time, now that time is past it is not by them they are remembered. Milton's poetry is read more than the *Areopagitica*. Marvell's pamphlets are read not at all, the political poems of Shelley and Byron are not preferred to their lyrics, the Houhynhims are more familiar to us than the *Conduct of the Allies*. *Robinson Crusoe* means more than the *True Born Englishman, The Lotus Eaters* than *Locksley Hall*. The writers who were most political in the last war are not the most famous, nor are the war records of Joyce, Lawrence, Firbank, Strachey, Garnett and Bertrand Russell the most inspiring. Realists, before they die for their country, are apt to consider too carefully what "dying" and what "country" ultimately mean. Zola was more political than Flaubert, Lamartine than Baudelaire, and the truth is that the value of political experience to a writer's art is indirect. Not Milton's polemical prose is the justification of his political life, but his character of Satan, his assemblages in Hell. And this is true to-day, so that a writer who cannot assimilate with genius the harsh fare of contemporary politics, had better keep out.

CHAPTER XIII

THE POPPIES

WE now come to the poppies, to the danger that is becoming known as " escapism ". This is not a significant word, for escaping in itself cannot be right or wrong, or worthy of comment until we know from what danger the escapist is fleeing, and whether flight is his best method of preservation. Escaping from a concentration camp or a burning building is admirable, escaping from responsibility, like the case who wrote to his psychiatrist that he was " only happy when he had cast off every shred of human dignity " is sometimes not. The word is usually employed by realists to beat romantics with, thus it was " escapist " to live at Tossa or Torre Molinos till 1936, but the centre of actuality shifted, and Sir Peter Chalmers-Mitchell, who retired to end his days in the sun, found himself, for a few hours in Malaga, in the intenser glare of History.[1]

[1] Expatriation is often beneficial, as a stage in which the writer cuts adrift from irritating influences. It is a mistake to expect good work from expatriates, for it is not what they do that matters, but what they are not doing. It gives them a breathing-space in which to free themselves from commercialism, family and racial ties, or from the " gentleman complex " which attacks public-school and university writers, just as the spectre of the " family business " haunts the American ones. Only occasionally

It is vain to accuse people of escaping from contemporary reality. Time is not the same for all of us, neither is our imagination's food nor our artistic material. We cannot all do our best work with the sun in our eyes. There is only one crime ; to escape from our talent, to abort that growth, which, ripening and maturing, must be the justification of the demands we make on society.

At present the realities are life and death, peace and war, fascism and democracy ; we are in a world which may become unfit for human beings to live in. A writer must decide at what remove from this conflagration he can produce his best work, and be careful to keep there. Often a writer who is escaping from his own talent, from the hound of heaven, will run into what appears to be reality, and, like a fox bolting into a farm kitchen will seek sanctuary in group activities from the pursuers outside. And after a time the hounds will be called off, the pursuit weaken, a signal that the Muses no longer wish to avail themselves of his potentialities. Thus among the hardest workers in political parties will be found,

does a writer make anything out of expatriation, Hemingway's *The Sun Also Rises* is such an exception. (Henry James was not an expatriate in so far as he repatriated himself as an Englishman—he exchanged American Society for international society and then settled down as an English man of letters.) It is important however to distinguish between the flight of the expatriate which is an essential desire for simplification, for the cutting of ties, the writer " finding " himself in the hotel bedroom or the café on the harbour, and the trajectory of the travel addict, trying not to find but to lose himself in the intoxication of motion. " How narrow is the line ", as Nicolson wrote of Byron's last journey, " which separates an adventure from an ordeal, and escape from exile."

140

like Rimbaud at Harar, those whom the God has forsaken.

To-day the old-fashioned boltholes of writers who do not wish to undertake the responsibility of creating a work of art, are not easy of access. Drink is available, and on the whole artists who drink to excess do so out of the consciousness of wasted ability, for drunkenness is a substitute for art, it is in itself a low form of creation. But it is not drink which is the temptation, since it is only a symptom of the desire for self-forgetfulness and the same is true of drugs, which play small part in the literary life in England, though among French writers opium has made headway.

More serious addictions are those to the harmless activities of day-dreaming and conversation. Day-dreaming bears a specious resemblance to the workings of the creative imagination. It is in fact a substitute for it, and one in which all the difficulties are shelved, all the problems ignored, a short cut ending in a blank wall. The same is true of conversation; a good talker can talk away the substance of twenty books in as many evenings. He will describe the central idea of a book he means to write until it revolts him.

Even as journalism brings in quicker returns than literature, so the profits of conversation are more immediate than those of journalism. A good talker is paid almost before he opens his mouth by the silence he commands, the luxury of his décor, the selected company who have been asked to meet him. The only happy talkers are dandies who extract

141

pleasure from the perishability of their material, and who would not be able to support the loneliness of other forms of composition, for most good talkers, when they have finished, are miserable, they know that they have talked too much, that they have thrown away material that should have a life of its own, in noises on the air.

Than good conversation nothing is sooner forgotten, and those who remember it do so unconsciously, and reproduce it as their own. Coleridge, Swinburne, Wilde, Harry Melville, Vernon Lee—not much survives now of the conversation of these mighty-mouthed, international talkers. They are at the mercy of a few indolent, forgetful, and envious listeners. If one tries to record the spoken word of one of these chrysostoms it becomes apparent that thirty per cent of their talk is a series of reassuring and persuasive qualifications, a buttonholing of the listener ; it is the ardour of the talker's wooing which convinces the audience of the splendour of his talk. This is not true of the talkers of the old school, like Bernard Berenson, who use their golden tongues for denunciation, but modern conversationalists make too free a use of the glad eye. They are apologetic, not only because they monopolise and individualise in an age opposed to these things, but because they are taking part in a ceremony of self-wastage, and because their audience knows it.

Sometimes when in flight from the demands of talent, from the bite of the gadfly, writers will seek refuge in gentility, in ancestor-worship, or by becoming members of an unliterary sporting class. They

142

will breed bulldogs, hunt, shoot, attend race-meetings, and try to lose contact with other writers, except those whose guilt is of equal standing. This instinct to hide themselves in a world where books are unheard of in no way resembles the artist's desire for " *luxe, calme, et volupté* ", for a lavish, ostentatious life, but is a particularly English affliction, and it is no exaggeration to say that every English writer since Byron and Shelley has been hamstrung by respectability and been prevented by snobbery and moral cowardice from attaining his full dimensions. It is this blight of insular gentility that accounts for the difference between Dickens, Thackeray, Arnold, Tennyson, Pater, and Tolstoy, Flaubert, Rimbaud, Baudelaire, Gide, it is the difference between being a good fellow and growing up.

There remains one other major escape, religion. It is not so common now for writers to join a church. I know two Anglo-Catholic and one Roman Catholic convert among the writers of to-day. All three are people of exceptional sensibility, poetically-minded writers for whom the ugliness of materialism is a source of horror. Are they escaping from their talent, or from conditions which would have rendered impossible the use of that talent ? It is too early to say. Religious faith involves the surrender of the intellect but not the surrender of the sensibility, and under its protection that may continue to develop. Yet joining a church implies regression for an intellectual writer, it is a putting on of blinkers, for a writer is hiding under the skirts of one of the great reactionary political forces of the world, and the poet drawn to the confessional and the smell of incense finds himself defending the garotte and Franco's Moors. Churches are the retreat of artists with æsthetic appreciation, delicate humour, ethical sensibility, and a sense of spiritual reality, but without the enquiring mind, the constructive intellectual fearlessness which is the historic factor in western civilisation, and which has moved far onwards from religion.

But in vain we discuss the nature of the poppies which put writers to sleep, or try to restrict their use. If they are indulged in by people who are seeking to escape their talent, we must find out why they are escaping. Many escape for psychological reasons which belong to their childhood, and with which this book is not competent to deal. But in writers who have dried up, who have put their hobby before their vocation, who now are doing well in the city or who collect first editions or old dust-wrappers, who run chicken-farms, or set and solve Greek cross-word puzzles, who write detective stories, or who have transferred their sensibility to cheese and old claret, there is one fact in common. They have all been promising.

Promise ! Fatal word, half-bribe and half-threat, in childhood round its exact meaning centred many tearful interviews. " But you promised you wouldn't ", " but that wasn't a promise ", " Yes it was—you haven't kept your promise ", till the meaning expands, and the burden of the oath under which we grew up becomes the burden of expectations that we can never fulfil. " Blossom and blossom

144

and promise of blossom, but never a fruit "—the cry, first heard in the nursery, is taken up by the schoolmaster, the friendly aunt, the doting grandmother, the inverted bachelor uncle. Dons, with long reproachful faces will utter it, and the friends of dons; the shapes and simulacrums which our parents have taken, the father-substitutes and mother-types which we have projected, accuse us, and all await our ritual suicide. Whom the gods wish to destroy they first call promising.

Young writers, if they are to be good, require a period of between three and seven years in which to live down their promise. Promise is like the mediæval hangman, who, after settling the noose, pushed his victim off the platform, and jumped on his back, riding as a death jockey, his weight acting as a drop, and his arms preventing the unfortunate from loosening the rope. When he judged him dead he dropped to the ground. Promise is that dark spider with which many writers are now wrestling in obscurity and silence. Occasionally they win, the load of other people's wish-fulfilments is cast off, and they produce a book; often after a struggle for breath they are stifled for ever. Let us go over to them for a moment, the writers on whom the executioner calls in the small hours.

Two o'clock. You won't accomplish anything now. Do you remember all the things you wanted to be? How Granny loved you! How we pinched and scraped to keep you at Oxford—and then those horrible bills! They killed Granny, you know, though we didn't tell you at the time. Now you're old enough to know. It wasn't that she minded the money—it was the thought you could ever do anything dishonourable. You did promise, you remember? That you could give all those bad cheques! Your father never got over it. Oh, we were all so proud of you. How could you, how could you, how could you!

Three o'clock. "We always hoped you'd write. A serious book, I mean. We can't count the kind of stuff you're doing now. I know an academic degree is not the real justification for three years here. There are many people whose careers after leaving college bring us more distinction than anything they achieve while they are up. We take a long view. But I think you'll agree we were very patient with you and I doubt if the stuff you are turning out now will prove we were right. Still we must be tolerant. I had hoped great things for you, and I dare say I was rather silly. Anyhow I shall always be glad to hear from you.

Why didn't you write to him? He would so have loved a letter. He often spoke of you before he died. I may say he was deeply hurt at what he considered, rightly or wrongly, your ingratitude. He had been fond of you in spite of everything. If you'd even troubled to send him a postcard! Why didn't you? Why didn't you? Why didn't you?

Four o'clock. Teeth hurt? I don't envy you at forty. Just as you're going to sleep you give a kind of twitch all over and wake up! H'm—a kind of noise like a clock makes before it strikes goes off at the back of your nose? That's bad! Your heart seems to miss a beat and you sit right up in bed with a jerk? Your blood beats too fast? Your mind races along? You can't breathe properly? Your bladder troubles you? A kind of dull aching pain somewhere in the side? You think it must be the spleen? H'm—And a funny kind of dry cough? That all? Oh yes—and a feeling like someone blowing up a balloon at the back of the nose? I wonder if you have some near relative or great friend whom I could talk to, just to check up on your family history. Your mother? Good. Well, Mr. Shelleyblake, if you don't mind waiting in here I think I'll, try and get right through on the phone to her.

Five o'clock. *How old are you?* H'm, I see. Just about half-way. And you've done what? H'm. Well, I must be off. Another patient. Sleep well, see you to-morrow, same time, same place.

. . . .

Sloth in writers is a symptom of inner conflict, especially that laziness which renders them incapable of doing something which they are looking forward to. The conflict may or may not end in disaster, but their silence is better than overproduction, which must so end, and the slothful writers, Johnson, Coleridge, Greville, in spite of the nodding poppies of conversation, morphia, and horse-racing, have more to their credit than Macaulay, Trollope or Scott.

CHAPTER XIV

THE CHARLOCK'S SHADE

SEX, the charlock's shade, is not the danger that it was. The Baudelaire, squandering his fortune, and ruining his health for a coloured mistress, is seldom met with; the temptations of writers to-day are group-temptations, in which the Cynaras and the Jeanne Duvals play little part. However, for a writer to be too fond of women is not uncommon, and then it may be found that they make crippling demands on his time and his money, especially if they set their hearts on his popular success. The charlock, or wild mustard, throws a more baleful shade on the young shoot when it is the love that dare not speak its name.

Many writers have been homosexual or gone through a homosexual period, and, although from a literary standpoint it is enriching, it is important to grasp the limitations of homosexuality, and to plan production accordingly. Thus a male homosexual, if cut off by his attitude from experience with women, will have difficulty in depicting them. This is not of consequence if he is, for example, a critic, and a poet also is free, since he works at that intense and sublimated level at which passion is general, and the

nature of such passion without importance. But most
writers are not poets and critics, and for novelists,
short-story writers and playwrights, difficulties arise.
Thus homosexual novelists are able to create mother-
types, and social mother-types (hostesses) and occasionally sister-types (heroines) but they have trouble
with normal women and make them out worse or
better than they are. They are forced to describe
something they know little about because so much of
life is concerned with it. Courtship, marriage, childbearing and adultery play a major part in existence,
a knowledge of the relations between men and women
is vital to a novelist, and a comparison of, say, *War
and Peace* with novels written by less normal authors
will show how few acquire it. Natasha, the heroine
of *War and Peace* is a delightful creature, but she is
capable of running away with a man whom she does
not love, and leaving a better one, after a single
meeting, because he looked at her in a certain way.
But she remains delightful because Tolstoy continues
to find her lovable for being human. If Natasha had
been one of Proust's heroines he would have turned
her into a monster, she would have been analysed till
nothing remained of her but lust and self-interest.

Nor is Proust's method, that of giving the male
characters in his life girls' names, and putting them
as girls into his novel, satisfactory. Their real sex
protrudes, they have no plausible relationships with
other characters in the book (Albertine is unreal when
she confronts Charlus or Swann or the Duchesse de
Guermantes, there is an ambiguous cloud over her
relations with the author), and they are incapable of

childbearing, home-making, husband-cheering, the drabber functions of woman. There is no solution for these problems. Nothing, for example, will make the two amorous young girls in *The Importance of Being Earnest* either young or amorous. The homosexual writer, until he can live differently, must construct his books so as to avoid situations where a knowledge of women is required, just as stammerers avoid certain words and substitute others. Otherwise the equipment of the homosexual writer, combativeness, curiosity, egotism, intuition and adaptability, leaves nothing to be desired.

The clasping tares of domesticity represent the opposite danger, and they too are less formidable than they were. The harried author sitting in a garret surrounded by screaming children, with duns at the door and a sick wife nagging from the bed is a thing of the past. But there remains some substance in the vision. The initial difficulty is in the sensitive writer's inability to live alone. The more he is alone the more he falls in love, if he falls in love he is almost certain to marry, if he marries he is apt to take a house and have children, if he has a house and children he needs more money, must do uncongenial work and deny himself the freedom which may have inspired him.

The homosexual is unable to treat of a section of the life of human beings, but, in return, he is free from the limitations of that life. He is apt to have a private income, he renews himself by travel, he has time for old friends and for the making of new ones, and as he grows old remains isolated, free from responsibilities and ties, and if he has been able to break free from the parasitism which is the weakness of homosexuals, he is detached. If he has joined the creative class, he is likely to become, like Gide, the " lonely old artist-man " that Henry James called himself.

In recent times the balance of literary success late in life is in favour of the childless writer. Children dissipate the longing for immortality which is the compensation of childless writer's work. But it is not only a question of children and no children, there is a moment when the cult of home and happiness becomes harmful, and domestic happiness one of those escapes from talent which we have deplored, for it replaces that necessary unhappiness without which writers perish. A writer is in danger of allowing his talent to dull who lets more than a year go past without finding himself in his rightful place of composition, the small single unluxurious " retreat " of the twentieth century, the hotel bedroom.

The fertility of the writer is often counterchecked by the happiness of the man. They do not want the same things, and where their desires conflict, the writer-self will be the one to suffer. The " animal serenity ", the " broad human touch " which Maugham envies in great writers, in Tolstoy, and perhaps, in Thackeray, and Dickens, can only be obtained by a series of experiences, which have extinguished the lesser writers who have attempted them. As far as one can infer from observation it is a mistake for writers to marry young, especially to have children young, for early marriage and paternity are a cure for loneliness and unhappiness more drastic than the

151

evil they set out to remedy. Writers choose wives for their beauty, not for their money nor for their appreciation of art, and the baby is even less capable of seeing the artist's point of view. As Tennyson put it—

> O love, we two shall go no longer
> To lands of summer across the sea ;
> So dear a life your arms enfold
> Whose crying is a cry for gold.

Thus there would seem little to choose between the tares and the charlock. The homosexual avoids domesticity, he pays a price, but pays it with his eyes open, the normal writer walks into a trap. Most young writers are weak, and know little about their weaknesses or their predicaments. They make a rush for the solution which promises them an immediate advantage, and are not apprehensive of its after-effects, if they find the years when they come to London after the cosiness of the university unendurable, they marry the first person whom they can. They work hard to make money, grow torpid with domesticity, and their writing falls off. After seven years or so they divorce, their talent is given another chance which (it depends on how they marry again), may or may not be taken.

In general it may be assumed that a writer who is not prepared to be lonely in his youth, must, if he is to succeed, face loneliness in his middle age. The hotel bedroom awaits him. If, as Dr. Johnson said, a man who is not married is only half a man, so a man who is very much married is only half a writer. Marriage, for an artist, can only succeed where there is enough money to save him from taking on uncongenial work, and, with a wife who is intelligent and unselfish enough to understand and respect the working of the unfriendly cycle of the creative imagination. She will know at what point domestic happiness begins to cloy, where love, tidiness, rent, rates, clothes, entertaining, and rings at the doorbell should stop, and she will know that there is no more sombre enemy of good art than the pram in the hall.

Some critics hold a mystical belief in talent. They think that it must come to fruition, that " if it is in you it's going to come out ", that real talent cannot be depressed by illness or poverty nor destroyed by success or failure. They even think that people die at the right time, that Keats and Shelley had nothing more to say, that Marlowe or André Chénier met their violent deaths at the appropriate moment. This kind of romantic fatalism is based on an optimistic nature and a refusal to face facts. If Milton had been drowned like *Lycidas*, there are people who would have said that he would never have written anything else. But talent is something which grows, and which does not ripen, unless there is the right kind of soil and climate. It can be neglected or cultivated and will flower or die down. To think that artists will muddle through without encouragement and without money, because in the past there have been exceptions, is like assuming that salmon will find their way to the top of a river to spawn in spite of barrages and pollution. " If it's in you it's bound to come out " is a wish-fulfilment. More often it stays in and goes bad.

Less advice and more money is what every artist demands from society and the idiocy of society in refusing these demands, except to servile and indifferent performers, is largely responsible for the line up of artists against that society to-day.[1] Capitalism is expelling the artist as Spain expelled her Jews or France her Huguenots, and the effects will soon be apparent, for the French nobles who had Voltaire flogged acted with similar foresight.

[1] I should like to see the custom introduced of readers who are pleased with a book, sending the author a small cash token, anything between half-a-crown and a hundred pounds. Authors would then receive what their publishers give them as a flat rate and their " tips " from grateful readers in addition, in the same way that waiters receive a wage from their employers and also get what the customer leaves on the plate.

CHAPTER XV

THE SLIMY MALLOWS

OF the enemies of literature, success is the most insidious. The guides whom we have quoted, whose warnings come through to us from various parts of the field, are unanimous against this danger. Pearsall-Smith quotes Trollope. " Success is a poison that should only be taken late in life and then only in small doses." Maugham writes,

> The common idea that success spoils people by making them vain, egotistic, and self-complacent is erroneous ; on the contrary it makes them, for the most part, humble, tolerant, and kind. Failure makes people bitter and cruel. Success improves the character of a man, it does not always improve the character of an author.

Success for a writer is of three kinds, social, professional, and popular. All three bring money, but in none of them is money the most important thing. Success is bad for a writer because it cuts him off from his roots, raises his standard of living, and so leads to overproduction, lowers his standard of criticism, and carries with it the germ of its opposite, failure.

Social success was the variety which most appealed to writers up to the slump, for social success, besides gratifying the snobbery which is inherent in romantic

155

natures, also provided them with delightful conditions, freedom and protection in large country houses.

There are writers for whom such success is beneficial, who find there the material they need, and the leisure to absorb it ; their public is also found among the world of fashion. Thus if Proust had been a social failure, if Pope had never been asked to a ball, nor Henry James presented to a duchess, *The Rape of the Lock*, *The Côte de Guermantes*, *The Ambassadors*, would not have been written. It is clear that social success is good for some writers and bad for others ; only because we envy it more than other success do we denounce it more often. It is good for writers if they are dandies or lyricists ; if they have suffered from poverty to the extent of being warped or weakened, rather than braced or steadied by it ; if they are homosexuals who need a frame to expand on, a beanstalk to climb up, or the kind of backing which will impress, and so free them from the domination of middle-class parents ; it is good for satirists and playwrights. Congreve, Gay, Wilde, were all the better for " being taken up " for they were taken to the field best suited for the flowering of their gifts, nor would Donne and Jeremy Taylor have written great prose if they had delivered their sermons to a slum parish. It must be remembered that in fashionable society can be found warmhearted people of delicate sensibility who, forming permanent friendships with artists, afford them ease and encouragement for the rest of their lives, and provide them with sanctuary. Lady Suffolk's friendship with Pope, Lord Sheffield's with Gibbon, Horace Walpole's for Gray,

156

Lady Gregory's for Yeats, Lady Cunard's for George Moore, acted as conservatories where the artist's talents ripened at a suitable temperature, neither forced too quickly, nor exposed to the rigours of the Grub Street winter. That Milton or Blake or Keats or Hopkins did not require such friendships does not discredit those who do.

But apart from these especial intimacies, or from such a comfortable greenhouse as was Holland House, there is little to be derived from an indiscriminating indulgence in fashionable society. That society is hard-hearted, easily bored, and will exact from a writer either a succession of masterpieces, or a slavish industry in keeping it amused at its own level, while he, in return, acquires an appetite for a set of external values, which, besides being hard to gratify, creates professional hostility and excludes him from a larger world in which he might be happily employed. The people for whom social success is dangerous are the realists, who have no place among such unreality, the militants, whose weapons rust in that atmosphere, or writers like Bennett who have already found their material, and can only deteriorate when transplanted.[1] The best thing that can happen for a writer is to be taken up very late or very early,

[1] Thus a writer not intended for social success was Swift, and it is interesting to notice what snobbish intoxication, what unpleasant vanity creep into the *Journal to Stella* at the height of his fashionable period. Johnson's comment on Addison's marriage to Lady Warwick may also be considered : " The marriage if uncontradicted report can be credited, made no addition to his happiness, it neither found them nor made them equal. . . . It is certain that Addison has left behind him no encouragement of ambitious love."

157

either when old enough to take its measure, or young enough to be dropped by society with his life before him. Married writers in particular are tormented by the contrast between the world they dine in and the world in which they wake up for breakfast, nor are the relations between writers' wives and worldly hostesses over cordial.

In any case the danger to-day is past. Fashionable society is not the temptation that it was, when it represented a cultural standard. The singing birds no longer nest in the great country houses, the Henry James and Robert Brownings of to-day are not met at lunch in Belgrave Square. " Cliveden's proud alcove " has no Pope to sing it. Maugham has shown that it is possible to possess and not be possessed by society. Forster that it is easy to do without it altogether, and Moore has summed it up, " Well-mannered people do not think sincerely, their minds are full of evasions and subterfuges . . . To be aristocratic in Art one must avoid polite society." A young writer must be careful not to pay society more attention than it pays him, he may satirise it, but is advised not to celebrate it, nor become its champion, for the moribund will turn on their defenders.

Professional success, the regard of fellow-artists and would-be artists is a delight, for it is absurd to assume that good writers cannot be famous in their lifetime. There have always been a few thousand judges of good literature, and these judges have recognised talent however unusual and uncontemporary, just as they have accorded to masterpieces of the past an appreciation independent of fashion.

Thus, nobody could be more forgotten than the poet Campbell, yet the other day John Betjeman pointed out three lines from the Battle of the Baltic which he admired.

> . . . When each gun
> From its adamantine lips
> Spread a death-shade round the ships
> Like a hurricane eclipse
> Of the sun.

Yet Tennyson, according to Palgrave, singled out the " death shade " for praise when he was compiling the *Golden Treasury*, even as he admired Marvell's *To His Coy Mistress* or Cowper's *Poplars*, poems outside the range of Victorian sensibility. These celebrators of the unfashionable best are the custodians of taste, the bodyguard of talent, like Maurice Baring, who has kept alive, in *Have You Anything to Declare*, French poetry that would be lost to English readers were it not for his impartial ear. In the same way Strachey wrote about Racine, Pearsall-Smith about Sainte-Beuve and Madame de Sévigné, writers who tend to be ignored owing to the cult of more violent-sensations, and Diderot, St. Evrémond, Shenstone and Cowper have been preserved.

If a professional success is painful in that it arouses the envy of the ex-artists, a popular success is fatal. Much has been written on the subject; I will try to summarise what I feel.

Success to-day is a kind of moving staircase, and once on it, it seems difficult for a writer to get off, for he is carried upwards, whether he writes well or not, encouraged by publicity, by fan-mail, by the tributes of critics and publishers, and by the friendly clubmanship of his new companions. The fan-mail gives the writer the sense of a mission. " Well, if I have made them forget their troubles for a moment, my stuff must be some good." Publicity also seems innocuous, since once a writer is " news " he continues to be news independently of his own wishes, and it helps to sell his books. As for the critics, their habit of praising a first book and damning a second can be put down to a personal grievance. " I regard every attack ", a writer once told me, " as worth about sixpence a word."

To-day a popular success may depend on the entertainment value of a writer or his political quality or his human touch. Those with the human touch never recover ; their sense of a mission is overwhelming. Not reviews, not the contempt of equals nor the indifference of superiors can affect those who have once tapped the great heart of suffering humanity, and found out what a gold-mine it is. Writers who have a political success may keep their heads, for they may still turn out a political disappointment.

The experience of Gide illustrates the full cycle. The greatest living French writer, he went " Left " and his Journal, which records the process, is an admirable piece of writing, showing the preoccupation with ideas at a level deeper than politics, which is the artist's role. In his next book, the voyage to Russia, he is enjoying the extra-literary success which his conversion to communism has brought him, the homage of the younger generation. The book is full of charm and energy, contains much praise and considerable blame of the Russian regime, some of it justified and some due to the writer's disappointment at not finding the earthly paradise restored in a country surrounded by its enemies. His criticisms awoke the extra-literary hatred of the party whose extra-literary friendship he had enjoyed. A literary public would have pronounced him right on some points, unfair and perfectionist on others ; a political-public simply abused him. The result was that in his next book he becomes more bitter and hostile, exhibiting the traits of which he was unfairly accused in the first. His mistake was to go beyond the artist's role, and become political investigator.

The entertainer, on the other hand, suffers from no criticism at all. No one has ever told P. G. Wode-house which is his best book or his worst, what are his faults or how he should improve them. The fate of the entertainer is simply to go on entertaining, till he wakes up one morning to find himself obscure.

The axiom which applies to popular success is that for every admirer gained by any means except the legitimate quality of a writer's art, that writer gains an enemy. It is an unconscious enemy, just someone who feels uneasiness at seeing the writer's name in the publisher's advertisements, who turns the other way from his picture in the Tube, one of those who voted against Aristides because he was tired of always hearing him called " the just ".

Every admirer is a potential enemy. No one can make us hate ourselves like an admirer—" de lire la secrète horreur du dévouement dans des yeux "— nor is the admiration ever pure. It may be *us*

161

they want to meet but it's *they* they want to talk about.

Popular success is a palace which is built for a writer by publishers, journalists, admirers, and professional success-builders, and in which a silent army of termites, rats, dry rot and death-watch beetles are tunnelling away, till, at the exact moment at which it is completed, it is ready to fall down. The only hope for a writer is that although his enemies cannot be seen, there is one that can be heard. He must listen for the death-watch, listen for the faint toc-toc, the critic's truth sharpened by envy, the embarrassed praise of the sincere friend, the silence of gifted contemporaries, the implications of the don in the manger, the visitor in the small hours. He must dismiss the builders and contractors, elude the fans with an assumed name and dark glasses, force his way off the moving staircase, subject every thing he writes to a critical supreme court. Would it amuse Horace or Milton or Swift or Leopardi ? Could it be read to Flaubert ? Would it be chosen by the Infallible Worm, by the circulating libraries of the dead ?

To refuse publicity that does not arise from the quality of his work, to beware of giving his name to causes, to consider his standards and the curve of development which he feels latent within him, yet not to indulge in gestures which are hostile to success when it comes, must be the aim of a writer.

Failure is a poison like success. Where the choice is offered, prefer the alkaline.

There is one kind of behaviour that is particularly

dangerous on the moving staircase. That is to attempt to ascend it in groups of four or five, who lend a hand to each other, and dislodge other climbers from the steps. It is natural that writers should make friends with their contemporaries of talent and express their mutual admiration, but it leads to a succession of services rendered, and however much the writers who help each other deserve it, their gratitude, frequently proclaimed, arouses the envy of those who stand on their own feet, who succeed without collaboration. Words like " logrolling " and " back-scratching " are soon used and the death-watch ticks overtime. Such writers must remember that they write for the reader, and the reader is the most unloved person in the world. No jokes must be made that are not explained to him, no relationships mentioned in which he is not asked to share. His capacity for being hurt, for feeling slighted, and excluded, for imagining that he is being patronised, is infinite. Like his capacity for revenge.

Success is most poisonous in America. According to Van Wyck Brooks, " The blighted career, the arrested career, the diverted career are, with us, the rule. The chronic state of our literature is that of a youthful promise which is never redeemed." He calls American literature " one long list of spiritual casualties ". Hemingway gives an account of the diseases of American authors which is worth comparing with our own analysis of spiritual tares.

> We do not have great writers. Something happens to our good writers at a certain age.

You see we make our writers into something very strange, we destroy them in many ways. First economically. They make money. It is only by hazard that a writer makes money, although good books always make money eventually. Then our writers when they have made some money increase their standard of living and they are caught. They have to write to keep up their establishments, their wives, and so on, and they write slop. It is slop not on purpose but because it is hurried. Because they write when there is nothing to say or when there is no water in the well. Because they are ambitious. Then once they have betrayed themselves, they justify it and you get worse slop. Or else they read the critics. If they believe the critics when they say they are great then they must believe them when they say they are rotten and they lose confidence. At present we have two good writers who cannot write because they have lost confidence, through reading critics. If they wrote, sometimes it would be good and sometimes not so good and sometimes it would be quite bad, but the good would get out. But they have read the critics, and they must write masterpieces. The masterpieces the critics said they wrote. They weren't masterpieces of course. They were just quite good books. So now they cannot write at all. The critics have made them impotent.[1]

It is not only authors who are killed by criticism but the critics as well; they seem, like the scorpion, able to destroy themselves with their own venom. But Hemingway's point about the critics is true. The praise from a critic is inflated by hope as often as his censure is distorted by envy, for his longing for perfection or his desire to be a John the Baptist drives him prematurely to recognise Messiahs, and his disappointment, thereby, becomes correspondingly aggravated. Also, as Desmond MacCarthy has remarked, there comes a moment when every clever

[1] Scott Fitzgerald ?   Thornton Wilder ?   Glenway Westcott ?

young man prefers to display his cleverness by expos-
ing a writer's faults rather than discovering his virtues.
That moment is most apt to occur in the early thirties,
which is a bad time all round, both for creators and
critics, or it may occur when the critic is in the early
thirties and the writer in the early forties. Butler
said a writer should write only for people between
twenty and thirty, as nobody read or changed their
opinions after that. Those are the years when the
artists are promising and the admirers full of admiration ; by the time the artist has ceased to be promising and become a good writer, the admirer is a critic
whose judgments are flavoured by his own self-hatred
or who, seeing the author as a symbol of his own
youth, refers all his later books back to his earliest
ones. When an admirer says, " Ah, yes ! But if
only he would write another *Prufrock* ! " he means,
" If only I was as young as when I first read *Prufrock*."
The sour smell of the early thirties hangs over most
literary controversy.

The shock, for an intelligent writer, of discovering
for the first time that there are people younger than
himself, who think him stupid, is severe. Especially
if he is at an age (thirty-five to forty-two) when his
self-confidence is easily shaken. The seventh lustre
is such a period, a real menopause for artists, a serious
change of life. It is the transition from being a young
writer, from being potentially Byron, Shelley, Keats,
to becoming a stayer, a Wordsworth, a Coleridge, a
Landor. It would seem that genius is of two kinds,
one which blazes up in youth and dies down, and the
other which matures, like Milton or Goethe, through

165

a long life, putting out new branches every seven years. The artist has to decide which he is likely to be. Often he has not decided, and finds himself exhausted by the sprint of youth, and unfitted for the marathon of middle age. Consequently a great many writers do die between those years ; some commit suicide, like Hart Crane, Harry Crosby, Philip Heseltine ; others die of pneumonia or drink or have nervous breakdowns. Others become specialists in other arts or in hobbies verging on the arts. Writers become painters, or painters writers, or renew themselves through someone from whom they can obtain self-confidence and encouragement, and a vicarious youth. Eventually, though critics are unfriendly, creation difficult, and the future monotonous or uncertain, a new position is established, and the young writer of promise becomes a master in his prime, one who can pass into old age, as a sage, a prophet, or a venerated, carefree and disreputable figure.

Hemingway, before he blames a critic again, should enquire if he is going through a " difficult period " for which allowances should be made ; sometimes it is a whole paper that seems affected, and which attacks young writers with the indiscriminate malice of rotting ambition.

But English criticism, unless it proceeds from some such gloomy sepulchre, is unfair only in that it is overkind, for a critic is subject to temptations of his own. Through praising their books, he gets to know more and more writers, and once he knows them finds it embarrassing to alter his opinion. Critics in

166

England do not accept bribes, but they discover one day that in a sense their whole life is an accepted bribe, a fabric of compromises based on personal relationships, and then it is in vain to remember that, like James's old man of letters, " our doubt is our passion, and our passion is our task ".

CHAPTER XVI

OUTLOOK UNSETTLED

THESE are the dangers and temptations of writers to-day. What consolations can be offered them ? What positive advice will procure for a new book a decade of life, and assure for its author a vicarious contact for another ten years ? We have seen that realism, simplicity, the familiar attitude to the reader, are likely to grow stale, that imagination, formality, subtlety, controlled by an awareness of the times we live in, are due to return. But besides the language in which it is profitable to write, we can also learn something of the forms which have vitality, and are assured of a future. Many writers have no feeling for the live or the dead form, and still attempt those which are doomed to failure. The record of literature is that of great writers perfecting a form, imitators bringing into disrepute that perfection, and a new writer arising to perfect another.

Thus *Paradise Lost* dislocated the English language for a hundred years, for it became impossible to write blank verse which was not an imitation of Milton as Young and Thomson discovered. Ultimately Cowper broke away, and after him Wordsworth and Tennyson. Since then, poets have been trying to escape from

Tennyson, by going back to the blank verse of the Elizabethans. Coming after Milton, Pope was the first poet to dodge blank verse, and bring to perfection a new form, the couplet, and this couplet in its turn paralysed the poets of the eighteenth century, till it was adapted by Crabbe and Byron. Blake and Collins meanwhile had broken free from the couplet, and made possible the rebellion of the romantics, who may be said to have held their own until *The Waste Land.*

A writer has to construct his shell, like the caddis worm, from the débris of the past, and, once there, he is safe, despite the jostling of contemporaries, till a younger generation dispossesses him, or until the vicissitudes of taste crumble it around him. He may attempt a new form, or he may revive an old one. But the revival, if it is to succeed, must not be premature.

What are the forms available at the moment ? The novel, the play, the poem, the article, the short story, the biography and the autobiography are the most fertile.

From the novel, dominant literary form of the last hundred years, has emerged masterpiece after masterpiece. But there have been a number of bad novels and from them certain facts can be deduced. Firstly, that bad novels do not last ; there is no point, therefore, in writing one unless it comes up to championship standard. And the novel is not a suitable form for young writers. The best novels (of Stendhal, Flaubert, Proust, James, etc.) are written from early middle age onwards. It is unsuitable because the

169

construction of a long book is exacting for young writers, whose novels begin well and go off, and who lack staying power, and because to write a novel an author must have experience of people as they are, and have resolved the contradictions in his own nature ; he must be integrated, a machine for observation.

Young writers force on real people the standards, motives and behaviour which appeals to them in books ; they are split-men, at war with themselves, and uncertain of their philosophy. I know of admirable young novelists, but their development is difficult, for they begin as lyricists or satirists ; even *Wuthering Heights* is not so much a novel as a lyric flight of sublimated eroticism. The satire of Evelyn Waugh in his early books was derived from his ignorance of life. He found cruel things funny because he did not understand them, and he was able to communicate that fun. But the predicament of the humorist is that his sensibility, if it goes on developing, causes him to find fewer things amusing, " for all our wit and reading do but bring us to a truer sense of sorrow ". The English humorist must therefore either cease to be funny, and so lose his entertainment status, or abandon his integrity and, æsthetically stunted, continue to give his public what it wants. For this reason humorists are not happy men. Like Beachcomber or Saki or Thurber they burn while Rome fiddles, or, like P. G. Wodehouse, repeat themselves with profitable resignation.

The short story and the long short story are more fruitful. The short story avoids routine, it is the most fluid and experimental of forms, as Elizabeth Bowen says,

> Peaks of common experience soar past an altitude line into poetry. There is also a level immediately below this, on which life is being more and more constantly lived, at which emotion crystallises, from which a fairly wide view is at command. This level the short story is likely to make its own.

The long short story is one of the most rewarding and yet neglected forms in literature, whose abandonment is solely due to the animosity of publishers. While short stories can be published in magazines and then in book form, and so be paid for twice, long short stories of from twenty to fifty thousand words can be published nowhere. Yet *The Aspern Papers*, *Sylvie*, *Candide*, *The Alien Corn*, *A Lost Lady*, and *Death in Venice* show to what perfection it can be brought, and *Sylvie* and *Daisy Miller* prove it a medium of youthful creations.

The play is another form where revival seems possible, the length is right for young authors, the technical difficulties can be solved by good advice. There are in particular two forms of drama which can be reclaimed by art : the English comedy and the revue. The prose comedy of manners is one of the finest creations of English literature, the perfection of our native dandyism. In Congreve the English language reaches the farthest point to which it can be pushed in the direction of stylised, colloquial, contemporary elegance. It is the polished, racy talk of men in periwigs, with muffs, and long waistcoats. From that moment people were to shorten their wigs and subdue their clothing, to begin the retreat to bald heads, sock-suspenders, and undistinguished diction. The tragedy of Congreve was that although a young man, his mission was to bring an old form to perfection and then see it into its grave. His predicament was that he was of the past, the form he perfected, the comedy of manners, belonged in spirit to the reign of Charles II, and was haunted by that prince of dandies, Wilmot, Earl of Rochester. Rochester had already been taken by Etherege as the hero of his *Man of Mode* and it was his habit of making confidential, almost wistful jokes with his servant, which established the favourite relationship of master and valet which has been a feature of the English Comedy down to *Jeeves*. The shade of Rochester retarded Congreve as much as did that of Oscar Wilde the young writers of the 1920's.[1]

But to-day there is room for a revival of comedy. There is no dandyism of the Left. A play which is politically and socially true of its time and yet achieves the elegance of *Love for Love* or the beginning of the *Importance of Being Earnest* would be secure of a future. Another likely form is the intelligent revue, because short satirical sketches are easily written by young writers, and because a revue which flattered the intelligence of the audience would have an element of surprise. Most creative writing to-day is Left in

[1] How typical of dandyism, for instance, was his reserve. " He is comparatively reserved ; but you find something in that restraint which is more agreeable than the utmost exertion of talent in others " (Waller). After, in Mirabell, celebrating this, the aristocratic Congreve retired, and left the field to Addison and his *Cato*.

sentiment. It would gain by conquering those fields of comedy which are still feebly defended by Toryism in retreat, by dukes and butlers, and people who think the word Epstein a joke in itself, by men of pleasure turned sour, and baby blimps just cutting their water-wings.

The article has a future, especially in the form of the critical essay, the analysis of times and tendencies, and the skilled " reportage ". But articles which cannot be reprinted are not worth writing.

Poetry is full of vitality, but it is a mistake, since Eliot, to be a poet and not realise the extreme difficulty of writing good poetry. The moment a poet forgets this, he will be superseded by a prose writer. We have one poet of genius to-day, Auden, who is able to write prolifically, carelessly, and exquisitely, and who does not seem to have to pay any price for his inspiration. It is as if he worked under the influence of some mysterious drug, which gives him a private vision, a mastery of form, and of vocabulary.

But poets to-day have to keep in training. Poetry, to stand out, must be a double distillation of life that goes deeper than prose. It must be brandy as compared to wine, otherwise consumers will get their poetry from short stories and novels. This distillation of experience can only be achieved by a writer who maintains his sensibility and integrity at a high pitch and concentrates on the quality of his production. He must examine the meaning, weight, force, pace, and implication of a word he uses, calculate the impact of each line on the reader, know what concessions can be made to sound or sense, and only deliver the finished poem after a drastic trial. Otherwise, prose will catch up on him. As poetry stands, inspiration is not enough, dreams have had their day, lucky shots miss the target. A poet, with the exception of mysterious water-fluent tea-drinking Auden, must be a highly-conscious technical expert. Poetry is an instrument of precision. That is why societies in return must respect him as they respect scientists or all who make greater sacrifices than they care to themselves, in their interest. The poet is susceptible to the temptations which we have described by reason of his sensibility, but we must not bully him.

> " Popular, popular, unpopular,
> You're no poet," the critic cried.
> " Why ? " said the poet. " You're unpopular ! "
> Then they cried at the turn of the tide,
> " You're no poet ! " " Why ? " " You're popular ! "
> Pop-gun : popular and unpopular.[1]

A lyric poet has the advantage over a prose-writer that he is entrusted with the experience of the ages, he is not a political conscript, nor can he be accused of escapism, if he confines himself to celebrating the changing seasons, memories of childhood, love or beauty. The tyranny of form to which he is subject is compensated by his free access to material. Literary history goes to prove that lyrical poetry is the medium which more than any other defies time. Didactic poetry becomes unreadable ; epics are pillaged for a few similes ; plays for the songs in them ; novels and essays crumble, or ossify ; but ten minutes' extra thought on the choice of a word, or the position

[1] Not Lawrence : Tennyson.

of a stress, may make in the lyric a difference of a thousand years. There is no age or period at which great lyric poetry cannot be written. It is possible to argue that Homer and Virgil to-day would have written in prose, that Shakespeare would have written novels—but Sappho, even after the international situation had been explained to her, would have written verse.

One of the colophons of literature, one of those great writers who put full stop to a form of art, was Marcel Proust. The form whose consummation he brought about was the autobiographical novel. *The Way of all Flesh*, *Of Human Bondage*, *The Portrait of the Artist*, preceded it, after 1922 they could not have been written, and autobiographical novels written since then have not been by great writers. They are the green shoots which continue to put forth from a tree that has been cut down.

The result of the flight of all but the most obstinate from this dying form has been a return of emphasis to the autobiography, which has an advantage over the novel in that it demands no fictional gifts from the writer, and a disadvantage in that it permits no alibis ; the characters are not imaginary and the hero is the only character with whom the author dare find fault. Its ranks have been swelled on the other hand by the journalists who have used the form to describe their reactions to the great men they have met, and these have acted as a tonic to the form, as have also books about young writers' war experiences. An interesting contribution was Harold Nicolson's *Some People*, which, disguised as short stories, is an autobiography where each episode represents a hurdle taken by the author on his way to maturity. Cowley's *Exile's Return* is another example of the planned autobiography (the only kind now worth writing), and in England I find it a temptation not to mention Orwell and Isherwood again. Closely related to reportage-autobiography is ideology-autobiography, in which an author looks back on himself in relation to the ideas of his time, a classic example of which is *The Education of Henry Adams*. There is room for many planned books of this sort for writers who can analyse themselves in relation to their environment, and avoid padding, but the journalism must be kept out—so must the ideology, for the faults of these books are already apparent.

To write well, and to go on writing well, depends on one's sense of reality. There is such a thing as literary health, and so far we have considered only literary diseases. If a writer is not writing as well as he would like to, or as often as he would wish, he should give himself an examination. Is he satisfied with his reality ? Is he " *dans le vrai* " ? If not, when and how has he departed from it ? Reality is a shifting thing. I take it to mean the nature of things as they are, and as they will be. It is life, and the future, however unpleasant, and not death and the past, however desirable. What people want to happen is real if it can be willed to happen, and there are realities of the imagination—such as the belief in a future life, or in a perfectible human society, which transcend at times the physical realities of death or annihilation. But for a professional writer it

176

means the realities of his time, the ideas and the actions which are changing the world and shaping history. The most real thing for a writer is the life of the spirit, the growth or curve of vision within him of which he is the custodian, selecting experiences propitious to its development, protecting it from those unfavourable. When he fails to do this something seems to rot, he becomes angry, frightened, and unhappy, suffering from what Swift called " that desiderium which of all things makes life most uneasy".

The spiritual reality of the artist may come in conflict with the historical reality of his time, and true to his own reality, he may even have to sacrifice it through his opposition to the external world, and so find that not life but premature death is required of him. There is no mysticism in this. We create the world in which we live ; if that world becomes unfit for human life, it is because we are tired of such responsibility. Genius is important in creating that world and therefore will be among the things to suffer. There are destructive elements—war, plague, earthquake, cancer, and the dictator's firing squad are among them—which take no account of the unfinished masterpiece, or the child in the womb. They are real and their reality must never be under-estimated, but there is also a reality of will and spirit by which, within the unchanging limitations of time and death, they can be controlled.[1]

[1] The Spanish poet Lorca was shot because he fell into the power of an element which detested spiritual reality. Yet Lorca fell into that power because he lived in Granada. Had he lived in Barcelona or Madrid he would be alive to-day like Sender or Alberti. But he lived in reactionary Granada, a city of the past,

Having satisfied himself of how he stands in relation to his time, and whether his talent is receiving proper nourishment, an ailing writer will enquire about those other sources of creative happiness, health, sex, and money.

The health of a writer should not be too good, and only perfect in those periods of convalescence when he is not writing. Rude health, as the name implies, is averse to culture and demands either physical relief for its bursting energy, or direct action. Action to the healthy man seems so desirable that literary creation is felt to be shaming, it is postponed till action has engendered fatigue, which is then transmitted to the reader. Also, in " this England where nobody is well ", the healthy writer is communicating with a hostile audience. Most readers live in London, they are run-down, querulous, constipated, soot-ridden, stained with asphalt and nicotine, and, as a result of sitting all day on a chair in a box and eating too fast, slightly mad and sufferers from indigestion. A writer, except on holiday, should not be fitter than his public, or too well for reading and meditation. The relationship of an author with his reader is the barometer of his æsthetic health. If he flatters or patronises, is hostile or pleading, then something is going wrong with him.

A preoccupation with sex is a substitute for artistic

of gipsies and bullfighters and priests, and he made his best poems about bullfighters and gipsies. That element in him which sought the past, which drew him to the mediævalism of Andalusia, contained the seed of his own death, placing him, who was no friend to priests or feudal chiefs, in a city where the past one day came to life, and was deadly.

178

creation, a writer works best at an interval from an unhappy love-affair, or after his happiness has been secured by one more fortunate. So far as one can generalise it would seem that the welling up of the desire for artistic creation precedes a love-affair. Women are not an inspiration of the artist, but a consequence of that inspiration. An artist, when his talent is uncoiling, has the desirability of any object fulfilling its function, but he also has a certain clear-headedness. His habits become moderate, he drinks less, because drink has no longer a psychological appeal. He does not lack confidence, he lives contentedly within his income, and he sees love and friendship as delightful things, but without their glamour. It is after creation, in the elation of success, or the gloom of failure that love becomes essential.

Economic health is a necessity. A writer suffering from financial difficulties is only good for short-term work, anything long will remain unfinished. And if he has too much money, unless he has had it all his life, he will spend it, and that is also a substitute for creation. Every writer should, before embarking, find some way, however dishonest, of procuring about four hundred a year with the minimum of effort. Otherwise he will become a popular success, or be miserable. Success he will take in his stride, for fewer writers are marred by it than are discouraged by failure. It is wholesome magic.

> Gently dip, but not too deep
> Or else you make the golden beard to weep.

Failure on the other hand is infectious. The world is full of charming failures (for all charming people

179

have something to conceal, usually their total dependence on the appreciation of others) and unless a writer is quite ruthless with these amiable footlers, they will drag him down with them. More dangerous are those who are not charming, the trapped foxes who bite the hand that would set them free, worst of all, the Kibitzers, the embittered circle of scoffing onlookers—

> The common rout
> That, wandering loose about,
> Grow up and perish as the summer fly
> Heads without name, no more remembered.

It is by a blend of lively curiosity and intelligent selfishness that the artists who wish to mature late, who feel too old to die, the Goethes, Tolstoys, Voltaires, Titians and Verdis, reach a fruitful senescence. They cannot afford to associate with those who are burning themselves up, or preparing for a tragedy, or whom melancholy has marked for her own. Not for them the accident-prone, the friends in whom the desire for self-destruction keeps blistering out in broken legs, or threatening them in anxiety-neuroses. Not for them the drumming finger, the close-cropt nail, the chewed glasses, the pause on the threshold, the wandering eye or the repeated " um " and " er ".

We create the world in which we live, and the artist plays a dominant role in that creation. By extension he can live in any world which he has created. At present, some artists are creating a militant world, others a pacifist one, and it is not only artists who are creating worlds, but capitalists and dictators. There is doubt about which world is

best as there is doubt about which world will triumph.
If a fascist world wins we may expect a black-out of
art, as under Attila. A communist world may make
experiments in intolerance, and then grow tired of
them. Or nothing may happen during our lifetimes,
and a few drops of patronage still be wrung from a
barren capitalism. Honours will be conferred on the
adroit, smart luncheon parties given, medals awarded.
Or a world revolution may establish conditions in
which artists will reach through their own merit the
public from whom they have been isolated.

Within his talent it is the duty of a writer to devote
his energy to the search for truth, the truth that is
always being clouded over by romantic words and
ideas, or obscured by actions and motives dictated by
interest and fear. In the love of truth which leads
to a knowledge of it, lies not only the hope of humanity
but its safety. Deep down we feel that, as every
human being has a right to air and water, so he has a
right to food, clothing, light, heat, work, education,
love and leisure. Ultimately we know the world will
be run, its resources exploited and its efforts synchron-
ised on this assumption. A writer can help to liberate
that knowledge and make clear the impediments to
human goodness and human improvement, the love
of power and money, the short-sighted acquisitive
passions, the legacies of injustice and ignorance, the
tiger instinct for fighting, the ape-like desire to go
with the crowd. A writer must be a lie-detector
who exposes the fallacies in words and ideals before
half the world is killed for them. It may even be
necessary for the poet to erect a bomb-proof ivory

tower from which he can continue to celebrate the beauty which the rest of mankind will be too guilty, hungry, angry or arid to remember. There is room in the arts besides the militant novelists and journalists for the " necessary lovers ", but the success worshippers, those for whom life is a Perpetual Party, a buffet where one swigs, if fortunate in the draw, for eighty years and then grudgingly makes room, are as out of favour as those who justify abuses as our christian burden " in this Vale of Tears ". The artist of to-day must bear a wound—" cette blessure ", according to. Gide, " qu'il ne faut pas laisser se cicâtriser, mais qui doit demeurer toujours douleureuse et saignante, cette blessure au contact de l'affreux réalité."

PART III

A GEORGIAN BOYHOOD

> Yet hark how through the peopled air
>   The busy murmur glows,
> The insect youth are on the wing
> Eager to taste the honied spring
>   And float amid the liquid noon.
> Some lightly o'er the current swim
> Some shew their gayly gilded trim
>   Quick-glancing to the sun.
>
> GRAY.

> "What sort of a thing is Tydeus?"
> "Tydeus rose and set at Eton: he is only
> Known here to be a scholar of Kings."
> [West to Walpole: Walpole to West,
> October, 1735.]

> Altro dirti non vo'; ma la tua festa
> Ch'anco tardi a venir non ti sia grave.
> LEOPARDI.

CHAPTER XVII

CREDENTIALS

TILL now this has been a book of criticism, and written with a critic's privilege, the privilege which enables him to assume equality with those he criticises, and to take their books to pieces as if he were their equal in stature. But this equality is a fiction, just as it is a fiction that a juryman is superior to the temptations and stupidities of the prisoner he judges, or qualified to convict a company director on a point of law. A critic is a product of his time who may affect impartiality but who projects his doubt and aspiration while claiming authority over the reader. Every critic writes as if he were infallible, and pretends that he is the embodiment of impartial intellectual sanity, a reasonable though omniscient pontiff. But the preacher of the loftiest sermon is only human, or subhuman, without his surplice, and now is the moment to step down from the pulpit and disrobe in the vestry. This autobiography is intended to be such a disrobing, and is meant to be an analysis of the kind of grounding in life and art which the critic received, of the ideas which formed him in youth; the education, the ideals, the disappointments, from

185

which are drawn his experience, the fashions he may exhibit and the flaws he may conceal.

The critic is an instrument that has made certain observations ; before the reader can judge of the value of them, he must know something of the accuracy of the instrument, and allow for the margin of error. We grow up among theories and illusions common to our class, our race, our time. We absorb them unawares and their effect is incalculable. What are they ? In my case, I am trying to find out, hoping that anything I find, however personal, may prove of use. To do so I have to refer to something which I find intolerable, the early aura of large houses, fallen fortunes, and county families, common to most English autobiographers. If the reader can stomach this, I will try and make it up to him.

CHAPTER XVIII

THE BRANCHING OGHAM

I HAVE always disliked myself at any given moment; the sum of these moments is my life.

The first occurred on the morning of the 10th of September, 1903, when I was born at Coventry, where my father had gone to look after a body referred to as " the Volunteers ". My father was in the army. His father was a retired admiral who lived at Bath where he had married a daughter of Charles Kemble, the rich broad-church Rector who restored Bath Abbey in the Victorian taste, and inhabited what is now the Spa Hotel. The admiral was born in 1816 and had done much of his sailing on wooden ships, he was older than my grandmother, older than the rector, his father-in-law, and died in 1900, with some reputation for good looks and bad language.

Meanwhile the rector's fortune (the Kembles were nabobs of the Indian tea trade) had vanished among his eleven children, his rectory had become a school, his country house been sold. He left a book called *Sermons from a Closed Pulpit* and a church he had built at Clapham. The fifty thousand pounds he contributed to the restoration of the Abbey was a bitter memory to his grand-children and formed the

basis of a grudge against society. I never had a
chance ! Both my great-grandfathers, the Rector,
and the Admiral's father, who succeeded Beau Nash
as Master of Ceremonies, have monuments in Bath
Abbey, and that corner where stand in incongruous
harmony the Roman Bath, the Gothic church and the
eighteenth-century Colonnade is not less sultry for
enclosing my roots.

In 1900 when my father's regiment was in Ireland
he married my mother, the daughter of a Colonel
Vernon of Clontarf Castle, outside Dublin. The
Vernons were a branch of the Vernons of Haddon
Hall who had come over to Ireland with the Duke of
Ormond in the reign of Charles II, and been given
Clontarf, then a castle of the Templars. They were
a race of small, dark, fiery people, proud of their
Anglo-Norman descent, and their position in the
sporting Church-of-England squirearchy, the land-
lords of the Pale.

I was christened Cyril Vernon Connolly, Cyril after
my cousin, Cyril Cattley, discoverer of the orchid,
whose functions were extended by Proust.

My earliest memory is of a chemist's shop in Bath
with coloured bottles in the window and a circular
air-cushion with a hole in the middle. This rubber
mystery excited me beyond words. What was it
for ? I never knew except that it must be for something quite unimaginably disgusting and horrible. I
knew it and It knew it, and It knew that I knew it.
It was vice made visible. And It was for Me !

My father's regiment went to South Africa, and
my memories became exotic ; arum lilies, loquots,

eucalyptus, freesias, are the smells which seem to me divine essences, something remembered from another life. The freesias grew wild in the grass, and those long thin stems, with their wayward creamy blossom, and the fragrance, half wild and half sophisticated, were my first clue to the meaning of the universe. I remember also Cape Point, the walk to the sea through clumps of rushes and over white sand feathered with the tracks of lizard, and around me, the indescribable sensation of sun and wind and space and salt. And at Montagu there was an island in the river on to which I used to be hoisted, clutching a stinking meercat's skin, lord of a rock on which a bird deposited the shells of crayfish, an Ithaca twelve feet long.

We lived at Weinberg; there were chameleons in the garden and squashed apricots; on Sundays the Regiment had church parades, and there were smells of pine and eucalyptus, paint blisters, and hot tar. I had already got used to being an only child, and enjoyed playing by myself. I had a dog called Wups, and a cat called One-Eye, and a crowd of other animals, some toys, and some imaginary. I derived enormous pleasure from animals and something approaching ecstasy from the smells of flowers and fruit, and from scenery.

Already my life was a chain of ecstatic moments, I invented happy families of tops and fir-cones, or made overtures to the sacred personages whom I learnt about from *Line upon Line*, Isaac on his way up the mountain to be sacrificed, the child Samuel, David, and Benjamin. But what mattered most to

189

me was the apprehension of visual beauty—to stand among the arum lilies, faintly scented, thick in texture, and break off their leaves, or among the brittle lines of sweet pea, or with a watering-can, by the rose-beds smelling the wet earth, pouring out the spraying water, these were experiences, like climbing a willow tree near the stables where the green and edible willow branches, hung down like the reed curtains in Spanish doorways, by which my existence was transformed. In vain Captain Scott shook hands with me on his last voyage to the South Pole, in vain I visited the giant tortoises, and the fleet at Simonstown or saw the Regiment parade on Minden Day, my relations, sadistic, with One-Eye and Wups, and æsthetic, with pale cones of the silver fir and the gummy blue cups of the eucalyptus, were all that concerned me.

I was twice in South Africa; when I was five, and when I was six. In between we went to Ireland and stayed at Clontarf, and at Mitchelstown Castle in Cork, which left a deep impression. The castle was an enormous eighteenth-century Gothic affair, which belonged to my great-aunt Anna, who had once been besieged there by the Fenians; there was a lake in the grounds, and a wishing well. It was winter and there were icicles along the lake. I wore brown gloves on week-days and white ones on Sundays, and held an icicle, the first I had seen, with its mysterious purposeful pointed whiteness, in my white glove. Of the rest of the visit I remember little. Lord Kingston had long been dead, but my grandfather was there, terrifying. " Where is Grandpapa ? " I asked my nurse one morning. " He's busy." "What's he doing?" "He's doing his duty." This answer, which would have covered the activities of all Irish landlords at that date, I took to mean that he was in the lavatory (Have you done your duty to-day?), and was more frightened of him than ever, except when he would come in with his gun and a huge stiff dead grasshopper two feet long in his hand, waving it at me and saying " snipe, snipe."

This was my first visit to Ireland, since babyhood, and besides the love of the beautiful, a new passion awoke in me. I became a snob. The discovery that I was an earl's great-nephew was important to me, but I made another. My mother's favourite sister had married a rich man. Aunt Mab was beautiful, but she also had special smells, smells of furs, and Edwardian luxe. Uncle Walter gave me a steam train and a watch for Christmas. Wherever we went with Aunt Mab there were presents and large houses, and the appeal her wealth made to an imaginative child was irresistible. Bishopscourt, Loughananna, Rochestown, Marlay, the names of her houses, for she moved every six months, held a poetry for me. They meant security and romance, fires and potato cakes, footmen, horses and the soft aquatinted Irish winter.

> Cold grew the foggy morn, the day was brief,
> Loose on the cherry hung the crimson leaf;
> All green was vanished save of pine and yew
> That still display'd their melancholy hue;
> Save the green holly with its berries red
> And the green moss upon the gravel spread.

★   ★   ★

In 1910 I was sent home from Africa for good. My parents stayed on, and I went with my nurse to join my father's mother and sister in Corsica, where they had a villa. By now I was an æsthete. I adored my mother, but otherwise lived in a world of my own. Sunsets were my preoccupation. I saw all words, people, numbers and proper names in colours or notes of music, and there was a different colour for every day of the week which I tried to paint but failed. I remember being ill with fever, and the taste of the orange-leaf tea I was given to bring my temperature down, and I added the taste of these leaves to my ecstasies, with walks in the " maquis " and sessions by the tank where I sailed my prickly pear leaves in the evening.

Then there was the sea itself, though, like Petronius, I cared only for the sea-shore. One evening I was taken out in a boat to see the French destroyers fire their torpedoes. The lurid Mediterranean sunset, the ships, the noise, the rolling, were not to my liking. I cried louder as each torpedo went off, and from that evening I date a horror of battleships, bands playing, noises, displays of arms, and all official functions.

I also discovered friendship in Corsica and fell in love with a child called Zenon, a Pole, three years older than myself. He had dark eyes, a fringe of brown hair and adored fighting. He made cardboard swords and shields for us, on which he used to paint coats of arms, and we would hack at each other till they were broken. From that moment I have seldom been heart-free, and life without love for me has seemed an operation without an anæsthetic.

I have been inclined to regard that condition as the justification of existence, which takes priority over other ideologies.

> Love the most generous passion of the mind,
> That cordial drop heaven in our cup has thrown
> To make the nauseous draught of life go down.

From Corsica we went to Tangier, where I fell again, this time for a handsome bearded Moorish guide called Salem. We showered presents on each other, and I still have a beautiful drum he gave me. Then we returned to Bath, where I went to school as a day boy. It was the hot summer of 1910 and we wore dark blue cockades for the general election, except the dentist's son, who was a liberal. He seemed to me to smell quite different from the other boys. Oily.

I was then nearly seven and from that moment my character began to deteriorate. My grandmother spoilt me. I have since observed that it is a pleasure of grandparents to spoil their grandchildren. They revenge themselves in that way on their children for the insults they have suffered from them. My grandmother was only playing her biological role. The tragedy was that I found it out, and recognised my victim. To this period I trace my worst faults. Indecision, for I found that by hesitating for a long time over two toys in a shop I would be given both, and so was tempted to make two alternatives seem equally attractive ; Ingratitude, for I got so used to having what I wanted, that I assumed it as a right ; Laziness, for sloth is the especial vice of tyrants ; the Impatience with boredom which is generated by devotion; the Cruelty which comes from a knowledge of power, and the Giving way to moods; for I learnt that sulking, crying, moping, and malingering, were bluffs that paid.

The people I had been in love with before, my mother, my nurse Betty, Wups, One-Eye, Zenon, and Salem or Selim (the spelling varied) were people who loved me, but we loved as equals, conscious of each others' rights. Sufficiently provoked One-Eye would scratch, my mother rebuke, Betty spank, Zenon, Wups and Salem slink away. Now for the first time I learnt of unequal love. I was not in love with my grandmother, she was in love with me, and I would take advantage of her like a little Nero. *Sic ego perire cœpi.*

At school I was popular, for I had embarked on the career which was to occupy me for the next ten years of " trying to be funny ". I was neither good nor bad at games; my favourite exercise was to take a short piece of pointed wood in my hand and walk for hours through the long summer grasses round the playing fields, calling at imaginary ports, tunnelling the hay, chewing sorrel, and following my faint tracks in the silver grass as a liner follows a trade route. Inside my desk a cardboard shoebox per-forated with holes supported a brood of looper cater-pillars. Who can forget that smell of caterpillars, the smell of wet cardboard, drying leaves and insect excrement, the odour of northern childhood? It was on one of these long summer cruises, in a patch of cow-parsley, that I realised my own identity; in a flash it came to me that my name and myself were

194

something apart, something that none of the other boys were or could be, a kind of divine " I am that I am " which I should carry all through life and at last deposit on my grave, like a retriever with a bit of stick.

I was still in love, as I had been since I first saw, in Little Arthur's History of England, the picture of the Princes in the Tower—those two royal princes, so sweetly embracing, so soon to be smothered—what only child could look at them without a disturbance, or read of Arthur himself, walking beside the gaoler, on his way to have his eyes put out ? Indeed, like many children, I had fixations on the kings of England. With their remote grandeur and their drooping black moustaches they were like my great-uncles, huge brooding stylised figures who awoke a sense of guilt.

My great friend was a boy called Foley. I remember leaning out of the dormitory window with him, watching the fireworks on a summer night, while the rockets went off and we heard the inevitable Gilbert and Sullivan from the distant military band. That summer I seemed to be initiated into the secrets of preparatory school life. I came to know the smell of the class-rooms, of slates, chalk, and escaping gas, and to fear the green baize door which separated the headmaster's part of the house from the boys. On the one side, silence, authority, the smell of savouries ; on the other noise and freedom.

At night we made " tabernacles " by stretching the sheets up over the top of the beds, and I would lie in the evening sunshine playing flicking matches between the fingers of my right hand and my left, or arching my hands into swan-like shapes that swooped up and down above my head. When I was ill there were cracks in the ceiling to map and explore, and patterns in the wall-paper. I learnt the rhythm of the seasons : summer, which is the time for overdoing things, the recoil of creative autumn, the vibrant coma of winter, and the lowering spring. I began to enjoy my work and win prizes. I acted in a play and wrote facetious little Leacockian sketches. I declared a re-bellion against the masters, and returned a prize to one of them saying none of us would ever speak to them again. This was part of my insensitive teasing, but he took it seriously and looked hurt. I was so spoilt that I felt bored and disappointed with myself, and tried to take it out on whom I dared. Otherwise I was a typical schoolboy, with a red cap, a belt with a snake (which I slept with under my pillow), a cricket bat, a knowledge of the tracks made by wapiti, skunk, raccoon and wolverine, and a happy bitchiness which endeared me, as it was intended to, to my superiors. I went in brakes to watch matches and came home summertipsy in the dusk ; I adored sausages and Sunday breakfasts, said my prayers, bickered with other boys on walks, cried " quis " and " ego ", and was conceited and bright in the way in which so many small boys are, and which, alas, proves such a false dawn of intelligence.

I can never remember not being able to read and was already deep in " Natural History ". I could reel off the habits of aardvarks, aye-ayes, and Tasmanian Devils, and I knew (from *The World of*

Wonders) about the great Tun of Heidelberg, the Upas
Tree, and the Pitch Lake of Trinidad. I collected
stamps, pressed flowers in blotters, and adored chess.
For lighter reading there were fairy stories and non-
sense books. I enjoyed Burnand, Mark Twain, and
Stephen Leacock, but wept at the humiliations of *Vice
Versa*, or the suffering of the Yonghi Bonghi Bo. My
thrill of the week was to visit a little shop on Lansdowne
Hill in the early dusk of winter afternoon and receive
a rolled-up bundle of " Comic Papers ", *Chips* and
Comic Cuts, the *Rainbow*, the *Gem* and the *Magnet*—
I hold them, as I did with everything, to my nose,
the smell is excruciating—damp paper, newsprint ;
I feel I shall burst. Ahead of me stretches the evening
with my grandmother ; the gas lit, the fire burning,
the papers unrolled and untied, the peace and security
of the literary life, though even then I am depressed
by the knowledge that nothing I shall find inside will
come up to the sensation of opening them. As with
Leopardi's peasants, the eve of the Festival will always
bring me more happiness than the Feast itself.

There was one other lesson I learnt, living with my
grandmother. Hitherto I had been in exotic surroundings or in Ireland. But my grandmother was
poor, and we lived in rooms ; sometimes they were
by the seaside in the isle of Purbeck, where balls
bounce on the porphyry pavement, and a horse-drawn
tumbril dragged the long-robed bathers far out into
the string-coloured sea ; sometimes they were in
London, sometimes in Bath—but they were always
middle-class. I came to know the world of the realist
novel, the fuggy rooms with plush sofas and anti-

macassars, gas mantles, kettles on the hob, and their landladies, overfamiliar women with common voices, and ripe bosoms sprayed with jet. I came into contact with the lower classes too, for we used to visit one or two old servants to whom my grandmother had made pensions. One, Old Sally, who lived in an alcoholic bed-ridden fug, distressed me particularly. Here were horrible things, illness, poverty, old age, and I felt I must make every effort to avoid coming into contact with them.

I now made the comparison, as many a small boy would :

England = Grannie, Lodgings, School, Poverty, Middle Class.

Ireland = Aunt Mab, Castles, Holidays, Riches, Upper Class.

Ireland, therefore, became desirable, and England sordid. This division, however unreal it may seem, had importance for me, it conditioned my childhood, and made me a hybrid. I could not consider myself upper class ; yet I was not altogether middle class. I had fallen between two standards of living. With the upper class I felt awkward, dowdy and introspective, and a coward. With the middle class I felt critical, impatient and sparkling. This class distinction, the line between Kensington and Belgravia, is a source of anguish. To be half and half was as uncomfortable as having one shoulder higher than the other.

Meanwhile my mother returned, and tried to repair the damages to my character. She disapproved of the school in Bath, where I was always ill. I had whooped my way through the coronation summer, I had come out in measles and german measles, and chicken pox, and, after a recurrence of malaria, I was removed. My mother came down to see me while I was ill, and brought a trunk of toys, all the composition animals whom I adored in the holidays, with their house of parliament and their cricket elevens. I was ashamed of them and refused to play, for already my solitary only-child world seemed disgraceful to my social school-world, even my mother's presence in it seemed incorrect. She took me away to Ireland : and Bath, that beautiful, relaxing town where the Abbey chimes played *The Harp that once through Tara's Halls* with morbid sweetness, as one watched the county cricket matches, knew me no longer.

Clontarf was a paradise, for in the gallery was a pitch for the kind of cricket I played, bowling a marble with my left hand to my right hand which held a toy animal as bat. A book standing up was the wicket. When an animal was out another took its place. Animals that were solid like the elephant, or streamlined like the seal, made the best bats ; animals like the giraffe, whose legs broke when they hit out, were less successful. Books were filled with their batting averages, and my celluloid seal, besides being the best cricketer, was also a potent voice in parliament, and taken every night to bed with me.

My grandfather tried to give me real fielding practice on the lawn but I was frightened. There is a two-handed sword in the castle, reputed to have been used by Brian Boru in his battle there against the Danes, with which my grandfather and my great-uncle would pretend to chop off my head. Their sombre jesting accentuated my cowardice, but I became interested in Brian Boru, and so was led to cultivate my Irish side. I wanted to learn Gaelic, and I read history books from the nationalist standpoint. Shane O'Neill, Owen Roe O'Neill, Wolfe Tone, Lord Edward Fitzgerald were my heroes, and I learnt to sing the Shan Van Vocht. The last intellectual to stay at Clontarf had been Handel, whose bedroom was my nursery, and I began to be considered " Queer ". The introduction—" This is cousin Cyril [my nephew Cyril]. (*p*) He's supposed to be very clever. (*pp*) His grandmother's spoilt him," depressed me. I responded as usual by showing off and " trying to be funny."

I went on " trying to be funny " till I was seventeen. This horrible process was my defence mechanism. It was the shell I was secreting as a protection from the outside world : by making people laugh I became popular, and I became feared as well. " Go on, be funny ! " some boy would command, and I would clown away or recite my poems and parodies, with their echoes of Mark Twain and Stephen Leacock. " Connolly's being funny," the word would go round, and soon I would have collected a crowd. I revelled in this, and would grow funnier and funnier till I passed quite naturally into tears. " Connolly's not funny now. He's gone too far," and the group would break up and leave me, except for some friend who remained to puzzle over the psychology of the manic-depressive. " But you were being quite funny a moment ago." " Oh, Boo-Hoo-Hoo. I wish I was dead." " Oh, shut up, Connolly." " Oh, go away. I hate you." Then a master would come by and comfort me. I would be handed, still hysterical, to the matron, and the inevitable case-history would be gone over. (*p*) " It's his grandmother. (*pp*) She spoils him."

But I could not be funny in Ireland. My wit was the opposite of the native sense of humour, my jokes, a combination of puns and personal remarks interlarded with the wisecracks of the day, (" Oh, go and eat soap " was a favourite) were beyond the Irish, who saw only the humour of situations, and could not appreciate a *calembour*. They began to tease me about being English, which I gathered meant possessing a combination of snobbery, stupidity, and lack of humour, and was a deadly insult. There were many stories of social triumphs at the expense of England—especially against unpopular viceroys, like Lord Aberdeen. The Irish were a superior people. Better born, but less snobbish ; cleverer than the English and fonder of horses ; they were poorer no doubt, but with a poverty that brought into relief their natural aristocracy. And, above all, they were loved, (for " being Irish " meant belonging to the Protestant Landed Gentry), by about four million devoted bog-trotters, who served them as grooms, comic footmen, gardeners and huntsmen.

And the real Irish—what had happened to them ? They were my first lost cause, and I worshipped them with passion, reciting the ' Dead at Clonmacnois ' to myself in a riot of grief.

In a quiet watered land, a land of roses,
Stands Saint Kieran's city fair
And the warriors of Erin in their famous generations
Slumber there.

There beneath the dewy hillside sleep the noblest
Of the Clan of Conn,
Each below his stone with name in branching Ogham
And the sacred knot thereon.

Many and many a son of Conn the Hundred Fighter
In the red earth lies at rest ;
Many a blue eye of Clan Colman the turf covers,
Many a snow-white breast.

Even to-day such verses typify Ireland, the soft
constipating weather, the unreality of that green
cul-de-sac turned away from Europe, where the
revolutions lead backwards, and the Present is the
victim of the Past.

In the meanwhile what of Clan Colman ? Great-
Uncle Granville made a list of chieftains for me.
They were not all extinct ; behind the Anglo-Norman
families of the Pale, the Fitzgeralds, de Burghs,
Tristrams, Talbots, and Plunkets, lurked the remnant
of an older race—the O'Grady of Killyballyowen,
the O'Gorman, the O'Connor Don, the Magillicuddy
of the Reeks, the O'Reilly and the Fox. These were
the legitimate rulers, the heirs of Shane and Owen
Roe. I begged Uncle Granville to point them out
to me. To serve the O'Gorman ! To speak Gaelic,
wear a saffron Irish kilt, and sing the Shan Van Vocht !

In the curragh of Kildare
And the boys will all be there

with the O'Connor Don ! The parliament of animals
became supporters of the movement and the great

202

'seal himself, a fine cricketer and a generous statesman added the letters D.A.I. (Dublin and Irish), after his name. I planned a restoration of the monarchy, and pestered Uncle Granville about the claims of various families. Who should be considered the rightful king of Ireland, the successor of Brian Boru ? Naturally all Connollys, O'Connors, and O'Connells, through Conn, the King of Connaught. That pointed to Edward Conolly of Castletown. But his family had taken the name Conolly, and were really Pakenhams. Besides, his Gaelic . . . ? The O'Briens were Uncle Granville's candidates for the vacant throne. They had a Gaelic motto and were descended from Brian Boru himself through the kings of Thomond. Lord Inchiquin had the best right to the crown of Tara. For my part I had no personal ambition, nothing to hope from the New Court.

> It was friends to die for
> That I would seek and find.

and my day-dreams ended in my being sacrificed for the new king, like little Arthur.

This Irish nationalism may seem an extraordinary phase, but it must be remembered that there are still hundreds of thousands who believe in it. Gaelic is now compulsory in Ireland, and I believe Lord Cullen of Ashbourne wore a saffron kilt in Richmond Park. Monarchy has lost ground there since 1912, but at that time the revolutionary movement was unknown to me. My own feelings were romantic and literary, in fact English. Ireland represented glamour and luxury, and I tried to make a religion out of them. Of course, I was a failure with the Irish. I never could learn the Gaelic Alphabet, nor for that matter could I talk with an Irish brogue, and the only Irish people I knew were the housekeeper at Clontarf and her husband.

My cousins were healthy, destructive, normal children. I was lonely, romantic, and affected, and already the friction between extrovert and introvert was set up. I was extremely shy, for the effort to accommodate my inner life to my outer one proved harder and harder. I was sentimental at night and facetious in the morning. Between morning and evening my personality would swing from one mood to the other as I watched my wisecracking morning self with its defiant battle-cry " Oh, go and eat soap," turn by degrees into the tearful Celtic dreamer, who believed in ghosts, and would go into a trance over a line of poetry at night. My appetite for Gaelic and ghosts waxed and waned with my craving for titles. There were evenings when I wanted to kill myself because I was not the O'Grady of Killballyowen. Why had not my father got a title ? It was heartless, anguishing—why be born, why live at all if I could not have one ? Nobody understood me. Nobody cared, and I would scream and scream, with real tears, and screams that grew more and more artificial as I had to raise my voice to carry to the dining-room. Nobody loved me, nobody understood me, nobody would give me what I wanted, there was an Elemental under the bed. I could die for all They cared. Wur ! Wur ! Wur ! till at last my mother appeared in evening dress, and would sit with me, smelling of chocolates.

The fever I got from time to time was a recurrence of malaria, and was enough to cause anxiety—the anxiety enough to procure me privileges. Nobody could be certain if I was shamming. And in the morning, when my night fears had been discussed and I would come down in an atmosphere of sympathy it was " Oh, go and eat soap," or " Stick him with a fork."

Such were these early excesses that to-day I cannot listen to any discussion of titles or open a peerage without feeling sick, as from the smell of rubber steps and stale whisky on the stairway of a Channel boat. I shall never be able to breathe till they are abolished. Nor has being understood proved reassuring.

In the end I compromised with the brogue. I pretended that I had got rid of it except in moments of great excitement and I would even pretend to lose my temper so as to try out a few phrases, though I was careful to do this when no Irish boys were in the room. My history books taught me to abominate England, for I read *Tales of a Grandfather* at the same time, and it never occurred to me that the England I hated, the oppressor of the Celt and the Gael, the executioner of Fitzgerald, Emmet and Wolfe Tone, was made manifest in my grandfather, who owned streets in Dublin, and a shoot in Kerry; that the Anglo-Irish were themselves a possessor class whose resentment against England was based on the fear that she might not allow them to go on possessing.

CHAPTER XIX

WHITE SAMITE

THE new school my parents chose for me was on
the coast. At first I was miserable there and
cried night after night. My mother cried too at
sending me, and I have often wondered if that incu-
bator of persecution mania, the English private school,
is worth the money that is spent on it, or the tears
its pupils shed. At an early age small boys are
subjected to brutal partings and long separations
which undermine their love for their parents, before
the natural period of conflict, and are encouraged to
look down on them without knowing why. To owners
of private schools they are a business like any other,
to masters a refuge for incompetence, in fact a
private school has all the faults of a public school,
without any of its compensations, without tradition,
freedom, historical beauty, good teaching, or communication between pupil and teacher. It is one
of the few tortures confined to the ruling classes and
from which the workers are free. I have never met
anybody yet who could say he had been happy there.

Yet St. Wulfric's, where I went, was well run and
vigorous, and did me good. We called the head-
mistress Flip and the headmaster Sambo. Flip,

206

around whom the school revolved, was able, ambitious, temperamental, and energetic. She wanted it to be a success, to have more boys, to attract the sons of peers and to send them all to Eton. She was an able instructress in French and History, and we learnt with her as fast as fear could teach us. Sambo was a cold, business-like and dutiful consort. The morale of the school was high, and every year it won a shooting trophy and the Harrow History Prize from all the other preparatory schools. Inside the chapel was a chaplain, inside the gym a drill-sergeant, and there were a virid swimming-pool, a cadet corps, carpenter's shop and riding class.

The school was typical of England before the war; it was worldly and worshipped success, political and social; though Spartan, the death-rate was low, for it was well run, and based on that stoicism which characterised the English governing class, and which has since been under-estimated. " Character, character, character," was the message which emerged when we rattled the radiators, or the fence round the playing fields, and it reverberated from the rifles in the armoury, the bullets on the miniature range, the saw in the carpenter's shop, and the hoofs of the ponies on their trot to the Downs.

> Not once or twice in our rough island's story
> The path of duty was the way to glory

was what we had to learn, and there were other sacred messages from Kipling or Newbolt.

Muscle-bound with character the alumni of St. Wulfric's would pass on to the best public schools, cleaning up houses with doubtful tone, reporting their best friends for homosexuality and seeing them expelled, winning athletic distinctions—for the house rather than themselves, for the school rather than the house, and prizes and scholarships and shooting competitions as well—and then find their vocation in India, Burma, Nigeria, and the Sudan, administering, with Roman justice, the natives for whom the final profligate overflow of Wulfrician character had been all the time predestined.

After I had spent one or two terms at St. Wulfric's, blue with cold, haunting the radiators and the lavatories, and waking up every morning with the accumulated misery of the mornings before, the war broke out. My parents had gone to live in London in Brompton Square, and the holidays had become an oasis after St. Wulfric's austerity. In the big room at the top of the house with my grandfather's sea chest and the animal books by Ernest Thompson Seton, a fire and the view of the sea-green limes of the Brompton Oratory, or in the rosewood drawing-room with its vine-clad balcony, I could be happy. The square abounded with looper caterpillars, tight in the shallow earth wriggled the pupæ of the privet moth (in those that did not wriggle the icheumon was at work). On Sundays people made jokes about not going to church, but went, and the churches disgorged their top-hatted congregations into the Park, from whence they strolled back, myself in an Eton jacket moving in an Anglo-Irish phalanx, and imagining I was Charles Hawtrey, through gates and squares and crescents aromatic with Sunday luncheons, the roast beef, the boredom, the security of 1913. At night my fear of the dark was still acute. I had to have night-lights, and I had a terror of anything " going out "—I could not bear a dying fire or a guttering candle, or even a clock to run down—it seemed a kind of death-agony.

The rest of my time at St. Wulfric's was spent on a war-time basis. The school throve ; it's *raison d'être* apparent in the Roll of Honour. Old boys came down in uniform, and retired generals lectured to the corps, while the boys stuck flags into maps, gave Woodbines to the wounded soldiers, and learned to knit ; doing without more and more, as Flip's organising genius found its expression.

The master who took me in hand was Mr. Ellis. He was gruff and peppery with an egg-shaped bald head. He and Mr. Potter, the high-priest of the shooting trophies, were professional teachers, the rest makeshifts thrown up by the war. Ellis was pro-German ; the Germans deserved to win the war, he thought, because of their superior efficiency. The boys respected his point of view, to them, a German victory would have seemed natural, a chastisement on England for neglecting duty and discipline, and not listening to ' Lest we forget '. He made me enthusiastic over algebra, and as my enthusiasm grew I became good at it.

From that moment Daddy Ellis befriended me. He called me Tim Connolly and built up a personality for me as the Irish Rebel, treating me as an intelligent and humorous person, an opponent to respect. When the Germans conquered our decadent country through

209

their discipline and the superiority of general staff I should be one of the first elements to be shot.

My new personality appealed to me. I changed my handwriting and way of doing my hair, jumped first instead of last into the plunge-bath, played football better, and became an exhibit, the gay, generous, rebellious Irishman, with a whiff of Kipling's McTurk. Flip also admired the transformation and began to introduce me to parents as " our dangerous Irishman ", " our little rebel ". At that time I used to keep a favour chart in which, week by week, I would graph my position at her court. I remember my joy as the upward curve continued, and as I began to make friends, win prizes, enjoy riding, and succeed at trying to be funny again. The favour charts I kept for several terms ; one began at the top and then went downwards as term wore on, and tempers.

When angry Flip would slap our faces, in front of the school, or pull the hair behind our ears, till we cried. She would make satirical remarks at meals that pierced like a rapier, and then put us through interviews in which we bellowed with repentance— " It wasn't very straight of you, was it, Tim ? Don't you *want* to do me credit—don't you *want* to have character—or do you simply not care what I think of you as long as you can get a few cheap laughs from your friends and shirk all responsibility ? " On all the boys who went through this Elizabeth and Essex relationship she had a remarkable effect, hotting them up like little Alfa-Romeos for the Brooklands of life.

The only thing that would bring our favour back

(for, womanlike, Flip treated the very being-out-of-favour as a crime in itself, punishing us for the timid looks and underdog manner by which we showed it) was a visit from parents, and many a letter was sent off begging for their aid. I was restored, after a low period during which I had been compared, before the whole school, to the tribe of Reuben because " unstable as water thou shalt not excel ", by an enquiry from Lord Meath, the founder of Empire Day. Sometimes we could get back by clinging to friends who were still " in favour ". It might drag them down, or it might bring us up, and the unhappiness of these little boys forced to choose between dropping a friend in his disgrace or risking disgrace themselves was affecting.

I had two friends whose " favour " was as uncertain as my own, George Orwell, and Cecil Beaton. I was a stage rebel, Orwell a true one. Tall, pale, with his flaccid cheeks, and a matter-of-fact, supercilious voice, he was one of those boys who seem born old. He was incapable of courtship, and when his favour went, it went for ever. He saw through St. Wulfric's, despised Sambo and hated Flip, but was valuable to them as scholarship fodder. We often walked together over the downs in our green jerseys and corduroy breeches, discussing literature, and we both won, in consecutive years, the inevitable " Harrow History Prize ". There was another prize for having the " best list " of books taken out of the library during the term, the kind which might have been only invented to create intellectual snobs, and to satiate boys with the world's culture at a time when they were too young to under-

stand it.   The books were given out in the evening
by Flip herself, and a way by which it was sometimes
possible to get back into "favour" was by taking
out or returning one which caught her eye.   Old boys
who came down enquired, "What sort of favour
are you in?" and letters to those who had gone on
ended up, "I am (touch wood) still in good favour"
—"I shall have to do something, I'm losing favour"
—or "I am in the most awful favour"; unjust
as this feminine tyranny seemed at the time it was a
valuable foretaste of the world outside; even the nick-
name Flip suggested some primitive goddess of fortune.   Thus, although I won the prize through head-
ing my list with "Carlyle's *French Revolution*"—
and Orwell won it next, we were caught at last with
two volumes of *Sinister Street*, and our favour sunk to
zero.

We both wrote poetry.   At sunset, or late at night,
in the dark, I would be visited by the Muse.   In an
ecstasy of flushing and shivering, the tears welling
up as I wrote, I would put down some lines to the
Night Wind.   The next morning they would be
copied out.   Although the process of composition
seemed an authentic visitation, the result was an
imitation of Stevenson or Longfellow, or my favourite,
Robert W. Service.   I would compare them with
Orwell's being critical of his, while he was polite
about mine, and we would separate feeling ashamed of
each other.

The remarkable thing about Orwell was that he
alone among the boys was an intellectual, and not a
parrot, for he thought for himself, read Shaw and

Samuel Butler, and rejected not only St. Wulfric's, but the war, the Empire, Kipling, Sussex, and Character. I remember a moment under a fig-tree in one of the inland boulevards of the seaside town, Orwell striding beside me, and saying in his flat, ageless voice: " You know, Connolly, there's only one remedy for all diseases." I felt the usual guilty tremor when sex was mentioned and hazarded, " You mean going to the lavatory ? " " No—I mean Death ! " He was not a romantic, he had no use for the blandishments of the drill sergeant who made us feel character was identical with boxing, nor for the threats of the chaplain with his grizzled cheektufts, and his gospel of a Jesus of character, who detested immorality and swearing as much as he loved the Allies. " Of course, you realise, Connolly," said Orwell, " that, whoever wins this war, we shall emerge a second-rate nation."

Orwell proved to me that there existed an alternative to character, Intelligence. Beaton showed me another, Sensibility. He had a charming, dreamy face, enormous blue eyes with long lashes, and wore his hair in a fringe. His voice was slow, affected, and creamy. He was not good at games or work, but he escaped persecution through good manners, and a baffling independence. We used to mow the lawn together behind an old pony, sit eating the gooseberries in the kitchen garden, or pretend to polish brass in the chapel; from Orwell I learnt about literature, from Cecil I learnt about art. He occupied his spare time drawing and painting and his holidays in going to the theatre.

On Saturday nights, when the school was entertained in the big schoolroom by such talent as the place could offer, when Mr. Potter had shown lantern slides of *Scrooge*, or Mr. Smedley, dressed up like a pirate at a P. & O. gala, had mouthed out what he called "Poethry" there would be a hush, and Cecil would step forward and sing, "If you were the only girl in the World, and I was the only boy." His voice was small but true, and when he sang these sentimental songs, imitating Violet Loraine or Beatrice Lillie, the eighty-odd Wulfricans felt there could be no other boy in the world for them, the beetling chaplain forgot hell-fire and masturbation, the Irish drill-sergeant his bayonet practice, the staff refrained from disapproving, and for a moment the whole structure of character and duty tottered, the principles of hanging on, muddling through, and building empires were called into question.

On other Saturday nights gramophone records were played; when we came to "I have a song to sing O, sing me your song O" I would open a book which I had bought in the Charing Cross Road, at the prepared place and read:

> Far out at sea when the evening's dusk is falling you may often observe a dark-coloured bird with white under-plumage flit by just above the waves—another and another make their appearance, and you soon find out that a party of Manx Shearwaters have paid your vessel a passing call. They are nocturnal birds for the most part, spending the hours of daylight in their burrows, and coming out in the gloom to speed across the frowning waters in quest of food. There is something very exciting about the appearance of this singular bird. The noisy gulls which have been playing about all day drop slowly astern as the sun nears the west; the parties of Razorbills and Guillemots and Puffins have

214

sped away to their distant breeding colonies ; and the wide waste of waters seems unusually destitute and dreary as the night approaches, and the evening breeze fluttering in the sails, and through the rigging, is the only sound that breaks the oppressive stillness. But the hour of the Manx Shearwater's ghostly revelry has come, he holds high carnival over the waste of gray waters, flitting about in most erratic manner in his wild impetuous course, following the curve of every wave, dipping down into the hollows, where he is almost invisible, and then mounting the foamy crests, where you catch a brief glimpse of his hurried movements.

The combination of the music with this passage was intoxicating. The two blended into an experience of isolation and flight which induced the sacred shiver. The classroom disappeared, I was alone on the dark seas, there was a hush, a religious moment of suspense, and the Manx shearwaters appeared, held their high carnival, etc., and vanished. Then, the schoolroom where each boy sat by his desk, his few possessions inside, his charted ink channels on top, returned to focus. This experience, which I repeated like a drug, every Saturday, was typical of the period. For those were the days when literature meant the romantic escape, the purple patch ; when nobody who taught it would have questioned the absolute beauty of such a line as " clothed in white Samite, mystic, wonderful ! " We were still in the full Tennysonian afterglow and our beliefs, if the muse of St. Wulfric's could have voiced them, would have been somewhat as follows.

" There is a natural tradition in English poetry, my dear Tim, Chaucer begat Spenser, Spenser begat Shakespeare, Shakespeare begat Milton, Milton begat

Keats, Coleridge, Shelley, Wordsworth, and they begat Tennyson, who begat Longfellow, Stevenson, Kipling, Quiller-Couch and Sir Henry Newbolt. There are a few bad boys we do not speak about—Donne, Dryden, Pope, Blake, Byron, Browning, Fitzgerald, who wrote *The Rubá'iyát of Omar Khayyám*, and Oscar Wilde, who was a criminal degenerate. Chaucer is, mediæval but coarse, Spenser is the poet's poet, Shakespeare you will remember from your performance as the witch (' aroint thee, wretch, the rumpfed runion cried her husbands to Aleppo gone the master of the tiger, but in a sieve I'll thither sail and like a rat without a tail I'll do I'll do and I'll do '). Precisely. Milton was a great poet, he wrote *L'Allegro*, *Il Penseroso* and *Paradise Lost*; Keats wrote *The Ode to a Nightingale*; and Tennyson wrote *The Lady of Shalott*—and what else ? *Morte d'Arthur*, *Locksley Hall*, *In Memoriam*, *Break*, *Break*, *Break*, and *Crossing the Bar*. Longfellow wrote *Hiawatha*, Stevenson *Under the Wide and Starry Sky*, Kipling *Sussex* and *If* and *Gunga Din*, Quiller-Couch is a Good Influence and *Drake's Drum* and *Lyra Heroica* are by Sir Henry Newbolt.

" There are other good poems, *Chevy Chase*, *John Gilpin*, *The Armada*, *The Ancient Mariner*, *Grayselegy*. A poem is good either because it is funny (Ingoldsby Legends, Bab Ballads) or because it makes you want to cry. Some funny poems make you want to cry (the Jumblies, the Dong with a Luminous Nose) ; that is because you are not a healthy little boy. You need more Character. The best poems have the most beautiful lines in them ; these lines can be detached, they are purple patches, and Useful in Examinations. Gray's *Elegy* is almost all Purple Patch and so is the *Ode to a Nightingale*, especially

> Magic casements, opening on the foam
> Of perilous seas, in faëry lands forlorn.

When you come to a purple patch you can tell it by an alarm clock going off, you feel a cold shiver, a lump in the throat, your eyes fill with tears and your hair stands on end. You can get these sensations for yourself when you write poems like your *Ode on the Death of Lord Kitchener* or *To the Night Wind*.

" Nobody wrote so many purple patches as Tennyson, and he had character too (*Bury the Great Duke, Charge of the Light Brigade, The Revenge*). Kipling is the only great poet alive to-day. Poetry is romantic, purple—a help in time of trouble—or else it is clever and funny, like Calverley—or has Character. (Life is real, Life is earnest, And the grave is NOT its goal.) It is also something to be ashamed of, like sex, and (except with the chaplain) religion."

My experience with the Manx shearwater fulfilled these conditions. It was prose, so could not become poetry and truly purple, till heightened by music. It was romantic ; something out of the ordinary, remote, and false, for in real life I should hate tossing about the Hebrides in a small boat—and escapist, since I imagined myself away from my present surroundings, alone on the northern waters, and yet not alone, a Manx shearwater, playing with others of my kind. The twilight was " my " time of day (the time I felt most the poetical thrill), the waste of grey waters my weepy Celtic spiritual home.

217

Because poetry was associated with emotional excess, night and unhappiness, I felt disgusted with it by day, as by a friend in whom, when drunk, one has unwisely confided, and I never exhibited the Manx shearwater even to Orwell.

It will be seen that the thread running through this autobiography is an analysis of romanticism, that romanticism in decline under whose shadow we grew up. Romanticism I would call the refusal to face certain truths about the world and ourselves, and the consequences of that refusal. It is a refusal which can be both splendid and necessary, this pretence that truth is beauty and beauty truth, that love is stronger than death, the soul immortal, and the body divine, but in the hundred years that have gone by since the romantic revival we have had too much of it. By the twentieth century it's best work has been done and those of us who thought we were angels or devils have had a long struggle to free ourselves from such ideology. We have been the dupe of words and ideas, we have been unable to know when we are well off, we have expected too much from life, too many treats, and we have precipitated crises to satisfy the appetite for sensation acquired in childhood; the womb world of the hot bath and the celluloid duck has been too near us. The romantic's artillery is always bracketing over the target of reality, falling short into cynicism, or overreaching it into sentimental optimism, so that, whatever the achievements of romanticism in the past, to be a romantic to-day, knowing what we know about the nature of man and his place in the universe, is the mark of a wilful astigmatism, a confession of cowardice and immaturity.

If some of us lived in the world of romantic poetry, we all lived in the world of romantic love ; there was no sentiment in *Maud* or *In Memoriam* that to us seemed exaggerated, we accepted " being half in love with easeful death " as a matter of course, like the psychology of the *Belle Dame Sans Merci*. Love was a recurrent ecstasy which drove us to make sacrifices for an object which might or might not be aware of them. Reciprocation killed love faster than anything, then came Ridicule, it was only Ignorance in the Beloved, that could permit the emotion to last. The prosaic Sambo seemed to have a flair for detecting our romances, and he would try to expel the Cyprian by taps on the head from his heavy silver pencil.

> Always I long to creep
> Into some still cavern deep,
> There to weep and weep, and weep
> My whole soul out to Thee.

Such was my ideal, and if it met with any opposition I would answer in the romantic way with a spiteful poem.

The boy whom . loved for the last three years I was at St. Wulfric's was called Tony Watson. He was small, brown, wiry, good at games, untidy and silent, with a low brow, green eyes, and a fringe of rough short hair. I describe him because he is a type that has recurred through my life and which g(:s me into trouble. It is that faunlike, extrovert creature with a streak of madness and cruelty, not clever,

219

but narcissistic, and quick to adapt itself to clever people. In appearance it is between colours, with a small mouth, slanting eyes, and lemon-yellow skin.

By the time I was twelve all four types to which I am susceptible had appeared. I do not know whether it is glands, numerology, the stars, or only environment that disposes one to these fierce sympathies, inherited as if from another life, but I recognise my kindred forms by now with familiarity ; the Faun, the Redhead, the Extreme Blonde, and the Dark Friend.

The Fauns know their power, which a series of conquests have made obvious, and they derive a pleasure, which I mistake for reciprocation, from watching it at work. They are not people who grow old well, and the world is apt to turn against them. With the other types my relations are happy, I supply them with vitality and intensive cultivation, they provide me with affection, balance, loyalty, good taste. The Extreme Blondes are quiet, intelligent, humorous, receptive ; they have an impressive reserve against which I roll, like the Atlantic Ocean on the Cornish cliffs, confident that they will be able to withstand me. The Dark Friends are the most sympathetic, they have brown eyes and oval faces, They like my jokes, and look after me when I am ill, but it is one of the hardships of romantic love that it rarely is bestowed on people like ourselves, and the Dark Friends end by being Consolers. The Redheads have some of the quieting effect of the Extreme Blondes, but they may suddenly become as deleterious as the Faun. They are a special type,

220

not the dreamy, brown-eyed, long-faced auburn, nor the aggressive albino, but the gay Ginger Rogers.

Being an only child I romanticised sisterhood, I wanted an Electra, and longed for a relationship with sister types of the same age. I liked health and equality in women, an implicit friendship. The same was true with my imaginary brothers. The Dark Friends and the Extreme Blondes supplied this, the Redheads added an excitement which raised it to perfection. And then the exotic Faun would reappear and harmony would vanish. As in other only children my desire for a brother or a sister was so strong that I came to exist in terms of the couple; in whatever group I found myself I would end by sharing my life with one other, driven by an inner selection through a course of trial and error, till after forming one of a group of four or five, and then of a trio, I achieved stability as the half of a pair.

I called this search for the " *dimidium animae meae* " the Pair System, and was fascinated, when I read the Symposium of Plato later, to come across his theory that human beings had once been double, and were for ever seeking the counterpart from whom they had been so rudely forced. We were all one half of a Siamese Twin.

> The brothered one, the not alone
> The brothered and the hated.

But it is a romantic theory, and it is part of the romantic's misfortune that in the search for his affinity he is not guided by a community of interests, but by those intimations which are the appeal of a mouth or an eye, an appeal which is not even private, so that the spectacle is presented of half-a-dozen Platonic half-men trying to unite with the same indifferent body. Love at first sight—and the first sight is the supreme consummation for romantics—is an intuition bred by habit of the person who can do them harm.

Yet Tony Watson let me down lightly. He was a wild little boy, with plenty of character, but not of the right kind. He taught me to smoke, which I hated; to rag in the corridors at night, fighting among the coats hanging from their pegs, and to take part, on the downs, in gang warfare, which I adored. He moved in a fast set of hard-smoking and hard-swearing cronies, from whom he protected me. Our unlikeness made us over-polite. He accepted my devotion, even a poem beginning, "Watson, the silent, Watson, the dauntless" and showed me, in return, an extraordinary drawing, a Parthenon Frieze of sheets of paper stuck together that unfolded like a concertina, and revealed a long procession of soldiers—cavalry, infantry, artillery, wounded and dying, doctors, nurses, ghurkas, staff-officers and engineers on their way to the war.

The war for most of us was skin-deep. The *Titanic* had gone down, the passengers all singing, "Nearer my God to Thee"—that was terrible—and now the war : pins stuck in maps, the Kaiser dying of cancer of the throat, Kitchener drowned, ration cards, Business as Usual, a day when we were told of the Battle of Jutland, and another when we heard that a terrible thing had happened, a revolution in Russia, with a monster called Kerensky now in power. None of us, except perhaps Orwell, believed that England could

222

lose the war or that we would grow up to fight in it, but meanwhile Watson's exact and bloodthirsty pageant grew fuller, a page at a time, till it stretched, by 1917, the length of the schoolroom.

Tony shared my love of animals and drew for me pictures of foxes in lonely postures barking to the moon. I had several excruciating moments with him. Once we vowed blood-brotherhood in the Albanian way. Tony cut a cross on each left hand and we held the bleeding scratches together. Another time, left in the bathroom alone, he came up to me, wrapped in his bath towel, and pursed his lips for a kiss. My modesty made me flinch. He turned away and never tried again, while for weeks I lay awake angry and miserable. He slept in a dormitory called the Red Room, I was in a two-bedded one across the passage with the Dark Friend, his cousin, Frankie Wright. Tony would come over in the morning after a night of pillow fighting, gang reprisals, and smoking on the roof, and get into my bed, where my innocence hung round my neck like an albatross. Then the eight o'clock bell would ring and we would troop down to the plunge-bath. There was a smell of gooseflesh and slimy water. One by one, under the cold eye of Sambo, and to the accompaniment of such comments as " Go on Marsden, you stink like a polecat ", we dived or jumped in, until it was the turn of the group of water-funks, who shrank down the steps, groaning wer-wer-wer, while the sergeant-major waited to haul them out by a rope attached to a pole. When the last had been towed it was time to dress and go on the asphalt for gym.

Year by year the air, the discipline, the teaching, the association with other boys, and the driving will of Flip, had their effect on me. I grew strong and healthy, and appeared to be normal, for I became a good mixer, a gay little bit who was quick to spot whom to make up to in a group, and how to do it. I knew how far to go in teasing and responding to teasing, and became famous for my " repartee ". I had a theory that there was one repartee effective for every situation, and spent weeks in elaborating it. At that time the magic phrase seemed, " Dear me, how very uninteresting ! " If I had to choose one now it would be " This is a very bad moment for both of us." I kept a Funny Book which contained satirical poems and character sketches. I became good at history, that is to say I learnt dates easily, knew which battle was fought in the snow, and who was the little gentleman in black velvet. I read Dickens, Thackeray, Carlyle and Scott and got marks for them, and for pleasure John Buchan. It was time for me to go up for a scholarship. I had crammed Watson energetically for the common entrance, which he managed to pass, and when I saw him again in the holidays he was a dapper public schoolboy with his hair brushed back, a felt hat and a cane, and we had nothing to say to each other.

We still wrote letters however ; there was something harrowing about them, I looked forward to getting them, with their misspellings and drawings of animals coloured for me, but between the one who stays on at a school and the one who leaves it communication grows impossible. I felt like an old custodian guarding a crumbling shrine from an ignorant generation, and yet drawn away from it, and towards that generation. Tony began to feel forgotten by St. Wulfric's, and would reproach me with having a new best friend, then he began to forget it in his turn. " O last regret, regret can die "— our letters were full of protestations ; I kept his, for they were for me a religion, a religion of loyalty, of faith defying time, of friendship triumphing over distraction. If I failed him, I failed myself and love —yet I had to fail him, unless, at the age of twelve, I could learn to live in the past, a disconsolate widower. At last the letters, with their postscript of scribbled kisses by which we clung to a shrinking icefloe of common experience, ceased, and we breathed more freely. I was brotherless again.

I first went up for a scholarship with Orwell, at Wellington. I hated every moment, the blue-suited prefects bustling about the dismal brick and slate, the Wellingtonias and rhododendrons, infertile flora of the Bagshot sand. It was winter, and an old four-wheeler bore me from the examinations to my great-aunts, with whom I was staying. The musical groaning of the wheels and springs in the winter stillness had a profound effect, and I felt like Childe Roland, mystical and Celtic. Pines and heather seemed to have a message for me, to be the background for some great event as I trundled through them after the afternoon paper. Orwell got a scholarship, I did not, but the experience was considered good practice.

A year later I went up for Eton, which was very

different. Sambo took us ; he knew many people there, and we had tea with old Wulfrician boys and masters. I had a moment on Windsor Bridge ; it was summer, and, after the coast, the greenness of the lush Thames Valley was enervating and oppressive ; everything seemed splendid and decadent, the huge stale elms, the boys in their many-coloured caps and blazers, the top hats, the strawberries and cream, the smell of wistaria. I looked over the bridge as a boy in an outrigger came gliding past, like a waterboatman. Two Etonians were standing on the bridge and I heard one remark, " Really that man Wilkinson's not at all a bad oar." The foppish drawl, the two boys with their hats on the back of their heads, the graceful sculler underneath, seemed the incarnation of elegance and maturity.

There was no doubt that this was the place for me, for all of it was, from the St. Wulfric's point of view, utterly and absorbingly evil. I got in twelfth on History and English as Orwell, after Wellington, had done the year before. In case there was no vacancy I went up for one more scholarship, this time at Charterhouse, where we did the examination in a cellar during an air raid.

My last year at St. Wulfric's was rosy. I was in sixth form, which had a sitting-room of its own, with Ned Northcote, the captain of the school (Extreme Blond), Frankie Wright (Dark Friend), and Nigel Kirkpatrick (Faunlike). We were about as civilised as little boys can grow to be. We were polite and we hardly ever caned anyone. We wrote to each other in the holidays, we got on with each other's

226

parents, we went to theatres together, and had tea at Rumpelmayer's. Ned was captain of the eleven and Nigel of the football team. I was head of the sixth.

My lack of character was now a permanent feature. I was *unreliable*. For that reason I was head of the sixth but not captain of the school, I occupied already the position I was to occupy in after life, that of the intellectual who is never given the job, because he is brilliant but unsound. I was also a physical coward, though I learnt how to conceal it, a captain of second elevens, and a moral coward, in compensation, since, in an English community, moral cowardice is an asset.

Already I had accepted the theory that (1) Character is more important than intellect. (2) Intellect is usually found without character (Oscar Wilde). (3) Intellect, when found with character, is called Nous. (Intellect plus character = Nous plus gumption.) Character is desirable because it makes for success at school (winning colours and reporting best friend for homosexuality), prepares boys for the university, and is the foundation of success in business, politics, the army, the navy, the Indian and Egyptian civil services, and the African Police. But my analysis of success had disclosed another quality which seemed, in school life at any rate, to go as far. It might be called Prettiness. In the matriarchy of St. Wulfric's, it was not Character, but Character plus Prettiness that succeeded ; Colin and Nigel Kirkpatrick in their green kilts, even the outlawed Tony Watson, or Roy Brown with his treble voice ; they

were the favoured of fortune, petted when others were
scolded, permitted to wait at Sunday night supper
in their blue suits, introduced to the guests when
they brought the food into the room, and able to
stuff their pockets with potato salad when they took
it out.

Prettiness alone (Cecil) was suspect like intellect
alone (Orwell), but prettiness that was good at games
meant " Character " and was safe. Since I was not
pretty I worked hard to be charming, and the four
of us grew so civilised that we became inseparable.
We were a little clique at the head of the school, a
kind of " Souls " of St. Wulfric's, gay, powerful,
introspective and absorbed in each other's impressions. We took to visiting in our cubicles at night.
One evening, after lights out, Ned Northcote, and
Frankie Wright were in mine when we heard the
matron pass along.

> Stalk and sneak, stalk and sneak,
> Maud of the rubbery shoes.
> Sneak sneak every week,
> Maud of the rubbery shoes.
> Over the cubicle wings you go
> Hearing the Red Room whispering low . . .

I had once written to please Tony, and now it was
my turn to be caught.

Maud went into Northcote's cubicle. No sign of
him. She called out in a terrible voice, " Where's
Northcote ? " I answered from my cubicle, " I think
he went to the lavatory." We heard her go along
to open the door and lost our heads, like rabbits
chased by a ferret. Ned bolted the latch of my
cubicle with a toothbrush, and started to climb over

the partition into his own. But Maud came and rattled it. " Why is this door locked ? Open it this instant." I was afraid to. Silence. At last, with white face, Frankie opened it and she burst in. There was an eternity of waiting while our crime was reported, and then the three of us were taken down and caned by Sambo in our pyjamas. The locked door was evidence which our unromantic number could not palliate. It was Oscar Wilde over again.

The caning was only the beginning, next day our sergeant's stripes were removed, we were turned out of sixth form, and a period of miserable disfavour started, from which there seemed no hope of escape. But my scholarship was needed, like Ned's bowling, for propaganda ; gradually we were forgiven, and our disgrace forgotten, except by ourselves. For we never felt quite the same, we realised that there was a pitch of civilisation which once reached, brought down a Nemesis. Character was safest, we had seen the writing on the wall.

Before I went to Eton I had spent the Christmas of 1917 in Ireland, in my aunt's house at Rathfarnham. The Easter Rebellion had taken place since I was last there, and to be pro-Irish, pro-Celt, pro-Gaelic was no longer a harmless eccentricity. I used to go riding with a groom over the Wicklow mountains, and for the first time the Sinn Feiner of St. Wulfric's met his equal. Frank, the groom was supposed to command a company of the Irish republican army whom he drilled in the glens of Kilmashogue and up by the Hell Fire Club. I afterwards pretended that I had been present at these parades, but never met anyone with him except an old hermit. We went to the Abbey Theatre, and saw Synge acted, and heard " God Save the King " hissed, and to Clontarf for a pink-coated Christmas dinner, at which everyone told hunting stories in the brogue. I felt dowdy, awkward, and English again.

Otherwise my holidays had been uneventful. My great moment at home had been the purchase of a bicycle with three speeds, which I called the Green Dragon. I rode it over to where we lived at Crondall, and a few days later was allowed to go away for a night on it by myself. My mother and Uncle Granville saw me off. I bicycled that day from Farnham to Winchester, stayed at the George and went over the school and the Cathedral. The hotel people thought I had run away from somewhere, and were suspicious, for the sight of a tourist of thirteen booking a room and dining by himself, with a guidebook, was unusual. It was the first welling up of the love of travel that was to dominate my spare time for the next twenty years.

I was still ignorant of anything I had not read in a book, but just before I went to Eton a concerted attack was made on my modesty. My father struggled to explain the facts of life, and the chaplain at St. Wulfric's gave the boys who were leaving a seedy exhortation. Sambo was more precise. We were going into a world full of temptations, he said, especially the Etonians ; we must report any boy at once who tried to get into our bed, never go for a walk with a boy from another house, never make friends with anyone more than a year and a half older, or, eventually, younger, and above all, not play with ourselves. There was an old boy from St. Wulfric's who had done it so much that when he got to Oxford he had put, in a fit of remorse, his head under a train. That miserable boy, I afterwards learnt, had attended all the private schools in England.

Sambo gave a few examples of Wulfricians who had made good, and mentioned cases where those who were doing well, and were heads of houses, had been able to lend a helping hand to those floundering amid sexual difficulties due to lack of character. The other boys leaving looked at me curiously, for I was warned to be careful, since my literary temperament rendered me more open to " all that kind of poisonous nonsense ", and I was told that the boy with " character " in my election at Eton, who would, although not an old Wulfrician, keep an eye on me, was called Meynell. The Easter term over, we bade a tearful farewell to each other, Flip turned into a friend, and Nigel Kirkpatrick, Ned Northcote, Frankie Wright, promised to exchange letters with me from Marlborough, Repton and Radley. But it was three years before I wrote another letter.

CHAPTER XX

DARK AGES

IF we had written, our letters would have told the same story. The lively aristocrats of the cubicles and the sixth-form room were reduced to serfdom, cultivated Greeks pitched into the Carthaginian slave market. We began to adapt ourselves to our new indignity; C. V. Connolly, Esq., K.S., New Buildings, Eton College, Windsor.

The seventy Eton scholars lived together in a house, part Victorian, part mediæval, where they were ruled by the Master in College, who had under him the Captain of the School, and nine other members of sixth form, who wore stick-up collars, could cane, and have fags. The boys were divided into elections, according to the year in which they won their scholarship; the elections moved slowly up the school *en bloc*, and each represented a generation.

Below the top twenty came another thirty boys or so, who formed the bulk of college, and then the bottom twenty, about fifteen of whom were doing their compulsory year of fagging, and who, while all the others had rooms, lived in cubicles in Chamber.

The whole school, ruled in theory by sixth form and the Captain of the School, was governed by Pop, or the Eton Society, an oligarchy of two dozen boys who, except for two or three *ex officio* members, were self-elected and could wear coloured waistcoats, stick-up collars, etc., and cane boys from any house. The masters could not cane. They punished by lines, detentions, and " tickets " or chits of misbehaviour which had to be carried to the housemaster for signature. Serious offences, or too many tickets, meant being complained of to the headmaster, and might end in a birching.

This system makes Eton the most democratic of schools, for it is a school where all the prefects except the sixth form (who are only powerful in College) are self-elected. The boys have the government they deserve.

In practice Eton was not a democracy, for the system was feudal. The masters represented the church, with the headmaster as Pope ; the boys, with their hierarchy of colours and distinctions, were the rest of the population, while the prefects and athletes, the captains of houses and the members of " Pop " were the feudal overlords who punished offences at the request of the " church ", and in return were allowed to break the same rules themselves. Thus a boy had two loyalties, to his tutor, and to his fag-master or feudal overlord. Sometimes the " church " could protect a young clerk, making the lot of a serious little boy more bearable, in other houses the house-master was powerless, the " church " weak, and unable to control the feudal barons. At other times there were struggles between master and boy which ended in Canossa.

233

On the whole the feudal system worked well. The boys elected to Pop, those who combined goodness at games with elegance, vitality, and a certain mental alertness, were urbane and tolerant, it was among the house-barons that bullies and stupid types were to be found.

A fag in Chamber I was in the lowest ranks of serfdom. Though fagmasters were usually chivalrous to their own slaves, mine was not, nor had we privacy, for our spare time was at the mercy of our rulers, who could send us far into Windsor to buy them food and beat us if we made a mistake over it. I had not often been beaten at St. Wulfric's, at Eton it became a hideous experience, for even the little boy who was " Captain of Chamber " could beat us, not with a cane, but with a piece of rubber tubing. There was a " Chamber Pop " who also could beat one in a body for a breach of privilege.

I felt quite lost and friendless in this world, and sought out Meynell, who had no use for me. He was the familiar blend of character and prettiness, a tousled wire-terrier of a boy, tough, humorous, a natural leader and political commissar. We were all unhappy, and had such a feeling of persecution that we bullied each other to forget it. I was sixty-ninth in college order, and among the most bullied boys in my election, where Meynell was the ringleader. He invented tortures as a perpetual inquest to see if we had " guts ", and was much liked in the elections above him, who considered him a " good influence ".

Nobody would have believed that he could make me stand on a mantelpiece and dance while he

234

brandished a red-hot poker between my feet and said. " What is your name ? " " Connolly." " No—what is your name ? Go on. Say it." " Ugly." " All right, Ugly, you can come down." He was aided by a few boys who hoped that their sycophancy would save their skins, and by another bully called High-worth. Highworth was not a torturer like Meynell, but a conceited, rakish, conventional boy, who could not bear anyone to be eccentric or untidy. He should never have been in College, he was a natural Oppidan.

I spent much of my spare time in School Library, moping among the poets. I had discovered the Celtic Twilight, and in proportion as I was unhappy, I took it out on the *Lake Isle of Innisfree*, the *Little Waves of Breffny*, *Glencullen* and other escapist poems, to which I added the *Golden Journey to Samarcand*. I tried to make friends with one other bullied boy, but he reciprocated too violently, showed me poems, and sniffed at the back of his nose. Instead I fell for a boy called Wilfrid, the faun type over again with green eyes, nectarine colouring, who was quick to divine in the little black-gowned, dirty colleger a potential admirer, even as a beautiful orchid accepts the visits of some repulsive beetle. He was an Oppidan, good at games, and older than me. It was possible to see him leaving his classroom about once a week, or sometimes coming out of Chapel or at Absence, when the whole of Feudal society assembled in School Yard. If he was with anyone important he would cut me ; if not he would make a joke or two at my expense, while I grinned like a waiter. My day-dreams centred round him. I looked up his home address, found out about his family, and copied his initials on to bits of paper. It was something to be in love again.

The beatings were torture. We were first conscious of impending doom at Prayers, when the eyes of sixth form would linger on us. They had supper in a room of their own, and a special fag, " senior ", who was excused ordinary duties, like other police spies, was sent from there to fetch the " wanted " man. From Upper Tea Room " Senior " set out on his vile errand, past the boys chatting outside their rooms. " Who's ' wanted ' ? " " Connolly." At last he reached the fags who were shivering with terror—for this was always an agonising quarter of an hour for them— in their stalls in Chamber. Those who were sitting in their tin baths paused with the sponge in the air—they might have to get out again to dress. The talkers ceased their chorus simultaneously, like frogs, and fear swept over the wooden partitions. " It's Connolly." " Connolly, you're ' wanted '." " Who by ? " " Wrangham." " That's all right. He can't beat me, only tick me off. He's my fag-master." " He's going to beat someone. He's got the chair out."

The chair was only put in the middle of the room when beatings were to take place, and sometimes the fag was sent beforehand to get the canes with which he would be beaten himself.

The worst part was the suspense, for we might make a mistake the day before and not be beaten for it till the following evening. Or we could get a day's grace by pleading a headache and getting " early bed leave " or by going out to the shooting range, the musical society, or a mysterious evening service, held once a week to end the war, which was much frequented by guilty consciences, called Intercession. The huge chapel was dark and deserted, the gas mantles plopped, the stained-glass windows glittered, the headmaster droned the prayers from the altar. I too was praying. " Please God may Wrangham not ' want ' me, please please God may Wrangham not ' want ' me, or may he forget to-morrow, and I will clean my teeth. And make me see Wilfrid. Amen."

Often mass executions took place ; it was not uncommon for all the fags to be beaten at once. After a storm of accusation to which it was wiser not to reply, since no one, once the chair was out, had been known to " get off ", the flogging began. We knelt on the chair and gripped the bottom bar with our hands, stretching towards it over the back. Looking round under the chair we could see a monster rushing towards us with a cane in his hand, his face upside down and distorted. The pain was acute. When it was over some other member of sixth form would say " Good night "—it was wiser to answer.

These memories are associated for me with the smell of sixth form supper and with the walk back through the spectators to the bed that pulled down from the wall, the knowing enquiries of the master in college, a Jesuit at these executions, and the darkness that prisoners long for.

The Captain of the School, Marjoribanks, who afterwards committed suicide, was a great beater.

237

Meynell began to receive anonymous notes which made certain suggestions, and showed character by taking them to his fagmaster. The Captain of the School was told, and the culprit was ordered to confess ; nothing happened. Then another note arrived. The sender, clearly high in the school, was never found, but in one satisfactory evening Marjoribanks had beaten all the lower half of college. Thirty-five of us suffered. Another time we were all beaten because a boy dropped a sponge out of a window which hit a master, or we would be beaten for " generality ", which meant no specific charge except that of being " generally uppish ".

The result of this, combined with chamber beatings and bullyings, was to ruin my nerve. My work went off, and I got tickets which I had to present my tutor, in itself a torture. To this day I cannot bear to be sent for, or hear of anyone wanting to see me without an acute nervous dread.

My own election were broken under the strain of beatings at night, and bullying by day ; all we could hope for was to achieve peace with seniority and then start beating in our turn. But there was one ray of hope. The election now in power was a reactionary one, which would be succeeded by a gentler lot, and our own senior election, the year above us, whom we as yet hardly knew, contained heroic fighters for liberty and justice. It bristled with Pyms and Hampdens and the feudal system was powerless there.

I had another stroke of luck. After a " chamber pop beating " from Meynell and four other boys, he

238

began a heart-to-heart—" Ugly, why are you so filthy, what is the matter with you ? " After the tears which followed I succeeded in making him laugh, and revealed my capacity as a wit. I was able to expand it, and soon I could make not only Meynell laugh, but Highworth : they began to leave me alone, bullying me when they could not find anyone else, but even then sparing me, if I seemed unsuspecting and confident, and did not smell of fear. At last I made them laugh at the expense of their victims and my sarcasm became useful. One evening in my second term, after the Armistice had been signed, Meynell asked me to call him Godfrey. From then I was safe, my prayers at intercession were answered. I had become a bully too.

Highworth's father was a general, Meynell's a colonel, mine a major. We became the rulers of Chamber, in which Godfrey Meynell was the Hitler, Highworth the Goering, and I the Goebbels, forming a Gestapo who bullied everyone we could and confiscated their private property.

After two terms of being bullied, I had a year of bullying with occasional relapses, when, owing to my bad tactics, I let both Godfrey and Highworth combine against me. Yet we were fond of each other and our triumvirate was racked with jealousy. Highworth was a big neat handsome boy, good at games, a fast bowler, fond of girls and dirty stories. Godfrey was untidy, lazy, yet energetic, sentimental and self-reproachful, with a saving grace of humour, a border baron half-converted to Christianity, whose turbulent life fitted exactly into the pattern of Eton feudalism, for he was an example of character and prettiness in authority; his courage was tremendous, to play football under his captaincy, on a losing side, was a sensation. For an hour and a quarter he blamed, praised and appealed to our feelings, leading rush after rush against boys bigger than himself, poaching any kicks he could get, and limping off the field with his arm round my neck. " My God, you went badly to-day, Nolly—haven't you any guts—to think we lost to those bastards by three to one," and tears of rage would roll down his cheeks. " Next time we've got to win—we've just go to—understand, Flinch-face ? "

His personality dominated us because it was the strongest, and because it was the incarnation of schoolboyness; the five hundred years of Eton life had gone to make it, the Gothic windows, the huge open fireplace, the table in the middle of Chamber round which our life centred, had been brought into being for him. He was emotional and as Captain of Chamber, would " beat " me for untidiness, half miserable at having to flog his best friend, half pleased at fulfilling a Roman duty, only to suffer remorse at the condition of his own belongings. " God knows what I'm to do—I can't let you beat *me*—I haven't the authority—if I ask you to hit me as hard as you can I might lose my temper and knock you down. We'll have to make Wayne and Buckley tidy our stalls for us in future."

Godfrey's relaxation was reading Homer, he adored the Odyssey, for the Homeric world was one in which he was at home and the proverbs of " the wily

Odysseus ", to the disgust of the able but Philistine
Highworth, were never off his lips. " Oh, babababar-
baba bababababarbaba," he would storm ; " for God's
sake stop spouting Greek—I can't understand a fellow
with guts like you, Godfrey, wanting to quote that filthy
Greek all the time—and as for you, Cyril, you're worse,
—nine bloody beanrows will I have there and a hive for
the honey bloody bee—my God it makes me crap."

Between two such personalities it seemed that I
never would have a chance to develop, or find room
to reach out to the sun, but I had two pieces of
good fortune. Highworth was sent away for two
terms, and Godfrey got pneumonia. He was in the
sick-room for a month, and while he was ill his trampled
satellites plucked up their courage. I made friends
with three of them, and when he came back, we
presented a united front against further bullying.
Godfrey himself was deeply altered by his illness,
his mischievous restlessness left him ; being ill for
so long, and perhaps discovering how little he was
missed, and how well people got on without him,
how transitory was power, had changed his character. For the rest of his time at Eton, (he left early
for Sandhurst), he was hardworking and modest. He
never recovered his leadership, but became liked by
all those who once had gone in fear of him. The
border baron, the prince of the dark ages, had undergone a change of heart, a genuine conversion.

Godfrey afterwards joined his father's regiment,
went out to India, and had himself transferred to the
Indian Army, for he disliked the social side of army
life, and wanted to be in closer contact with the men

he loved. From there he went with his ghurkas to Waziristan, still reading Homer, and was killed in action on the frontier, winning a posthumous V.C.

> Liquenda tellus et domus et placens
> Uxor . . .

Encased in the shell secreted by my cowardice, I have thought about his death on that untenable hillside, outnumbered, putting heart into his troops by assuring them that help would reach them, though aware that help could not, and dying covered with wounds after fighting all day.

Such an end seems remote from the literary life, yet it was the end of one my own age, with whom for four years I had been shaken about like stones in a tin. To a parent passing through College there must have seemed nothing to choose between Godfrey and myself, two small boys in Eton jackets cooking their fagmaster's sausages, both untidy, noisy, and mouse-coloured, and yet in each a fate was at work; two characters, reacting differently to the same environment, were shaping our lives. The qualities I admire are intellectual honesty, generosity, courage, and beauty. Godfrey was brave. I was not.

Such was the reward of leadership, the destiny of character, not the position of business responsibility which St. Wulfric's promised, but a premature and lonely death with the barren glory of a military honour.

*　　*　　*

The boys with whom I now made friends were Charles Milligan, Kit Minns, and Jackie O'Dwyer. Charles became of morbid interest through being caught smoking, which made him seem romantic and subversive. He was the Extreme Blond, with delicate features and an air of neatness and languor. Minns, a peaceable Oriental-looking boy, surprised the Gestapo by refusing to be bullied. He was quiet and good-natured, but when threats or force were employed he would not move. The Gestapo were puzzled; we felt like hunters up against a new animal, for Minns was invincible, not through his badgerlike strength, but because he knew he was right. For the first time we felt guilty, aware that our bullying proceeded from a sense of inferiority deepened by sexual ignorance, and confined ourselves henceforth to the official victims.

O'Dwyer was nearly always in tears, but he was Irish like myself, and I secretly made friends with him. We arranged that if he stood up to the Gestapo I would try to prevent him being punished. The moment came. Godfrey, as usual, was late for something in changing. " My God, I've lost my braces." He looked round, then marched up. " O'Dwyer, give me your braces." " No." " Take off your braces and give them me at once." " No." This was unheard of : Godfrey glowered at O'Dwyer, who stood rooted to the spot with the tears streaming down his face. After a silence, Godfrey turned away and got the braces elsewhere. Another serf was on the road to emancipation. Not unnaturally our election had a bad name, though no one knew what was going on in it.

I was now fifteen, dirty, inky, miserable, untidy, a bad fag, a coward at games, lazy at work, unpopular with my masters and superiors, anxious to curry favour, and yet bully whom I dared. The

law of the election system was that we spoke only
to the boys of our own year; we could be beaten for
speaking first to a boy in an election above, and
could enforce the same discipline on those below.
All our election were formal with the year that had
arrived beneath us. I got a bad report and was
described as " cynical and irreverent " " *tu ne cede
malis* ", wrote Mr. Stone, " *sed contra audentior ito* ".

My parents were upset, heads were put together,
and the blame was thrown on Orwell, who was supposed
to be my " bad influence ", though now I hardly
saw him. We had been for walks on Sundays,
but we belonged to different civilisations. He was
immersed in *The Way of all Flesh* and the atheistic
arguments of *Androcles and the Lion*, I in the Celtic
Twilight, and Lady Gregory's resurrected Gaelic
legends. His election found us (Meynell excluded)
brutish and savage. They were anxious to talk to
their junior election, and attack in that way the
reactionary " election " system, but they did not
know how to begin for we were hardly the material
on which liberal opinions could be tested.

The moral leaders of my senior election, known
as " the caucus ", were Denis Dannreuther, Roger
Mynors, Robert Longden, Gibson and Cazalet. Orwell
was rather aloof, and Farlow, the most original and
vigorous member, too rough and cynical, for the lofty
inner ring of whiggery. One day at the end of my
sixth term I found myself " staying out " in the sick-
room with Roger Mynors. Day by day we made
friends, discovering in each other the inevitable
passion for the Isle of Purbeck, for chalk streams and

geography, and for the first time I underwent the civilising influence of my senior election. They were a remarkable set of boys, and included a batch of five scholar athletes, animated, unlike the rulers of college, by post-war opinions. They hated bullying, beating, fagging, the election system, militarism, and infringements of liberty, and believed in the ultimate victory of human reason. They were polite to each other, and formed an oasis of enlightenment, with one set of baby reactionaries underneath them, and another, more dangerous, in the year above.

Mynors did not drop me when we came out of the sick-room, and an epidemic of mumps thinned out my election, enabling Charles Milligan, Jacky O'Dwyer and myself to push forward together. Jacky was clever, lazy, good at games, and attractive. He represented a type which is found in every school, the genial kind of boy whose life is a succession of enthusiasms ; for dab cricket, for learning all the peers by sight, the variations of the house colours, the results of the Harrow matches, or the batting averages of the eleven. He was sunny and tolerant, suspected of " not going hard " in the more painful sports, and like myself, greedy. We ate quantities of bananas and cream, and all day played a game called " passage fives " under a white fused light in the echoing mump-stricken corridor. Roger Mynors walked about with me and called me the " little ray of sunshine ". The affectionate and civilised head boy of St. Wulfric's showed himself again, and that Easter, after my fourth term, I wrote O'Dwyer a letter. The dark ages were over.

CHAPTER XXI

RENAISSANCE

IT was now the summer of nineteen twenty. I was no longer a fag, and had a room of my own. Neither a ruler nor a worker, I formed part of the central bourgeoisie of College. I first saw Nigel by the letter slab, and from that moment I was as much changed as Godfrey by pneumonia. The " pair system " reappeared in my life, the faun, the dream brother. That afternoon we played in a knock-up cricket match, and each made twenty-five. Nigel had all the familiar features, dark hair, green eyes, yellow skin, and a classic head with the wistfulness of a minor angel in a Botticelli, but, being a colleger, he was not stupid like Wilfrid or Tony; in spite of the year and a half between our ages, companionship was possible.

To say I was in love again will vex the reader beyond endurance, but he must remember that being in love had a peculiar meaning for me. I had never been kissed, and love was an ideal based on the exhibitionism of the only-child. It meant a desire to lay my personality at someone's feet as a puppy deposits a slobbery ball; it meant a non-stop day-dream, a planning of surprises, an exchange of con-

246

fidences, a giving of presents, an agony of expectation, a delirium of impatience, ending with the premonition of boredom more drastic than the loneliness which it set out to cure. I was now entering adolescence and was long to suffer from that disfiguring ailment. My sense of values was to be affected, my emotions falsified, my mind out of focus, my idea of reality imposed on reality, and where they did not tally, reality would be cut to fit.

Nigel was in my sub-junior election. This meant that, although I could be seen about with my junior election, I could not be seen with him. One way I could talk to him was by availing myself of co-ordinated visits to the shooting gallery, glimpses on the way to meals, leaving chapel, at absence, or other ceremonies of the community. The other was to frequent my junior election, and make use of the etiquette by which they were allowed to go about with him. This meant altering my ideas about the election system, in fact, ceasing to be a reactionary. The change in emotional life led, as is often the case, to a new political alignment.

I first made friends with the two civilised members of my junior election, Peter Loxley and Walter Le Strange, and through them was able to see something of Nigel, and his red-haired friend Freddie Langham. At the same time, growing more liberal, I became more acceptable to the election above. Denis Dannreuther and Robert Longden took me up, and afterwards Farlow and George Wansbrough. At the end of the term I sat next Nigel at a house-match. (I could not give a picture of Eton

247

if I did not emphasise how much time was devoted to planning meetings with people of another year or in another house ; the intrigues were worthy of Versailles or Yildiz.) At the house-match I asked Nigel who he liked best in the school. Langham ? " Second best," Loxley ? " Fourth best," and so on. He also asked me. We realised that we had both omitted " first best " and that the only people we had not mentioned had been each other. I experienced the thrill not untinged with apprehension by which the romantic recognises reciprocated love.

Then came Camp, where my father, who lived near, gave dinner-parties for Godfrey, and my new friends, Mynors, Runciman, Wansbrough, Longden, and Dadie Rylands. Our house was a refuge from Camp and, making up my little dinner parties, I tasted the joys of being a political hostess, and laid plans for the future.

The Christmas term of 1920 I was launched. Looking back at my schooldays I am conscious of a rhythm about them, every year culminated in the summer term ; it was the term when things happened, the climax of emotions, successes, and failures. I never felt well in the summer term. The Thames Valley climate was lowering, I was enervated by the profusion of elms and buttercups and sheep-turds, the heat and the leisure. The summers at Eton were too pagan, one collapsed half-way through. Those hot afternoons when the " toc toc " of bat hitting ball resounded, and I sat in the shade with a book, or wandered through the deserted buildings, where the chalky sunbeam lay aslant the desk, were deleterious. Christmas terms meant consolidation, and new beginnings; Easter was a season of promise; the games that I was good at were fives and squash; I liked the Easter terms best. Christmas was a primitive, Easter the quattrocento, and summer the decadence.

To this day I can tell whether a person is school-minded: whether they are cowardly, gregarious, sensitive to pupil-teacher relationships, warm, competitive and adolescent—or whether they are school-proof. The art of getting on at school depends on a mixture of enthusiasm with moral cowardice and social sense. The enthusiasm is for personalities, and gossip about them, for a schoolboy is a novelist too busy to write. Orwell, for example, or Runciman, who divided the world into two groups, the stupids, and the sillies, lacked the ape-like virtues without which no one can enjoy a public school. I had them, and from now on was happy and successful. I joined the College Literary Society, for which we wrote poems, and criticism.

I had two friends in super-senior election who belonged, Dadie Rylands and Terence Beddard, whom I called, as one was so much more censorious than the other, the Old and the New Testament. Dadie was a charming, feline boy; he lent me modern poetry to read, in the Chap Books which were then coming out. He liked Rupert Brooke and introduced me to the Georgians. My possession of these Chap Books awoke in Highworth envy tinged with incomprehension. " My God, Cyril—if I'd known you were going to turn into a bloody æsthete, and go bumsucking after

249

people like Rylands! There's Godfrey turned pi as hell and all the rest of our election without any guts —and now you start letting your hair grow long and reading those bloody chapbooks. Rupert Brooke! Ow boo-hoo boo-hoo, stands the church clock at ten to bloody three and is there honey still for bloody tea!" After this I lost my temper, and for the next year never spoke to him. Handsome and neat as ever, with several cricket colours, and many Oppidan friends, he had hopes of getting into Pop, and yet was bewildered, isolated from the rest of us by his lack of adolescence.

One day I wrote a pines-and-heather poem myself for the Literary Society, which was favourably criticised. The last couplet was:

And, winging down the evening sky,
The herons come to the heronry.

Dadie said that by accident I had written a couplet as good as anything in Rupert Brooke. Godfrey took me aside and said that he wished he could have written the poem, that it expressed everything he felt and that he did not know anyone else could feel. Even Terence Beddard, a dandy with a romantic side, and a gift for satire, was impressed—but Highworth never saw it.

Terence and I did classics up to Headlam in the same division, we satirised Georgian poetry and the literary society in our spare time, and invented a Georgian poet called Percy Beauregard Biles. Terence was a Byronic character, the first one I had met, he was a Mercutio, a foppish, melancholy and ironical person. I used to go along to talk in his

250

room and we discovered a common interest in Nigel. By then I liked Freddie Langham almost as much, he was more engaging, intelligent, and whole-hearted than Nigel, who could embarrass me by displaying a sentimentality which I shared. He was also weepy, and religious. We sometimes walked across School Yard at night and lay on our backs looking up at the buttresses of the chapel, for it was a discovery of mine that the height of the Gothic could be appreciated in that way.

" I suppose we are the only people in college," said Nigel, " who ever look at the stars. The others are all fools. We are the only two who are humble."

By the next term Terence had left. He had had great influence on me, bringing out a side, Don Juan with a touch of Wilde, whose development made my life more interesting, but also more theatrical and egocentric. For years afterwards I wrote to him, about " Le Rouge et Le Noir " as I called Freddie and Nigel. Nigel sulked that term, and was more religious than ever. My friends were Denis Dannreuther (the head of senior election), Charles Milligan, and Freddie Langham; the Dark Friend, the Extreme Blond, and the Redhead, were rallying.

Denis was an exquisite classical scholar, one of those rare people who combine a brilliant and logical mind with genuine moral feeling, and become more than a careerist. We talked ethics and college politics, for the political situation was fascinating. There was party government in the struggle between pre-war and post-war—between right and left. The armistice and the end of the war had released a wave of scepticism and revolutionary feeling over Eton where a book like *Eminent Victorians* was absorbed. The Left Wing, or Liberals, as we called ourselves, in opposition to the Reactionaries, had a clear view of the situation.

(1) The war and the corresponding increase of militarism had affected the freedom of Eton boys. Emergency measures had been enforced and not repealed, lights went out earlier, discipline was stricter, and privileges had been given up in the crisis which had not been restored. The tightening up of discipline involved a cynical view of boy nature, which, especially in College, was to be deplored. Those responsible were the ushers, among whom were certain Vile Old Men, who wished to wrest from the boys all liberty and independence, and who were aided by our vacillating Master, who extorted information about boys' morals from hysterical confirmation candidates, and practised other jesuitical abuses. Behind him was that fine casuist, the Headmaster, and the Old Tugs—old collegers who belonged to the stoic generations, the pillars of the *ancien régime.*

(2) The corner-stone of this régime was the election system, which did not exist in the houses, was of recent origin, and was harmful in that it created a false authority, separated people who ought to be mixing with each other, prevented a " bad " election being improved by a " good " one, and created a sense of guilt in those who had innocent relationships outside. The theory that the election system prevented bullying was untrue, since bullying, like immorality, was commonest among boys of the same

252

age. The election system must be abolished, from the top, and boys be allowed to talk to whom they liked. The danger of immorality would be less in this daylight, than in the present atmosphere of privilege and intrigue.

(3) Corporal punishment was a relic of barbarism. It was as bad for those who administered as for those who received it. That also must be abolished from the top, while mass floggings, and generality beatings were inexcusable.

(4) The fagging system must be modified, the summoning of boys in Chamber to distant parts of college, the last one to arrive being sent off to Windsor for a walnut cake, made too great inroads on their time, and the knight-and-squire relationship between fagmaster and fag was sentimental.

(5) The privileges of College Pop or Debating Society were invidious. There was too much canvassing and blackballing, the elections made too many people unhappy.

(6) Games and colours were over important. Their influence was exaggerated, and must be fought. They should not be competitive or compulsory.

(7) The Corps was a joke; it had no business to be compulsory, and any tendency to increase militarism among a war-weary generation must be exposed and ridiculed.

(8) Boys must be appealed to through reason. They must be given the benefit of the doubt; their fundamental goodness and good sense must be believed in, however contrary to appearances.

To this the reactionaries replied as they always

have; that human nature could not be changed, give people an inch and they would take an ell, that "one must draw the line somewhere", that if games and discipline were relaxed orgies would break out, that corporal punishment was the only check on self-satisfaction, and answered a bully in his own coin, that boys were conservative and hated giving up any of their hard-won privileges, that life was a Vale of Tears in which liberalism did not work.

At that time College Pop, unlike School Pop, still had debates, and some of senior election had been made members of it. There had been two classic debates, on the election system and on corporal punishment, that had almost ended in blows. The liberals at the bottom, Denis, Farlow, Roger Mynors, Bobbie Longden, and Gibson had been supported by Clausen and Christopher Hollis, the liberals at the top. The election in between, that would shortly be coming into power was reactionary, except for Rylands, and one or two others who were non-political.

As the last liberals left the top of the school, and my reactionary super-senior election came into office, the position of the liberals in senior election, and the few others, like myself, Charles Milligan, Le Strange, and Loxley, grew unpleasant. Reprisals were due, and our protectors were leaving. Without Beddard and Rylands I had no friends among those coming into power, and at the age of seventeen I received a beating for "uppishness". Here are two letters of the time.

Easter, 1921.

MY DEAR TERENCE,

Home and Morbid. Since I wrote I have become clean
gone on Nigel again. It's really too awful. I told you
his attitude this half has been sulky with flashes of nice-
ness—well, Monday I lectured him about it, and got out
from him the fact that he despised me. B, that his ideal
was to be completely indifferent—this he kept up con-
tinually till on Thursday afternoon I got him alone in
Lower Tea Room and discovered that " he was aiming at
obtaining spiritual perfection, and that he regarded me as
a distraction to be avoided, that I brought along other
distractions (Loxley and Le Strange) and tried to talk
about nothing with him and Langham."

All of which is true. I spent the last three days trying
not to show him (Freddie) that I liked N. more (which I
did since last Monday). N. told me that he thought it
impossible to like everyone, and that he wanted to cut
down his acquaintances to a small and select circle, and
he did not want me to be one, but he was afraid my personality was too strong. Well, I then had him on toast. I
said that he must have a pretty rotten sort of perfection
if it had to be guarded from plausible antichrists like me
(that is his unexpressed idea of me), that he treated me
like a muck-heap in the corner of his room which he
shunned instead of trying to clear up—that he was running
away from temptation instead of fighting it, that he was
completely selfish, and instead of trying to make others
better was only trying to safeguard himself—as for his
beastly set, he, I suppose, believed in the parable of the
good Shepherd ? Yes he did—Well, which did the shepherd
admire most, the 99 good sheep or the wandering one ?
He had to admit he would admire the 99 more. But
which did he like most and take most steps over ? Moreover who did he suppose liked the shepherd best, the 99
good sheep or the wandering one ?

He had to give in and admit he was quite wrong and
unchristian . . . I showed him that, temporarily at any
rate, I preferred him to Langham. This morning I found
him in Lower Tea Room and said goodbye, he asked me

255

to write to him and seemed to have forgiven me. Now I can think of no-one else. Do you know the Greek epigram " delicate are the fosterlings of Tyre but Myiscus outshines them as the sun the stars " ; it seems to me that suits him, there is a husky look about him which the name Myiscus brings out and his good looks are typical sun products, not rosy or effeminate. Langham is now very nice and attractive but relegated to second place, and now I am not glad at getting home but sorry at not seeing N. I am altogether rather fed with last half—I talked exclusively to a set consisting of Dannreuther, Minns, Milligan, Eastwood, Langham and N., with no one else have I talked anything but trivialities. I got on badly with N. and quarrelled with Highworth. However I got my first " stinker " (Distinction in Trials) the story of which I must tell you when I have more time. I never dreamt I could go clean gone on the *same* person. Wish me luck in my new venture. I hope I can get him gone on me again, but I dread lest I should then cool myself. N. despises you I think even more than me. χαῖρε.

Tuesday.

MY DEAR TERRY,

I wrote you two letters lately. Re N. I think it was being treated the right way set me gone on him again. What I like is a winning fight—well at first I got that, then nothing to fight for, then a losing one. Now I am straight again. It is not true to say the unattainable is the spice of life, it is attaining the unattainable. I never enjoy doing a thing until I have made sufficient difficulties— given that I am colossally conceited, I only realised it lately. Tuppa (Headlam) and Crace both saying I was v. able bucked me up enormously. I used to think I could never do more than obtain a superficial knowledge of a few things. Now I think there is *nothing* I cannot do, though very few things worth taking the trouble to (don't end sentences with prepositions).

You ask how life is ? Chaos. I am in the state of mind of not being able to get at anything, the only thing that is true is that (*a*) everything is true (*b*) everything is false.

Tuppa's formula of Some People . . . Others . . .

seems to be the only generality worthy of acceptance. I am house-hunting for a way of life, it is fun in a way but the agents do not know what I want, and the houses that sound most attractive are hideous to look at close, others are beyond my income.

I wrote to N. and sent him my photo, with a lot of explanation of my present state, which seems to worry him. I said I thought I lived for the best form of happiness : learning to appreciate the first rate and know the sham, learning to look for beauty in everything, sampling every outlook and every interest (bar stinks and maths), trying to stop people being lukewarm and liking the second rate, trying to make other people happy, but not doing so at the cost of my own happiness, or concealing it when I am being generous. Publishing all the good I do. I suppose I am too cautious to risk investing in treasure in heaven. Roughly these are my ideals. I said how much more I liked him than I used to, and that he must treat me as a nice dog, not worship or despise, but sympathise. I said I really had no aim in life (by the way I am trying to analyse after doing anything my motives for doing it and so deduce what my outlook is—unwilling to accept my own introspective failure). I think the fact that one does things and cannot analyse motives or reconcile them to averred principles goes a long way to proving fatalism. I love extremes, either I would be a Catholic fatalist, or an atheist. (I did not say that to N. at the time.) I began " Dear Nigel " and signed my photo " Cyril ". I got :

Dear Conolly, I feel very honoured that you (then in pencil) *consider me worthy of ink. You see that I don't think you are. I did not ask for the picture, but as you have sent it there remains no other course for me than to say " Thank you "* (you notice the improvement in style on the last letter !). *By the way I wish you would leave paragraphs in your so-called letters.*

I want you to understand that I consider your spiritual welfare a thing that it is my duty to improve. I will allow that I have felt a certain amount of pitying affection for you. I saw last half that you were a waste paper basket for wrong

*ideas and that something ought to be done for you. I should
have tried to do this had I had a chance of seeing you alone
and discussing. But you, quite blindly and utterly incapable
of putting yourself in my position, always brought company
with you and went into Langham's room, where your frivolity,
barely keeping within the bounds of decency, was to me so
utterly despicable and repulsive to my principles, that I was
bound to adopt the attitude which you called a pose. If it
hadn't been for Langham I might have quarrelled with you
quite nastily—but of course you are not appreciating anything
I say. Think of all the millions of times last half you came
into MY stall ALONE.*

*If you come next half alone I shall not generally consider
you a distraction, but you must be quite prepared to be sent
away, and I want you to understand you are not going to
come before either my work or my religion and I want you to
realise that anything in the nature of company or popularity
is quite repugnant to me. Langham is quite nice and sociable,
but as yet I do not know much about him and am beginning
to wonder if there is much beneath the surface. Be it far
from me to worship you ! You state that you have no aim
in life as yet and are trying to find one, well why not take the
plain one with which you have been fed from your youth up.
(A. Because it is plain. B. Because I have been fed
with it from my youth up.) I.E. The Christian One. You
can form a pretty average good ideal from this I should have
thought. Of course you must know all about it and you can do
this by systematic bible reading. Form your principles on
what you read, and do everything on principle. Imagine your
ideal, which after all is set down in the N.T. You need not
call it God, if you dislike the word, but think of it and act on
it always. If you like, take it as a matter of interest. Think
how frightfully dull your present aimless life is* (is house-
hunting dull ?) *compared with what it might be. If you
have an aim in everything you do you will find you have an
extraordinary pleasure at every success achieved, renewed confidence, and firmer principles. For instance I can assure you
I gain real genuine pleasure in turning you out of my stall
when I want to talk to you, but have some work to do. In
your condition you are perfectly lonely and whenever you are*

in trouble you have nothing to fall back on, no one to help you, and you act on inspiration. When I am in trouble I always know what to do through my principles. I consult with God and so am acting definitely, and not in an aimless helpless way.

Try this, will you? Call it imagination at first if you like, but if you are sincere you will soon be convinced that it is more than that.

You must see for yourself how thoroughly unsatisfactory your present state is.

Now I am sure you will laugh at me for all this.

N.

A wonderful letter for a boy of fifteen and I think he means it. I wonder why he is so deliberately rude and impersonal. I don't think his ideal is so very good, he says God is his principle while the Christian idea is God is Love. His is more Petrine than Joannine Christianity. I think unless I can make him take an interest in poetry, painting, etc. he will become an awful Puritan. If he cares only about religion he will become narrow-minded too. I know he does despise all popularity, but then he is good-looking enough to be able to. The only respectable Christianity is Broad Church or R.C., and here we have a modern P. father in embryo. Moreover he talks as if he will drop Freddy as soon as he is sure there is nothing in him, though Langham likes him best in the election. I want to make Langham interesting and wrote to him telling him to go to the National Gallery before he answered. He has not answered but I think he is too young to enjoy writing letters.

I am becoming quite a Socrates in the lower half of college. I do want people to like talking religion and morals, to read good books, like poetry and pictures, and think for themselves. N. merely retires further into his shell as when he wouldn't answer my questionnaire for my religion chart. You see I think my ideals are superior to his. Of course they are founded on the assumption that there is no conscious immortality, that happiness is the mean between good and evil (in their usual sense) that the greatest happiness is to be found in novelty. I think self-

259

sacrifice is the greatest happiness when you are at an age to appreciate it, at present it must be ostentatious and announced to everyone. I think in Art it is at first necessary to accept the decisions of others. I have to go before a picture and say " that is a great picture, I must learn to like it ", till, aided by my own good taste, I do like it. I think my ideals have deteriorated. I used to think Perfection the aim of life, now I think it is Perfection in Happiness. Adversity is like a purge, it is good for you at the time and you are the more able to enjoy life when you have done with it, and it gives me a chance to demonstrate my atheism. I think I must try and be a stoic in adversity, and Epicurean in prosperity. Baudelaire says somewhere :

> From the crude ore of each minute
> Draw the pure gold that is in it.

Gangue is the word for " ore ".

I would love to have tea with you at Rumpelmayer's when you come back on the 24th when I go to stay with Loxley in town. I am so hard up for a sufficiently debauched confidant that you must excuse these long rambling epistles. Biles has written a bawdy ballad in exile. It begins—

> O to be back at school again
> To gossip and laugh and swear—

I must go to bed now. A Riverderci.
PS.

> Is it so small a thing to have enjoyed the sun
> To have lived light in the spring
> To have loved, to have thought, to have done,
> To have advanced true friends, and beat down baffling foes?
> That we must feign a bliss
> Of doubtful future date
> And in pursuit of this
> Lose all our present state
> And relegate to worlds yet distant our repose?

The summer of 1921 my life was once again changed by Nigel. At first we got on well. We agreed that

I should introduce him to art while he would convert me to religion. But the relations between adolescents are variable, and Nigel, who had overreached himself with religion, that summer cared only for cricket, and despised all who were not cricketers. One day we quarrelled. I said our friendship must be all or nothing; he said, " Very well, I choose nothing," and I left his room. After a day I tried to make it up. " Nothing " was not having the effect I hoped for. Nigel was brutal and called me a dirty scug (boy without a colour). I left him in a hysterical mood and broke a chair in Upper Tea Room. Then I went to Freddie and Denis for sympathy. I was fond of Nigel, and fond of myself, and he had injured both these idols.

The rest of the half I kept on making overtures to him, which he rudely ignored. Sometimes I was rude too, and used to seek him out in order to cut him. He would make loud personal remarks, and kick Walter Le Strange if he was walking with me, for he had now got a cricket colour and made Oppidan friends. The effect of this quarrel on me was threefold. I was unhappy, and for the first time in my life rebuffed; the guardian angel who looked after my relationships had forsaken me. My one ambition was to get over my feeling for Nigel, and avenge myself by making him regret having quarrelled with me. I wanted to become the most useful and desirable person in his world, indispensable to his vulgar ambitions, to which I would help him as contemptuously as Lord Steyne helped Becky Sharp to a new necklace. In my day-dreams I acquired

261

all the colours under the sun. I put him up for
Pop.

The three results were that I became more social,
that I worked harder, that I grew sceptical and
pessimistic about the world. I was determined that
Nigel must only see me with people he would himself
like to know. I hugged closer to Denis, and to
Farlow, who was my fellow history specialist. He
was robust, tough, cynical, good at games, energetic,
and vulgar. We were both absorbed in Renaissance
history and translated everything we learnt into our
own lives ; after reading Machiavelli I practised
Machiavellianism, drawing up analyses of whom I
should sit next, whom make friends with ; of how to
separate So-and-so, how to win over somebody else.
Every man had a price. It was necessary to discover
his ruling passion and play on it. The test of action
was whether it led to one's own advantage, i.e. was
justified by political necessity. One must learn to
keep " one's thoughts secret in an open face ".

Thus all college must be cultivated, for I could not
tell who might prove an asset in the humiliation of
Nigel—that humiliation which was to consist in
giving him the things he valued, and which I despised,
and in being the only person who could give them
him. He now went around with my enemy Highworth. They talked of cricket, and cast black looks
in my direction, so I made friends with Highworth
again. Machiavelli would have approved. Highworth, outwardly successful, was still bewildered,
and oppressed by the thought of the Vale or official
leaving poem he would have to write at the end of

the term. I offered to write it for him. I tried to make Nigel jealous by cultivating Freddie Langham, whom I liked more and more; I could not make friends with cricketers as College did not possess any, but I made up to our rowing men, two of whom were in the eight. Farlow had some rowing and football colours, and I felt less of a scug as I swaggered past Nigel's room with him.

It was the fashion to have photographs of friends signed and put on the mantelpiece. I had sent Nigel mine. He refused to give me his. I took one, and he said I had stolen it. I collected photos after that like an old hostess collecting celebrities. I cultivated anyone who was a rarity, or who had not been taken, persuading them to get done for me, and rushing off with the scalp. Machiavelli worked. I found I could charm people by asking them questions, and seeming interested in them, and at the end of the term was elected to College Pop.

The election had been stormy, it was through my friendship with the rowing men that I got in, for had I been put up by any of the liberals I would have been blackballed. The political situation was acute. Super-senior election were in power, and beatings were frequent. To our indignation they beat Orwell for being late for prayers, another member of senior election whom they considered uppish, and on the most flimsy pretexts, Farlow and myself. Orwell and Farlow were boys of eighteen; they were just outside Sixth Form, and were beaten by boys in their senior election, of the same age, as if they were fags.

The feeling ran so high against the Captain of the

School and the six other reactionaries in his election that they were cut to a man. Denis's speeches at college Pop debates were reinforced by the contempt of Mynors, the intransigence of Farlow, the indignation of Cazalet and Gibson. At the end of the term it was customary to pass votes of thanks on those who were leaving from College Pop, on the President Treasurer and Secretary, the Keepers of College Wall and Field. For the first time in their history these votes of thanks were blackballed. The genial ceremony collapsed, the Captain of the School, the Cadet officer of the Corps, the boys who beat Farlow and Orwell and Whittome on trumped-up charges for political reasons faced the unprecedented verdict. Name after name was read out, the vote of thanks proposed and seconded, the ballet box passed, the blackballs extracted, and the transaction noted down in the annals. At Farlow's leaving tea a day or two afterwards a lampoon of mine, which drew attention to the idiosyncrasies of the seven blackballed reactionaries, was sung with rapture. The Master in College protested against the breach of tradition, the Old Tugs got to hear of it, the Vile Old Men took it up, and there were whispers about Bolshevism, which almost reached the newspapers.

Meanwhile I had succumbed to the disease of scepticism. My health was excellent, but I could not get rid of ideas of mortality, futility, and death. What was the use of existence ? Why did one do anything ? All was vanity. Stupidity governed the world, and human life was a blot on creation. I searched the classics for confirmation of my scepticism and found

264

an overwhelming support. Job and Ecclesiastes and the author of the Wisdom of Solomon agreed with me, the Greek lyric poets and philosophers proclaimed it, Horace confirmed them, so did Voltaire and Gibbon and Villon and Verlaine. I wrote a paper on pessimism for the essay society. Only two kinds of thought existed, a pessimism which anticipated better things (Christianity) and my own, which did not. But if one thought this then one should kill oneself, which, of course, I was not prepared to do. Why not? Because of the consolations of friendship and learning, because suicide played into the hands of the Jealous God. One lived on to spite him.

For years I throve on this black doctrine, for although it originated with me owing to a rebuff from Nigel, and a Thames Valley summer, more virulent than usual, it happened that I had caught the fashionable malady of the period. Futility was the rage. With Farlow I concocted a play which was to expose history. We had been set a " work of the imagination " to show to housemaster and history tutor, and we collaborated on a revue about the Renaissance, interspersed with songs and satirical sketches which showed knowledge and reading, vast cynicism and an unsuspected talent for horseplay. The Popes, the Emperors, the Medici, the Doges, the Kings of France and England, the Constable of Bourbon, Calvin, Luther, Zwingli and Savonarola, the King of Spain, the Borgias, Leonardo and Michelangelo were treated to the same knock-about. It was the first creation of my new-born scepticism, and the most important. Nobody liked it but ourselves, least of all our tutors,

265

who refused to sign it, Mr. Gow making only the ambiguous comment ' perveni ad umbilicum,' and I had to write instead a little purple essay " On a Crucifixion attributed to Antonella da Messina ". But in the Specialists examination called the " Grand July " I did well and came out eleventh in the school. My gloom was not proof against this, although my philosophy withstood it. What did it matter, eleventh or eleven hundredth ? Was death deferred a day ? Would anyone care in a hundred years ? *Cui bono ?* " Can I forget Myiscus, who is in all beautiful things ? "

> Now years three and " halves " ten
> Have hastened by and flown
> And soon there will be other men
> But I shall be forgotten then
> My very name unknown.
> And no more careless evening hours
> Of slippered armchair ease
> No glimpse of tea things in the towers,
> No cans, no steam, no shouts from showers,
> No shorts, nor mudded knees.

as I made Highworth protest, echoing Mimnermus, in his commissioned Vale. At Camp that year my depression was entire, Nigel was not there, nor Freddie nor Denis, I was glad to be able to get away on a motor-bicycle and drink a glass of port with one of my rowing friends, at Ludgershall. I could only bear to talk to Jackie O'Dwyer ; even Farlow, in whose tent I was, lost patience with me, for like many Etonians, although cynical, he detested inefficiency. Nothing was worth doing, but it was not worth doing badly. We argued till he used to yell " Here, Private Connolly, you who appreciate the beauty of our English hedgerows, you who claim that pleasure and pain are the same thing, go and empty this bucket." I kept a volume of Gibbon in my uniform and read it when I could. My other bible was La Rochefoucauld, whom I remember reading when the Eight came back drunk from Henley. I found his opinions most reasonable, for I was one to whom the existence of good seemed already more mysterious than the problem of evil.

In an old French exercise book of mine, during this summer, Walter Le Strange, my Anglo-Irish æsthetic friend in Junior Election, was keeping a diary, a valuable contemporary document.

> June 9th. *In the afternoon repaired with Satyr and Apollo to the Stoa.[1] Pride was leading forth his chorus of Athleticism's devotees. " Ora pro nobis," he cried. " No anglo-catholicism " thought Man. Satyr fed him on strawberries while he read* Wuthering Heights, *and, that finished,* The Newcomes. *Discussions on Socialism and Tyrannus followed. Yesterday Man and Calm and Conservation and Calculus discussed Slavery and Fagging. Both are utterly foul. Everybody here seems to think*
> (a) *White men are better than others.*
> (b) *England is everything.*
> (c) *a " gentleman " is the* thing. *Also all or mostly all worship Athleticism.*
> Cynicus *and* Man *listened to a revue—" The Renaissance " —by Apollo and Cato, Apollo good, especially the lyrics, Cato inclined to drag but his horseplay satire superb. The conversation in Hall turned on the peerage. How ignorant they all are, even Pride.*

[1] The Stoa was the group of lookers-on at College cricket. They read and talked under the elms, which constituted ' taking exercise.' Pride is a boy called Drover, who leads his side out to field. I am Apollo, Man is the author, Tyrannus the Master in College, Cato Farlow; Rome Gibson; and Cynicus Orwell.

June 11th.

> *Barnaby bright*
> *Barnaby bright*
> *The longest day*
> *And the shortest night.*

A bright day indeed. The trees along the field and by Jordan looked splendid from the Stoa where I lay throughout the afternoon, near the Ball Alleys. Apollo was on my right. He too knows my loved acacia and has apostrophised it, he says, in verse. I am glad I did not try Shaw before. I am just in the state to understand him. Two years ago the preface to Androcles would have shocked me and upset me. A year ago I should have fallen too easy a prey to it. To-day I rejoice. Shaw wants just what I want. An equalising philosophy of life—politically and intellectually, morally, and socially a panacea, in fact an elixir. Stevenson's Velasquez is very interesting. I looked at the Prado reproductions with Apollo again to-day. How ravissant is Mercury and Argus. An English hamlet may be pretty, the country here—take Chamber Field overstrewn with buttercups and clover, or Fellows Eyot with its poplars—is beautiful. But O, for the Wicklow hills. I never realised till now the true glory of the sugar loaf—of Gilt Spear's top, or of the heights between Glencullen and the Scalp.

> *Evening full of the linnet's wings.*

Sunday. *Tea with the Alabasters. Then talk turned on the* Beggar's Opera, *which I have not seen. Apollo—with whom I walked in the evening—talked of introspection and confidences. Is introspection a good thing? I think it is. Why, I wonder, does one always feel a superiority to others? Not always, but frequently at least. Apollo, I fear, does it too much. Yet I like him.*

June 13th. *Apollo, Beatrice d'Este, Rome and I argued most of the afternoon about religion. Very interesting. The result : " Man must worship something by an inborn instinct." Surely he can drive this instinct out of him. Later on Satyr, Beatrice d'Este, Scaife and I gossiped with Rome. The conversation turning on Pride, Scaife gave demonstrations of his foul ways and words, whereupon Tyrannus entered and* in his hypocritical friendly way adjured Rome to cease. Rome with much coldness, though quite politely, dismissed him, and we continued our conversation. This evening, however, Greedy-for-Power " wanted " Rome and Scaife, accused the one of filthy talk and the other of encouraging it. Rome told the story of how it happened. He was dismissed. But— and I burn to think of it—Scaife was whipt—whipt like a mere slave—that is, an oppressed fag, or lower boy, by that unutterable brute, Greedy-for-Power, for a sin of which Rome had proved him guiltless. O may all tyranny perish. May everyone be free ! Let not the wretched new boy be oppressed and mishandled just for the convenience of the idle Capitalists, that is to say, the self-made priests of Athleticism, of the Public School Spirit of Imperialism.

June 27th. Peter came back to-night. Full of racing and tennis. I wish sometimes I could interest myself in such things. Of course not worship them. I have been reading the Loom of Youth. It is all so true in its way. Everything seems melancholy. Is life worth living ? Where can one get help ? One cannot paint for ever, it only makes you into that æsthete, loose tie, velvet coat sort of thing. Poetry makes you excited, or else sadder. O to do something ! But how can a Nobody do anything worth while ? Help is from within. Perhaps if one saw everybody as good. It is so hard—but it is beautiful. Therefore it is meet and right to do. " Les sanglots longs "—but they do it always. " I will arise and go now, and go to Innisfree . . ." O if only I could quit this place, with its society, its " gentlemen ", its absurd church. Where is a true religion ? O for peace. Even this journal is hypocritical.

July 2nd. There is only one God here. Athleticism and his law is " Believe—or Be Cast out." Even now I hear the shouts and cheers, as of barbarism. Baths are banged. Boys shout. Such a display of rowdyism I have seldom heard. The Mob ! The Howling of an Angry Mob. Awful. But a joyful mob is worse. The Eight have won the Ladies' Plate at Henley. Three of them are in College—" jolly boating weather—we'll cheer for the best of schools ". It seems sad to think that a great crowd of boys—of cultured boys— should pour out their spirits thus. O Athleticism ! Athleticism !

The din is now outside my door. Horror! Horror! Baths are banged and banged—cheers—cheers. So help me!

The noise has been quelled. It is sad that N. should have been so completely corrupted by athleticism. We were quite friendly once. But now he is so devilish superior. And rude, too. What have I done? I despise Athleticism—but not Athletics, yet I have never said he should not worship it just because I am interested in the things that really matter. Need he be so really uncivil?

July 3rd. A boiling Sunday. The heat was most oppressive. I talked chiefly to Cyril, Peter and Farlow. These questions of fagging and of College Politics are very interesting. So is reading the Greek gospel. Belief seems to be based on such slender grounds. It is extraordinary how unchristian are the lives of all those boys who " profess and call themselves Christians ", Drover, Maud, N. But there is an awful danger for us too. One is so inclined to become a Pharisee—an utter prig. The milder forms of this athleticism are not harmful for the young. They do no lasting good. But they tend to present happiness. But everyone seems to imagine that athletics mean success. Get a cricket colour and you are made for life. Half a dozen people come up to you. " I say, isn't it good for College having two Sixpennies." What could be more ridiculous? No one seems to take any interest in the fact that a Colleger has bought a Dürer, or that the Hervey English Verse Prize was won by a Colleger in C.

Drover's ignorance showed itself again yesterday. " Why Lord John Russell and not Lord Russell? " he asked. But I mustn't be a snob. The Hermit—it appears from a conversation of this evening—is an ultra-reactionary. He disapproves of boys in B playing ping-pong in sixth form passage.

Last Sunday Farlow gave a tea-party in Lower Tea Room, after which the party sang songs, including a topical one by Cyril. All very pleasant, but Drover made himself somewhat objectionable to his host. On the Friday evening there had been the usual College Pop election. Cyril got in. Peter was put up three times and blackballed, I ditto twice, Drover was put up and got seven (five excludes). All this gave us much subject for conceited conversation. Peter seemed rather sad not to have got in. I was also sorry for myself. Our conceit grew vehemently. On Monday, to the general consternation of many, Drover was awarded his College Cricket. This means he will be second keeper next summer, and so in a position to make even more of himself than at present.

.　.　.　.　.　.　.

That summer I went abroad for the first time. My father took me to Paris and the Belgian coast. We stayed off the Rue de Rivoli, and ate in restaurants with purple menus, screened from the pavement by tubs of sooty privet. I did not care for Paris, I was frightened by it, it was hot and I thought people's feet smelt, I only liked the Louvre, where I felt at home, Notre Dame, and Versailles, which, as I wrote at the time, " suited my mood ". " French revues are funnier than English," I wrote to O'Dwyer, " but after eight o'clock this town is as full of whores as camp was of wasps "—then I reverted to the interminable College politics. Drover, Nigel's great friend, in my junior election disliked me, and my cronies there, Loxley and Le Strange. There was a chance of him getting into College Pop. It was against my principles to blackball anyone, so somehow five people had to be found who would ; Cazalet and Farlow, alas, had left—" You have to remember, my boy," I enjoined O'Dwyer, " that you are Cazalet, and I am Farlow nowadays."

One event in Paris upset me. On a sultry evening, coming back to the hotel after dinner, I was stopped by a pimp with a straw hat and an umbrella outside the Café de la Paix. He offered to take me to a music-hall. I was too nervous to refuse, and he then informed me it would be " rather a rough kind of place, you understand ". I was now too frightened and excited to turn back and he took me to a brothel in the Rue Colbert. I was overcome with guilt and apprehension as I sat with the pimp in the little gilded *salon*, while he spoke to the Madame. The mechanical piano played, at last the girls filed in, and I was asked to choose two of them. Voiceless I pointed with a trembling finger. They stayed behind and a bottle of champagne appeared. We all had a glass, and then another bottle. Drink made no impression, I was paralysed with fear, partly of being hit on the head and waking up in Buenos Aires, partly of saying the wrong thing. Then it was suggested that I should go upstairs with the two ladies. It was then a new fear arose. How much was all this ? In a shrunken voice I asked for the bill. " *Quoi. Déjà ?* " " *Oui, oui, oui. Toute suite.*" I explained to Madame that I did not know if I would have enough money to pay. She was astounded. " But I thought Monsieur was a gentleman ! " When the bill arrived it was for almost ten pounds, mostly for champagne, and with a bonus for the pimp. I explained that I could not pay at once, that the ladies must leave immediately, that I would give her all the money I had (about four pounds), and find the rest within the week. I gave her my card, on which I had written the address of my hotel. My father was waiting up for me, and I told him I had lost my way.

The rest of my time in Paris was spent in anguish. At any moment I expected to see Madame and the pimp arrive to ask for me. Meals in the hotel were a torture which I could not bear, for I expected to see the pimp, with his umbrella, or Madame with my visiting card directed to our table by the concierge. No time of day was safe. I wrote to my grandmother who, I knew, was giving me five pounds for my birthday, and asked her to send it to Paris in advance, as the shops were better there than they would be in Belgium, and I wanted to buy some presents for my friends. It seemed as if her letter would never arrive ; my worst moment was in the Musée de Cluny, beside the crown of Receswinth. I went out and sat in a cold sweat on a bench in the garden.

Next day the money arrived and I rushed round to the brothel. It was eleven o'clock in the morning, no one remembered me, another Madame was on duty and listened in bewilderment while I explained, stuffing money into her hand, and wondering if it would seem impertinent to ask for my card again. At last I was out. I bought Charles Milligan, Denis, and Freddie a few cheap presents, and shortly afterwards attained my eighteenth birthday, still without having kissed anyone. The Belgian coast was a relief after the nightmare, and Bruges, like Versailles with its brackish canals and Flemish primitives, " suited my mood ", for I would try no more conclusions with the Present.

Boys do not grow up gradually. They move forward in spurts, like the hands of clocks in railway stations. Most of those in College advanced in this way, though in many the sap of youth ran down after their efforts. In my case the autumn of 1921 and spring of 1922 were a high renaissance. They were not the happiest days of my life, but I was as happy then as I am able to be.

I started the new term as " a bit of a chap ".   I was in a " mess ", that is to say I had tea in Charles's room with him, and Minns, and a fag to look after us, instead of having it in Tea-room.   This was an advance in civilisation, as one had privacy, and could have masters to tea, and get on better terms with them.   I was also in College Pop, and got my " shorts " for football, whereupon Nigel spoke to me again.   We were delighted to be friends, my scepticism was now permanent, but I had accepted the vanity of life and the worthlessness of human nature so fundamentally that I no longer felt bitter, or with a grievance against society.   " Our mess has china tea—down by the streamside " I used to sing, and we gave exclusive tea-parties.   Denis was in Sixth Form.   All the election above him had now left, except the youngest member, who was Captain of the School, a clerical reactionary, held in check by Denis, Mynors, Gibson and Longden.

CHAPTER XXII

THE BACKGROUND OF THE LILIES

SO far it would seem that work played a small part in our lives ; · this was not so, but for the first two years most boys did not enjoy their work, and found it a tedious drudgery. It was not smart at Eton to work ; to be a " sap " was a disgrace and to compete for prizes eccentric. Everybody used cribs, though the punishments for being caught were severe. For boys at Eton wanted one thing, popularity, and the flaw in the Eton education was that work was unpopular.

It is hard to see how such conditions arise. They are prevalent in most schools, although boys are more bored and more unhappy when they do not work. Even in College, among the seventy scholars, " sapping " was discredited, and we were infected by the fashion from without, behind which lay the English distrust of the intellect, and prejudice in favour of the amateur. A child in Ireland, a boy at St. Wulfric's, a scholar at Eton, I had learnt the same lesson. To be " highbrow " was to be different, to be set apart, and excluded from the ruling class, of which one was either a potential enemy or a potential servant. Intelligence was a deformity which must be concealed ; a public school taught one to conceal it, as a good tailor hides a paunch or a hump. As opposed to ability, it was a handicap in life.

At Eton this was emphasised by the stigma attaching to Collegers, which although an economic prejudice, was expressed as an anti-intellectual one and of which a ridiculous aspect was the contempt in which boys held masters, a relic of the eighteenth century, when boys brought their own tutors to Eton and treated them, as the term " usher " still indicated, little better than their servants.   In this direction the feeling was strong, masters who were old Etonians, who were rich like John Christie, or well-born like Georgie Lyttelton, escaped, but in general the boys assumed that most of the staff had never held a gun, or worn a tailcoat, that they were racked by snobbery, by the desire to be asked to stay with important parents, or to be condescended to by popular boys. An Eton division consisted of thirty boys, five of whom wished to learn something, ten of whom wished to do what everybody else wanted, and fifteen of whom spent their time searching for the usher's weak points, and then exploiting them with the patience of prisoners of war tunnelling out of a camp.   What Proust called the " *lâcheté des gens du monde* " was never so apparent as at Eton, where the life of a teacher like Aldous Huxley was made intolerable because of his defective sight.

The teachers in the middle parts of the school devoted themselves to cramming and keeping order ; inspired teaching, owing to the intransigence of the boys, could only appear at the top, where there were five real teachers : the Headmaster, Wells, Headlam, Marten, and Macnaghten. They are worth considering.

At Eton, as at other schools, there existed the ordinary education for the average boy, but there was also an inner culture, the eleusinian mysteries of learning, to which favoured boys were admitted, and which was maintained by teachers such as these, and by a few important outside figures, the Provost, Mr. Luxmoore, Mr. Broadbent ; the pure eighteenth-century Etonian tradition of classical humanism, which could be learnt nowhere else. Most of the boys went through the school without knowing of its existence, without having heard of esoteric figures like William Johnson Cory, or Mrs. Warre-Cornish, Howard Sturgis, or Austen Leigh, but by 1921 (the year for me when " modern history " begins), I was being initiated ; I would dine with the Provost and the Headmaster, or Mr. Headlam and Mr. Marten would come to tea.

The first of the big five a Colleger came up to, when about sixteen, was Macnaghten. Although a fine teacher, his teaching possessed the faults, or rather the literary vices of his time. He was an ogre for the purple patch, the jewel five words long, the allusion, the quotation, the moment of ecstasy. In fact he was embedded in the Milton-Keats-Tennysonian culture, that profuse and blooming romanticism of the " bowery loneliness ",

> The brooks of Eden mazily murmuring
> And gloom profuse and cedar arches

which had dominated English literature until the death of Flecker in Syria and Brooke in Scyros.

The Eton form was diluted with Pre-Raphaelitism. Watts' "Sir Galahad" hung in College Chapel, Burne-Jones and William Morris were Eton figures, and Mr. Luxmoore painted fastidious water colours of his riverside garden in which the fair Rosamund would not have disdained to take her medicine. He was a disciple of Ruskin, the forgotten man of the nineteenth century.

Another field for the Pre-Raphaelite influence was in translating. Homer and Virgil were the pillars of an Eton education; it would be hard to get more pleasure then or now than we obtained from reading them. But we read them with the help of two official cribs, Butcher and Lang for Homer, Mackail for Virgil. Lang believed that Homer must be translated into the nearest English equivalent, which was an Anglo-Saxon prose reminiscent of the Sagas. He tried to manage on a Bronze-Age vocabulary, and the Mediterranean clarity of the *Odyssey* was blurred by a Wardour Street Nordic fog. Homer, in short, was slightly Wagnerised. Mackail, who had married William Morris's daughter, gave to his Virgil an eightyish air, the *lacrimœ rerum* spilled over, and his Christian feeling about paganism, that it was consciously pathetic and incomplete, like an animal that wishes it could talk, infected all he translated with a morbid distress. Dido became a bull-throated *Mater Dolorosa* by Rossetti. His Translations from the *Greek Anthology*, one of the sacred books of the inner culture, the very soil of the Eton lilies, were more deleterious. They exhaled pessimism and despair, an overripe perfection in which it was always the late afternoon or the last stormy sunset of the ancient world, in which the authentic gloom of Palladas was outdone by that attributed to Simonides, Callimachus, or Plato. Meleager was the typical Pre-Raphaelite lover.

To put it another way, a sensitive Etonian with a knowledge of Homer and Virgil through these translations, and a good ear, would be unable to detect in poems like *Tithonus*, *Ulysses*, or the *Lotus Eaters* any note foreign to the work of Homer and Virgil. If he had been told that " a spirit haunts the year's last hours " was a word for word translation of Virgil, he would have accepted the fact. The two classics had been " romanticised " for him, impregnated with the cult of strangeness, of the particular rather than the general, and of the conception of beauty characteristic of the Æsthetic Movement as something akin to disease and evil.

Macnaghten accentuated this. He told us that the most beautiful word in the English language was " little ", he liquidated his " r's " in reciting, and intoned poetry in a special way . . .

and hear the bweeze
Sobbing in ver little twees.

Jolly good ! He would exclaim, and to hear him chant " Ah, poor Faun—ah, poor Faun " was a study in pity which made his severe and even harsh discipline appear the more surprising.

The other object of this inner cult was Plato. His humour and sophistry were the delight of those who

expounded them to the bewilderment of those who
learnt. His theory of ideas and essences, his conception of body and spirit, the romantic dualism
on which he insisted, were the ruling philosophy.
Platonism was everywhere, popping up in sermons
and Sunday questions, in allusions to Neoplatonism,
in essays by Dean Inge, at the headmaster's dinner-
parties, or in my tutor's pupil-room. Socrates roamed
through the classes like a Government inspector,
and Virgil and Tennyson withdrew before him.
But it will be remembered that Plato himself, in
the Republic, turned against the poets, and advo-
cated censorship and discipline. This contradiction
extended through our school-life and emerged in its
attitude to sex.

For there was no doubt that homosexuality formed
an ingredient in this ancient wisdom. It was one
forbidden tree round which our little Eden dizzily
revolved. In a teaching conscious, and somewhat
decadently conscious, of beauty, its presence in the
classics was taken for granted ; it was implicit in
Plato's humour and æsthetic. Yet Eton, like all
public schools, had no solution for sex. If boys had
intercourse between the ages of fourteen and eighteen,
no matter with whom or what, they had to go. The
School could do nothing for them. " Created sick,
commanded to be sound ", the majority floundered
through on surreptitious experiments and dirty jokes,
but there were always a number who, going further,
were found out and expelled.

The extent to which sex-life is necessary, and should
be permitted, to growing boys, remains uncertain.

The Eton attitude was in line with that of other authorities, and with the wishes of most parents, for the dilemma is inherent in all education, lurking in the playing-fields and vinegar-scented cloisters of our seats of learning as do, in the preaching of the careful Pater, the practices of Wilde.

The result was that boys learnt to walk a tight-rope ; the sentimental friendship was permitted in some houses and forbidden in others, allowed to some boys and denied to their fellows, or permitted and then suppressed according to the changing views and vigilance of the housemaster. No one could be sure on what ground they trod. There was Mac-naghten who, spartan in body as he was soft in mind, would give an annual and long-anticipated lecture attacking those friendships at a point in Plato's *Euthyphro* ; at the same time we were made to put into Latin verses a sentimental poem addressed by Dolben to the Captain of the Eleven. One thing was certain, the potentially homosexual boy was the one who benefited, whose love of beauty was stimulated, whose appreciation was widened, and whose critical powers were developed ; the normal boy, free from adolescent fevers, missed both the perils and the prizes ; he was apt to find himself left out.

There is much celibacy in public schools and where many housemasters are not married it is possible to say that their teaching will encourage continence officially, and homosexuality by implication, sending up to the universities, from whence they will immediately return as masters, that repressed and familiar type, the English male virgin.

Another effect of Macnaghten's teaching was to associate English literature with Latin verses. We came to think of poetry in terms of tags and useful epithets, and to think of the best poetry as being in the form of the sonnet or sixteen-line lyric. Macnaghten would not treat Latin verses as a cross-word puzzle; he insisted that we put feeling into them, that we exercised our dreams of literary composition through the medium of another language. In his taste, he was a true escapist; everything he admired reeked of the death-wish, port after stormy seas, holy quiet and romantic fatigue. No one who did his verses well wrote poetry afterwards. There would be one slim Eton-blue volume, with a few translations and a couple of epigrams, then silence. For the culture of the lilies, rooted in the past, divorced from reality, and dependent on a foreign tongue, was by nature sterile.

It may be wondered why I call Macnaghten a good teacher. The reason is, that, although he concentrated on moments of beauty, he did not neglect the drudgery approaching them, and because, although his taste was uncertain, he would permit no blasphemy. To laugh at anything he thought good meant punishment. He chastened the hooligans, even Highworth could but mumble, and he insisted on the modesty, the abnegation without which great art can not be appreciated. " Up " to him boys for the first time had the experience of literature, and felt every now and then, in the dusty classroom, the presence of a god.

Wells taught the classical specialists; he was a

fine cricketer and a judge of claret, a man of taste with a humour of understatement in the Cambridge style. The Headmaster was theatrical, he liked knotty points and great issues, puns and dramatic gestures. He was a worldly teacher, a Ciceronian, an All Souls Fellow, and we felt we were learning Divinity from a Prince of the Church. He was fond of paradoxes, and we learnt to turn out a bright essay on such a subject as " Nothing succeeds like failure ", or " Nothing fails like success ". The exaggeration of his teaching was repugnant to the classical specialists, and such was the moral weight of William Egerton, Denis, or Roger Mynors, that he became a naughty boy in their presence, although his entry into any other class-room would petrify us with fear.

His was the cult of that light verse which had always been the official poetry, for, despite Gray, Shelley, Swinburne and Bridges, the kind of poetry which Eton took to its heart was either the senti- mental lyric, the translation (of which Cory's *Hera- clitus* is the example) or the facetious. Praed, Clough, Calverley, W. S. Gilbert, and the sacred J. K. Stephen were the official bards, and if the Headmaster had had to include a living writer he would have added Father Ronald Knox.

Thus, although the *Eton College Chronicle* made an appeal to premature essayists, and the fourth leader of *The Times* was within the grasp of its editors, critical or creative writing there was none. Humor- ous " Ephemerals " had a sale, but in spite of tradition, and the encouragement given to them, the Arts at

Eton were under a blight. Three figures of the post-war world had been in College, Lytton Strachey, Aldous Huxley, and Maynard Keynes, but we would never have known it. They were not recognised, they did not form, like Maurice Baring, Arthur Benson, Percy Lubbock or J. K. Stephen, a part of the pale-blue canon.

Into this world the history teachers introduced a note of realism. Marten was a model of clarity and enthusiasm; he was the sanest of schoolmasters, but, for that reason, had less influence on us than a teacher like Headlam, who did not aspire to be impartial.

If the Headmaster epitomised All Souls, Headlam was typical of Balliol, but it was not Balliol that made him impressive, so much as the fact that in his class-room there was at last evidence of a Pre-Ruskinian culture, of the eighteenth century. His favourite writer was Horace, the book he gave us on leaving was *Boswell's Life of Johnson*. To us he was an enigmatic figure, he seemed to go some of the way towards futility, and yet while our conclusions from the axiom All is Vanity, were " nothing is worth while, except art ", " except friendship ", " except pleasure ", or " except wisdom ", his seemed to be " except success—except doing a job efficiently ". He appeared cynical, but that may only have been because he was un-Tennysonian. Although irritable in the early morning he was more tolerant than other masters; his tolerance at times seemed cynical, a product of disillusion, yet he hated idleness, dishonesty, and that frivolous complacency to which growing boys are addicted. He brought common sense, and reasonable worldly values into his relations with boys, with the result that his house was the best at Eton, and, as he surveyed the row of Pops with affected vagueness, he must have enjoyed the bewilderment of other housemasters.

All the history specialists imitated him, his affectations of saying " Erse " instead of " Yes " and " Toosda " for Tuesday, his apparent lack of interest in games and exercise (although he was a good fives player and his house held the football cup), his attitude of *nil admirari*. He was a Tory in politics, where again he seemed to stand for tolerance, efficiency, and a hatred of fuss. " You must learn that there is no justice in this world," he was fond of saying, perhaps setting the wrong boy a punishment to illustrate it, and " You must always remember that nobody is indispensable," was another of his maxims.

Was he a Balliol careerist, with the affectation of laziness and indifference that was considered the Balliol manner, and by which we were taken in, or a split-man, in whom an efficient and ambitious self was being watched by a cynical spectator ? Or was he an evocation of the eighteenth-century Tory, or of ancient Rome ? In appearance he was dark, handsome, and rather fat, not unlike the Roman poet whom he interpreted ; his expression was blasé and judicial, his voice and smile were charming, his eyes, sombre in repose, when angry, kindled into fire.

All masters lost their tempers ; there were some whose rages were comic spectacles, others who became maniacs, fascinating to watch, but dangerous if one

285

got in the way ; with the Headmaster or Macnaghten
there was a sensation of panic, owing to the severity of
the penalties they could enforce, but only with Marten
and Headlam did one get a feeling of shame ; they
were teachers whose rebukes of one boy enlisted against
him the sympathy of the class, and " To do poorly "
up to Headlam, or be " tiresome " with Marten, was
distressing, for at last we were attaining a level where
it was not unsmart to work.

In the æstheticism which was gathering round me,
part backwash of the nineties, part consequence of
my Celtic romanticism being worked upon by the
Pre-Raphaelite background of the Eton lilies, Headlam's sober intellectual energy, his Roman values,
offered a gleam of mental health.   But, to an æsthete,
what appealed in Headlam was his irony, his way of
making a reference to authority sound ridiculous (due,
one suspected, to an antipathy to the Headmaster
which was pronounced among the senior old Etonian
housemasters), and his fondness for what he called
gestures—" That would be a good gesture—the
Massacre of St. Bartholomew was a bad gesture."
The good gesture, the noisy piece of self-sacrifice, was
one of the few lines of conduct sanctioned by my
futilitarianism.   It must be like Sidney Carton's,
magnanimous, public, and useless.

By the time I had left Eton I knew by heart
something of the literature of five civilisations.   It
was a lopsided knowledge, since we were not taught
literature and the only literature that appealed to
me was pessimistic, but it is worth analysing, since,
although many of the books had been read for hun-

dreds of years, and others seemed my own discoveries, taken together, they give a picture of fashionable reading-matter after the war.

I was fond of the Old Testament, disliked the New. My favourite books were Ecclesiastes and the Wisdom of Solomon, in which I recognised the melancholy and tired distinction of an old race, the mysterious Ezekiel, and that earthy mystic, the first Isaiah. Job was too much thrust upon me, and the Lamentations of Jeremiah I found in faulty taste. All these I read with more pleasure in the sonorous Latin of the Vulgate. They were among the books I lived in through the winter evenings.

In Greek literature I had read the *Odyssey* with passion, but not the *Iliad*, I enjoyed Æschylus, particularly the *Agamemnon*, and Sophocles, particularly *Œdipus Rex*; Euripides and Aristophanes I disliked, and Plato, except his epigrams and the *Symposium*. I enjoyed the lyric poets, Sappho and Archilochus, and adored the Mackail selection of the *Greek Anthology*, Theognis, Plato, Callimachus, Palladas, and Meleager; I knew the sceptical epigrams by heart, and those about love and death and " the fate of youth and beauty ". In all my books I had written after my name " τίς τίνι ταῦτα λέγεις " (Who are you that say this, and to whom ?) Mackail's *Anthology* (in the one-volume edition with the long preface), might have been described as the Sceptic's Bible. I was also fond of the bloomy Theocritus, and the *Lament for Bion*.

In Latin literature I read Horace and Virgil, but did not enjoy them till later, for Horace, except by

Headlam, was not inspiringly taught, and Virgil associated with too many punishments, and, in his moments of beauty, with Macnaghten's vatic trances. Although I had learnt Latin all my life I still could not appreciate it without a crib, and it was the arrival at the end of my time of the Loeb translations, sanctioned by the authorities, that put its enjoyment in my grasp. Virgil and Horace, without them, had been too difficult, too tearstained. Horace was more connected with character than with prettiness. We were slow to appreciate him as a verbal artist

> Fortes creantur fortibus et bonis
> Est in juvencis, est in equis patrum
> Virtus

" Brave men are bred from the good and brave, there is in cattle, there is in horses," Headlam would rasp, " the virtue of their sires," and the history specialists, conscious that though not poets, they were the stuff about which poetry was written, seemed to preen themselves for a moment in the afternoon drowse.

My favourite was Catullus, whose poetry " suited my mood," and therefore the mood of the age. It was cynical, romantic, passionate, and bawdy, and I could substitute my name for his. " *Otium, Cyrille, tibi molestum est* ", " *Sed tu, Cyrille, destinatus obdura* ". I liked the world of Suetonius and Tacitus, but the Latin prose-writer for me was Petronius Arbiter. I had four editions of the *Satyricon*. The best I had bound in black crushed levant, and kept on my pew in chapel, where it looked like some solemn book of devotion, and was never disturbed. To sit reading it during the sermon, looking reverently towards the pulpit, and then returning to the racy Latin, " the smoke and wealth and noise of Rome " was " rather a gesture ".

I also liked Martial, crisp and Iberian, but resented the sanctimonious Juvenal, I was excited by the *Pervigilium*, I struggled through the convolutions of Apuleius, and admired the pagan chapters of the *Confessions* of Saint Augustine.

In French literature I cultivated the Troubadours but was disappointed, as I was by those four old bores, Montaigne, Rabelais, Boccacio and Burton. The deceptively simple verses of Villon I loved, with the Poussin landscapes of Chénier, and the garden sadness of Ronsard and Du Bellay. Then came a few lines of Racine, all Candide and Manon Lescaut, and an unrepresentative selection of Flaubert, Gautier, Hugo and Baudelaire, no Rimbaud, but a close study of Verlaine, Hérédia, and Mallarmé.

I was fortunate to read French with de Satgé, he loved literature, and working with him, I apprehended that remoteness of great poetry from life which is inherent in the exaction of the form, and creates literature, " la treille où le pampre à la rose s'allie."

In English literature I began with Spenser sleeping in his coils, I knew little Shakespeare, but I worshipped Hamlet, who seemed the Prince of Scepticism and Gestures, (" How now, a rat in the arras ! ") and Marlowe. Shakespeare's sonnets I absorbed. They formed, with Omar Khayyám, and the *Shropshire Lad*, some limited editions called " the Medici Books ", which, unhealthy though they were in bulk, one could yet obtain as prizes. Webster was my favourite

289

Elizabethan, then came Donne, and after him Marvell, Herrick, and Sir Thomas Browne. Milton was the poet in whom my appreciation culminated. Then came a gap until Blake, the *Marriage of Heaven and Hell*, and, still later, Tennyson and Matthew Arnold. I knew nothing of Pope, Dryden, and Crabbe, and I had a prejudice against the romantics; Keats turned my stomach, Shelley was ethereal, Byron vulgar and Wordsworth prosy. What I required from an author was the authentic romantic thrill, and the prestige of obscurity. After Tennyson was Housman, who came down to lecture on Erasmus Darwin, and then Bridges, Yeats, Brooke, de la Mare, Flecker, Masefield, *The Spirit of Man*, and a repository of Georgian cliché called *Poems of To-Day*.

In prose, after Sir Thomas Browne, came Boswell, Gibbon, and Sterne, then Pater, so clear in his thought, so evasive in his conclusions, in whose Sebastian van Storck, with his refusal " to be or do any limited thing," we recognised a fellow sufferer, then the usual modern mixture—Samuel Butler, Shaw, Compton Mackenzie, James Stephens, Belloc, Buchan, Conrad, Lytton Strachey, and Aldous Huxley. Orwell lent me *The Picture of Dorian Gray*. But I could not swallow it. It was not necessary.

I was as fond of painting as of poetry, and haunted the National Gallery. My taste was conservative. I knew of no French painter except Corot and it was typical of the civilisation of the lilies, the limitations of good taste, that I had such knowledge of the master-pieces of the past, yet remained at sea among the creations of the present.

CHAPTER XXIII

GLITTERING PRIZES

THE result of scepticism, of escaping from the world via the pursuit of knowledge, was that I won the Rosebery History Prize. This meant about twenty pounds' worth of books, but those available, with their horrible bindings, shocked me, and I obtained permission to get Medici prints. The Man with the Glove, Beatrice D'Este, and The Duke of Cleves now looked down on my bureau. After an intrigue with Denis I was given my " liberties ", the privileges (not wearing a hat, fagging boys, having supper by themselves) accorded to the next six in college, after Sixth Form. When a boy not in Division One (Sixth Form and Liberty) won the Newcastle, a classical prize, he was co-opted into it ; in getting the same reward for the Rosebery I had advanced the prestige of the History Specialists, a prestige which was rising at the expense of classics, languages, and science. Most of the important boys were history specialists, for history was easier and more interesting, it was the fashion, and Headlam's division had ended up by becoming a field of the cloth of gold for the feudal chieftains. Of the eleven hundred boys about twenty-five were in Pop, and eight

of these were " up " to him.   After I got the Rosebery
they began to notice me.

In every division there is room for one boy to
reconcile popularity with hard work.   He is the
brilliant idler, a by-product of dandyism.   " Petronius
deserves a word in retrospect.   He was a man who
passed his days in sleep, his nights in the ordinary
duties and recreations of life : others had achieved
greatness by the sweat of their brows—Petronius
idled into fame."   This archetype of scepticism came
to my aid ; by imitating his example, and doing my
work at night by candle, my days were free for social
intercourse.   I had an excellent memory, could learn
by heart easily, gut a book in an hour and a half of
arguments, allusions, and quotations, like a Danube
fisherman removing caviare from the smoking fish,
and remember them for just long enough to use in
a paper.   I was the perfect examinee.   The Oppidans
began to take me up.   I answered difficult questions
and discovered smutty passages for them, and if I
was caught reading a book in class, it would be
something as spectacular as the *Epistolæ Obscurorum
Virorum*.   Once a week we had to recite a few lines
of poetry that we learnt by heart ; most boys depended
on poems they had learnt before.

> Thereisswee musichere thasofterfalls
> Thanpetalsof blowroseson the grass . . .
> On the grass. . . .

At the end I would stroll up and recite, with modest
confusion, a long Greek chorus chosen for its pessimism,
for not to be born was best of all.

My strong point was still being funny.   I was

working hard enough to be permitted a licence, and I could make jokes about our subject—for the history we studied was the history of personalities—in which the Oppidans could join. I was at my best when being taken up, grateful but not servile, sunny but not familiar, and with the schoolboy's knack of living in the moment. I had the advantage of beginning at the top, the only Oppidans I knew were in Pop already, I had no inferior associates with whom I could be labelled, no ladders to kick down. Antony Knebworth was the first to make friends with me. He had won the other Rosebery prize, and was a Byronic figure of overpowering vitality, who with his friend, Nico Davies, seemed to make more noise than a whole division. He and Nico were the most successful type of normal schoolboy ; they were in all the elevens, ran their houses, were able and rather lazy at their work, conventional, intolerant, and sentimental ; they were easily moved to laughter, rage or tears, strict enforcers of privilege, and always appealed to by the headmaster when there was a question of Pop " using its influence."

A less schoolminded couple were Teddy Jessel and Edward Woodall ; they were dandies in the pure sense, with a sober worldly gravity. Jessel had a touch of the " Arbiter " himself, he was critical of errors of taste, especially on the part of the masters, whom he treated, with two exceptions, as a set of lower-middle-class lunatics. He disliked Collegers, they were dowdy and " pi ", and he was fond of remarking how their cleverness evaporated. " A brilliant scholar, won the Newcastle three times

293

running," he would exclaim, imitating a master's complacent tones, " and now he has passed second into the Office of Works." With me, however, he was more tolerant, Horace Walpole to Gray, Townley to Pontifex. The other important Pop was Alec Dunglass, who was President, and also Keeper of the Field and Captain of the Eleven. He was a votary of the esoteric Eton religion, the kind of graceful, tolerant, sleepy boy who is showered with favours, and crowned with all the laurels, who is liked by the masters and admired by the boys, without any apparent exertion on his part, without experiencing the ill-effects of success himself, or arousing the pangs of envy in others. In the eighteenth century he would have become Prime Minister before he was thirty ; as it was he appeared honourably ineligible for the struggle of life.

Relations with Oppidans were more superficial than with Collegers. They were extroverts and regarded friendship as a question of equality and shared interests ; only the Collegers treated it as a philosophy, an end in itself. · Meeting Oppidans was like going to smart luncheons where people seem more intimate than they are ; returning to College was going on from lunch to see a bourgeois intellectual friend of long standing. Friendship, among Oppidans, was a luxury—a touch of failure, inequality, absence, and it was over. In College it was a necessity, a religion invented by sensitive boys under hard conditions, and existed to combat them.

The term which was my happiest drew to an end. College politics were absorbing, and occupied people outside to the extent that we christened these busy-bodies " The College Investigation Society ", and wrote bawdy songs about them. Le Strange summed up the feeling of the minority :

Nov. 20th. *There are two great troubles : political and religious. What is one to believe? The religious services here are just awful. Singing absurd meaningless hymns among ugly windows and pictures, with hopeless tunes, and then the intoned droned prayers—all meaningless.*

If there is a God he can't be like the Yahweh of the Old Testament. Yet was Christ God? I think not. If there is no God—only a fiction of man's brain, what are we to do with life? Is there another life? Will it be a punishment or reward for this life? No! Then must we be good? Why not rest—peace is what I need. To get away from all the noise and squalor of the world out on to the hills—if there is any god it is Pan—but we cannot worship him except by letting ourselves be absorbed. He is deaf to prayers. He goes on his way regardless. There cannot be a benevolent God. It is impossible in all this squalor. Should one try to improve the squalor? Dorian Gray is an extremely interesting book but of course Lord Henry Wotton must be wrong. I have also just read Potterism. *It is dreadful the morbid state into which people get whatever they do. Either they become jingoists like Kipling or else they think of a vanished golden age—like those patriot poets in Ireland.*

All the questions of freedom—ethnologically, and of Dis-armament are so interesting, but the world is so parochial that one can never think of them.

All my time is taken up with talking of: Athleticism, College Pop, and Fagging. They all run into one another.

Peter and I were both elected to Coll. Pop at the beginning of this half, after being blackballed last summer. So was R. Cyril got in last half. We all arranged to keep Drover out. He was so awful, sarcastic, reactionary, etc. After all, he had his College Cricket, that was sufficient. Now he has got his Wall too. Poor R. has been turned out of that, he is a barbarian and to be foiled of his barbar triumphs must be hard. Everything here is done on an athletic standard. I

*am still in Lower College with those small boys, good enough
in themselves—But O! the ignominy of it. Thank God
Peter is also in L.C. O Peter is splendid! unselfish, generous. It must be wretched for him too. But I can't make
myself think of that.*

*I want to reform College when my time comes—to make
the fagging better if I can't abolish it, and corporal punishment too. Why should this heaven be made a hell just for
the sake of old traditions and to make the British public
school type? Ought I to keep Drover out? He has been
good to me—but his influence is bad in College. He stands
for Athleticism and Good Form and all the rubbish joined
with that. And still at the back of all these questions of reform
and improvement and an intellectual rather than an athletic
standard and so on, is the moral question.*

Is anything worth while?

*Should one live for the greatest happiness of the greatest
number, avoiding all classes and creeds—or live so as to get
the greatest peace for oneself. The second is so easy, and yet
conscience goes against it. What is conscience? Is it only
some hereditary tradition to be spurned with patriotism, etc.?
The English Gentleman. What an opprobrium that is. O
pray, if you have a God, for peace of mind. If we live for others
we spoil ourselves. If we live for ourselves we harm others.
The only course is to give oneself up to art or literature or such.
But then that doesn't pay, and I suppose—*Il faut vivre.

We shared Walter's contempt for the politics of
the world outside; politicians were monsters of
inefficiency and self-interest, we felt the general
post-war disillusion, and would have been surprised
and humiliated to be told, that, through the medium
of college politics, we had become politically-minded
ourselves. I was fond of quoting Halifax: "The
Government of the world is a very great thing, but
it is a very coarse thing compared with the fineness
of speculative knowledge."

296

My mother took me to Switzerland for the Christmas holidays. We spent them at Mürren. I was mad about ski-ing, the hotel was full of pretty girls. I skied, made friends and fell in love, but still managed to work for some part of the day. I had often met girls in the holidays, but when I was back at Eton they failed to retain their hold on the imagination; if I had asked them to come down to see me I would find excuses to put them off. Staying in the same hotel was Antony Knebworth and we saw something of each other. For the first time I was aware of that layer of blubber which encases an English peer, the sediment of permanent adulation. Antony was high-spirited, and even when he rearranged all the shoes outside the hotel's two hundred bedrooms he could do no wrong. The meeting had consequences for me. The alpine heights, unfriendly, like healthy climates, to forms of art, were also unsuitable for philosophic doubt. My scepticism retreated, the shutter between myself and the rest of the world was raised, and, under Antony's protection, I enjoyed a social success.

It was now decided I must try for a history scholarship; at first Cambridge was indicated. Most Collegers went on to Kings, where there were safe scholarships for them; Farlow was there, and Rylands, Walter Le Strange was going on, and eventually Nigel and Freddie. Some of us had been to Cambridge the term before to see the production of the *Oresteia*, and found it exhilarating and cosy, for, subject to a little permutation, the sentimental friendships from College continued unabated with undergraduates from other schools forming an audience, who, at a pinch, would contribute new blood to the cast.

On the other hand, Headlam advised Oxford, of which we had caught a glimpse on a wintry field-day, marching down the High while the old Etonians waved to us from their college porches. Denis and Roger Mynors and Bobbie Longden were going up for scholarships there, and besides Oxford was " better for history ". In the end I chose to try for Balliol out of admiration for Headlam, and as a gesture because it was the more difficult. For the same reason I concentrated on mediæval history ; we were taught European history from the Renaissance and " mediæval " history meant teaching myself, another " gesture ", and also provided that escape which I wanted my work to be. I was on the side of the underdog in history, I liked the past, the personal element, the Ages of Faith, the policies with no future. Most stimulating were the Dark Ages, there was " no damned merit " about them, they were obscure, their futility a standing criticism of humanity. I admired the Childerics and Chilperics of the Merovingian dynasty, the chronicles of Liutprand, the crimes of Brunnhild and Fredegonde.

Each night, by my outlawed candle, I read all Gibbon, all Milman's *History of Latin Christianity*. I specialised in the heresies of anarchists and Albigensians, but I was interested in them all, in the Manichæans, in the heresies of Abelard, of Frederic Stupormundi, the Flagellants, and in my favourite Neminians, who believed in a religion of " No Man ", because

298

" No Man living hath seen God ", and " To No Man is it given to escape Death ".

Reading late by candle was bad for the nerves, for it had to be hidden in one's bed or a chink of light might be seen under the door, and like many lazy people, once I started working I could not stop; perhaps that is why we avoid it.

The result of cramming was that a noise of any kind sent me into a temper, and the ordinary school-boy chatter drove me mad. I could only speak to Denis, Charles Milligan, and Jackie O'Dwyer; in other company I would glower and pull out a book. With the Oppidans my ill humour vanished, I became engaging and witty.

I now admitted to myself my ambition to get into Pop, and planned my campaign. My handicap was that I had no colour, nor was I in Sixth Form, from which a certain number of Pops had to be chosen. I could only hope to be elected as a wit. Although it was but a small section of Pop who thought me funny, they were influential. My tactics were to seem as important as I could in College, so that my Oppidan friends would not feel that I was too powerless in my own fief to deserve recognition abroad. There were two Pops already in College, the lion-hearted Gibson, a fellow history specialist, and Robert Longden, one of those boys whom the school delighted to honour. I liked both of them, and had known them for a long time. I would walk away with Gibson, arm-in-arm, from divisions, and seeing me with the only two " possible " people in College, the Oppidans felt they were safe in going about with me by themselves. I mention this in case it may be of use to others who wish to be elected to things. It was not difficult, for if the Oppidans saw me with the right Collegers, the latter saw me with the right Oppidans, and both felt pleased with their discrimination.

Beneath this lay my friendship with Teddy Jessel, which arose out of a certain boredom he felt at Eton through not being adolescent. I amused him because he stimulated me.

If I did get into Pop I told my conscience, my morbid spiritual director, I would make amends, for I should be free to talk to whom I liked, and no one could stop me. There could be no further social ambition. Meanwhile I watched my step.

The scholarship examinations came on. With Denis, Robert, and Roger Mynors I stayed in Balliol and did two papers a day, of which the most important paper was the English Essay. The subject was *Compromise*, which was a favourite of mine, for I had already written one essay on it, and had quotations ready by which I proved that compromises were failures, and that, even if they were successes, it was one's duty to remain uncompromising. The ages of Faith came to life under my pen. But as Denis and I walked about the Quad, or lunched with the Balliol contingent of Old Collegers, as we inspected the dingy rooms, with no pictures, and few books, whose furniture was a dark green tablecloth, burnt by cigarette ends, a blokey armchair, and a cold bedroom looking out on a Neo-Gothic quad, a doubt assailed us. Here we were, pouring out the content

300

of our well-stocked minds six hours every day. *And for what?*

The sheets had not been aired in my bedroom. I got rheumatism in my shoulder and could hardly hold a pen during the later papers. The dons impressed me, but the undergraduates I saw made me long to return to boyhood, to Charles and Jackie and Nigel and Freddie, my books and Medici prints, the view from my window of wine-dark brick, and the chestnut tree in Weston's Yard.

> College spirit [I noted down] is antagonistic to Balliol spirit in its suppression of the political, lack of emphasis on conversation, hatred of " giants at play " and in its attention to reading, and the reading of dead rather than living authors. It appears more akin to Cambridge, but with less emphasis on the bawdy Elizabethans.

We were all four school-sick (Oxford reminded me of Wellington), and happy when the train brought us back down the valley. The term ended in athletics. I went in for school fives with Longden, and then the scholarship results came out. Denis and Roger had got classical scholarships at Balliol, Robert at Trinity, and I had won the Brackenbury History Scholarship. There was excitement, the history specialists cheered, and a holiday was given. Then came the last Sunday, and the morning of the Pop election. I sat in my room with Charles. We had planned to go abroad together for Easter, our parents had given permission, and in a few days we would realise our dream of a visit to Provence. I longed to see Avignon, the scandalous history of whose popes was as real to me as the lines on my hand, for although

I had now been abroad twice, to Paris, and to Switzerland, I had never travelled alone before.

We knew that Gibson and Longden planned to put me up for Pop. The suspense grew heavy, our voices languished. Pop elections took hours, for the same boy would be put up and blackballed seven or eight times, a caucus of voters keeping out everybody till their favourite got in. Only the necessity of lunch ended these ordeals. Suddenly there was a noise of footsteps thudding up the wooden staircase of the tower. The door burst open, and about twenty Pops, many of whom had never spoken to me before, with bright coloured waistcoats, rolled umbrellas, buttonholes, braid, and "spongebag" trousers, came reeling in, like the college of cardinals arriving to congratulate some pious old freak whom fate had elevated to the throne of St. Peter. They made a great noise, shouting and slapping me on the back in the elation of their gesture, and Charles drifted away. I had got in on the first round, being put up by Knebworth, but after they had left only the smell of Balkan Sobranie and Honey and Flowers remained to prove it was not a dream.

At that time Pop were the rulers of Eton, fawned on by masters, and the helpless Sixth Form. Such was their prestige that some boys who failed to get in never recovered ; one was rumoured to have procured his sister for the influential members. Besides privilege—for they could beat anyone, fag any lower boy, walk arm-in-arm, wear pretty clothes, sit in their own club, and get away with minor breaches of discipline, they also possessed executive

302

power, which their members tasted, often for the only time in their lives. To elect a boy without a colour, a Colleger too, was a departure for them ; it made them feel that they appreciated intellectual worth, and could not be accused of athleticism ; they felt like the Viceroy after entertaining Gandhi. The rest of the school could not understand that a boy could be elected because he was amusing; if I got in without a colour it must be because I was a " bitch " ; yet by Eton standards I was too unattractive to be a " bitch "—unless my very ugliness provided, for the jaded appetites of the Eton Society, the final attraction !

When I went to chapel I was conscious of eyes being upon me ; some were masters, cold and censorious, they believed the worst ; others were friendly and admiring. Those of the older boys were incredulous, but the younger ones stared hardest, for they could be beaten for not knowing all the Pops by sight, and mine was a mug they must learn by heart. Everybody congratulated me. The only person not to was Denis. He himself had been co-opted in as future Captain of the School, and could not believe that my election to such an anti-intellectual and reactionary body could give me pleasure. I thought that it was because he was envious, since he had been elected *ex officio*. My intravenous injection of success had begun to take.

Before we went abroad I visited St. Wulfric's. I was now Old Wulfrician No. I whose triumphs were chronicled in the school magazine, but although Flip and Sambo were charming, I was uneasy as I surveyed the eighty little boys in their green jerseys and corduroy knickers. I taught the Sixth Form, I wandered round the classrooms and the playing fields, the drill ground, the gooseberry bushes, the chapel. It seemed inconceivable that I could have felt so deeply, that I could have been a boy there myself, that Tony Watson had existed, or the Manx Shear-water. Flip was confidential; I saw her angry with one or two boys, then when they had gone, she would laugh about them, and say what a lot of nonsense one had to tell them at that age, how difficult it was to keep them in order. Had I dreamt then about my favour-charts ? Had I imagined it all, like a savage who believes that a tree or an old bone is ill-disposed to him ? I could not be sure, for it was clear that the monsters whom I had feared when I was ten, had become delightful and reasonable people now I was eighteen—or would my " favour " change and Flip be revealed again as Avenging Juno ? I was bewildered.

All the boys seemed happy; there were several peers and a Siamese prince ; once more the School had won the shooting trophy and the Harrow History Prize. It was a mystery. I felt like the English lady at the Paris exhibition whose mother was taken ill in her hotel, and who came back with a doctor to find her name absent from the register, the rooms re-let, re-papered, refurnished, and the hotel staff adamant that mother and daughter had never been seen. I wired to Charles to fetch me a day early, and we crossed to Dieppe. Sambo's farewell was vivid. " Don't forget, Tim. A Balliol scholar has the ball at his feet." Already I felt embarrassed to know what to do with it.

We stayed our first night near the Gare St. Lazare and went to the Folies Bergères. In the interval we roamed about the Promenoir, and sat down at a table with two thin dark prostitutes. It was a great moment and seemed to wipe out my humiliation of the year before. We gave them drinks and were extremely polite, in the *Sinister Street* manner, for who knew, they might have as many different editions of Petronius as I ? We wore blue suits, camel's hair waistcoats, and dark blue overcoats with a waist at the back ; we smoked cigars, and drawled a little, for I was now in Pop, and Charles, in Sixth Form, was blonder, and neater, and vaguer than ever. He might have entertained prostitutes at the Folies Bergères all his life.

Suddenly Egerton and Rylands came up. We were uneasy and left our guests, for " Pussy " Egerton, now a scholar of Trinity, had been the Captain of the School, and in the Eleven ; he was " the hell of a chap " and the Colleger who had best fitted into the background of the lilies, correcting the headmaster, sleeping through difficult construes, to wake up and suggest an emendation with that bloom of laziness which was a trait in the " To him that hath shall be given " Eton type. Rylands, his great friend, was more exaggerated, more literary. He was going to be the Duchess in the *Duchess of Malfi* next year, he told us, and he talked of " Lytton " and " A.C.B."

Afterwards we went back to the hotel and lay

awake in the dark. My face itched, and I could feel lumps under my fingers. I scratched, and heard a noise in the silence. Charles was scratching too.

" Charles."

" Yes."

" Are you awake ? "

" Yes."

" So am I."

" Charles."

" Yes."

" Do you know how one catches it ? "

" Yes. I think so. From shaking hands—or touching them or drinking out of the same glass."

" My God—it's come out on my face already."

" And mine."

" I shook hands with mine."

" Mine wore gloves—I felt fairly safe."

" But don't you think she wore them because she *had it there* ? "

" Christ ! How awful—and my face itches too."

" Have you got anything we can put on ? "

" Only some Icilma."

" It's better than nothing—in the morning we can go to a doctor."

" Or should we go now ? "

We put on the light and looked at each other. Charles sat up in his white Egyptian cotton pyjamas. They were mosquito bites. We joked about them with nervous vigour, and caught the morning train to Avignon.

There is the first time we go abroad, and the first time we go to Provence. For me they almost coincided, and it would be hard to express what I felt that evening, in the garden above the Papal Palace. The frogs croaked, the silver Rhone flowed underneath, the Mediterranean spring was advancing. I have been back so many times, as a spring ritual, to that palace, to Hiely's restaurant with its plate-glass windows, to the Greek Theatre at Arles, the hills of Les Baux, the ruins of St. Remy, to the Rhone with its eddies and islands, and the cypress hedges where the cicadas charge the batteries of summer, that I can no longer remember what they looked like for the first time. I only know that they are sacred places, that the country between the Mont Ventoux and the Canigou, from Avignon and Vaucluse to Figueras and Puigcerdá, is the expression of the complete south, the cradle of my civilisation.

We hired bicycles at Villeneuve-les-Avignon, and visited Nîmes and Tarascon and Beaucaire. Then we had to make a decision. Should we go on to the Riviera, or down the east coast of France towards Spain ? Charles inclined to casinos, but we choose Spain because it was cheaper, and spent the next night at Narbonne. The town was gloomy, the the mistral blew, Charles broke the chandelier in our room and tried to hide the pieces. At the last moment they were found and a large item added to the bill. The mistral made travelling impossible. We sat in the train going past platforms where the acacias and cypresses were plastered back by the wind, and where even the names of the stations seemed fretted by the mistral ; Agde, Leucate, Fitou, Palau del Vidre. The lagoons fascinated us, for it was the country of *Mariana in the South.* The strip of sand, the reeds, the sea lavender, the wind and sun brought back South Africa ; there was the Mediterranean, a dark streak beyond the lagoons, like the edge of a pineta, and close at hand the stakes in the water, the white beds of flaking salt, the barren rocks of the Corbières. We reached the red soil of Roussillon, the fortress of Salses, the cathedral of Elne where a Byzantine empress lay buried, Collioure with its phallic church tower, dingy Port Vendres, Banyuls, and after many tunnels the frontier at Cerbère. We could go no farther without a visa.

Next morning we scrambled up to the top of the hill from the beach, blown flat against the ground by the mistral, but able to feel we had looked into Spain. Below us was an identical stony hillside dotted with asphodel, Port Bou with its cove, Cullera and Llansa, the mountain peninsula that runs out to Cadaqués, and the plain of the Ampurdán. For one moment we surveyed it, then we were blown off our feet. Unable to stay on in Cerbère, we retreated, still battered by the mistral, from the station, with its queues of Catalans, in berets and rope-soled shoes, with rugs slung over their shoulders, to the palms and cafés of Perpignan. I was getting school-sick for Eton.

> *Où sont les gracieux galants*
> Whom I saw last a month ago ?
> And here at Perpignan I want
> To see them all again, although
> 'Twas not with such an easy flow
> Of mutual intercourse enjoyed. . . .
> In fact I often was, I know,
> By ἔρις not ἐρῶς destroyed.

And how does my dear Denis fare
Called " proud " by Dadie, whom we met
The prey of the Folies Bergères
And wooed by many an Amoret
Who said " *Dormirez-vous*, you pet ? "
But Egerton, with visage *noir*
Repulsed the sirenaic set
Who circle in the Promenoir.

Our journeys back were unpleasant. We both ran
out of money and because of our tickets had to
return different ways. I travelled by Toulouse, carried my suitcase across Paris, got to London in the
evening, and rather than confess that I was penniless,
spent my last five shillings on dining alone in Soho
and then retired for the night to St. Martin's-in-the-
Fields. It was cold and uncomfortable, the people
coughing all round me, and wrapping themselves up
in newspapers, kept me awake. The next morning
I met Charles at Victoria. He was coming back by
Avignon, but had overslept and gone on to Marseilles,
where they had tried to make him pay the difference.
He had only a bag of dates on which he had been
living, and we took them to the Park and finished
them before going round to his home in Upper Brook
Street.

CHAPTER XXIV

VALE

WHEN we went back to Eton the news of our travels had preceded us. We were sent for by the Headmaster and rebuked for having visited the Folies Bergères, which was not the sort of place where Etonians go. Charles's visit in his sleep to Marseilles was misconstrued by his tutor, who asked him if he was aware that it was a centre of the white slave trade ? I had been staying on my way back with my aunt, and had packed the magazines which were by my bed, including a copy of *La Vie Parisienne*. My tutor was horrified, it was bad enough to have such drawings, he explained, what made it worse was that they were so " diabolically clever ". He also took away *Tristram Shandy* and an uncut Rabelais.

Denis, Robert Longden and Roger Mynors now formed the principal mess. Charles and I messed alone ; Denis was Captain of the School, but for the first month of my last term I lived among Oppidans. " Since God has given us the Popacy let us enjoy it," was my motto, after Leo the Tenth's. I was ashamed to hire classical records now from the music shop, and on summer mornings I would go down there with Edward Woodall and Teddy Jessel to play " Say it with Music ", while the music floated away on the sunlight and we commented on the looks of the passers by.

It was a custom to walk up to a hotel in Windsor and sit in the garden, drinking and smoking. These were serious offences, but the Pops took them for granted, and never went about without a full cigarette case. At lunch they sat beside their housemasters, breathing port and tobacco over them, and making patronising conversation. I soon discovered that my notion of being careful whom I went about with till I was in Pop, and then making friends with whom I liked was impracticable. The Pops clung together, as afraid of what the school thought of them, as the rest were of the Pops ; those who had nothing in common and disliked each other, hurried when they met, to link arms against an invisible danger.

Thus only boys in Pop were allowed to walk arm-in-arm. When I was not in Pop, but was walking with Teddy Jessel or Robert Longden I would notice the gesture, the arm first raised and then shot forward to bring the sleeve and cuff down within grip of the fingers, and then the whole arm inserted, like a bishop laying on hands, with a sacred stealing motion, through my own. It was a solemn moment when this public favour was conferred, but when I was in Pop and enjoyed the same privilege I found that my arm would not experiment, and was only at ease, when another braided Pop sleeve reposed in mine.

Soon everybody in College began to seem insipid and dowdy, for I saw them through Oppidan eyes, and only the fastidious Charles and the genial Jacky

311

were proof against that insolent fashionable stare. " How petty everything is," wrote Walter Le Strange. " Even people one would never suspect of it seem afraid of Cyril, speaking of him only in hushed whispers."

Some of the Pops had been worried about me not having a colour, and the Captain of the Boats was persuaded to give me a rowing one ; like any oligarchy the Eton Society went in terror of letting itself down. For a month I was a model member of that corrupt and glittering eighteenth-century clique, and I forgot for the first time that I was a highbrow, and that highbrows are cut off from the world.

During this month I managed to emancipate myself from the Irish bogey, through the Irish boys at school who were cousins of mine, and whom I met at my aunt's. Being in Pop was a distinction even the Anglo-Irish had to recognise, and one day I realised that I was the most important boy there, that they wanted to know me, not me them, that I need not rack my brains to think of something to say about horses, it was for them to try to talk about *She Stoops to Conquer*, in which I was playing an ostentatious role. A voice told me that Clontarf, rebuilt with livid stained glass in the Isle of Wight Gothic of the sixties round an ivied tower, was an ugly and unimportant house in a Dublin suburb, that History, after taking one look at the Vernons, had moved across the Channel, and that whoever might now receive her favours, it would not be the lately landed Anglo-Irish Gentry.

Alas, in my excursion into the ruling class I had

312

reckoned without my enemy—the Thames Valley summer. Buttercups, lilac, elms and steamy evenings, had returned and were preparing their annual coup. They used a roundabout method.

It was the privilege of College Pop that their letters should be stamped. One member offered to " keep the stamps ", and to him a fag would bring the letters in the letter-box, stamp them there, and enter the amounts due in a book. When he ran out, the stamp-keeper would go round and ask people for what they owed him. At that time I kept the stamps for College Pop, but I spurned the dunning of people for money, and announced that I would pay for the stamps myself. One or two conscientious boys gave something, the rest accepted this typical " gesture ", as a mixture of idealism, laziness, and the desire to show off. I soon ran out of stamps, and having letters brought to me to post, I remembered that any placed in the letter-box in the rooms of the Eton Society were franked in the same way. I sent the fag down with them. That afternoon, when the letters were collected, somebody in Pop chanced to go through them, and noticed that several were to the parents of Collegers. The old hostility broke out. " Why the hell should those bloody bastards in College post their letters here—why should we stamp letters addressed to all the bloody villas in Tooting, etc., etc."

The Pops assumed that they had been posted by Denis, whom they disliked, to oblige his friends, and made remarks about him. I heard of the proceedings, but at some time in the St. Wulfric's or Dark Ages period my nerve had gone. I felt the old panic

about " owning up ", " going straight ", " generality ",
and " being wanted "—I could not explain, only wait
for it to blow over. Eventually—by eliminations—
they discovered who it was. Nico Davies and Knebworth rebuked me in a friendly way. I tried to
apologise but was seized with a hopeless feeling of
guilt. How could I explain ? I had betrayed Pop ;
I had let down the friends who had made the experiment of electing me.

From that moment my vitality failed, as I had seen
it fail in others, I felt uneasy whenever I was with
Pop, and could no longer face the rakes of the Hotel
Garden. I made the mistake, common in youth, of
not realising that people can like one for oneself, and
overlook occasional lapses. I felt that the Members
of the Eton Society only liked me in so far as I con-
formed, while a maturer person would have known
that the affair was trivial, and that they liked me
because they knew I could never conform. Dis-
concerted, up to now, by success, my persecution
mania had found an outlet.

In College my self-confidence held out, but as I had
fallen victim to scepticism a summer before, so now
I succumbed to æstheticism. It was in the air ; the
season, the lime-flowered summer evenings undermined
me, and I fell. I wore, instead of a blazer, with my
grey flannel trousers, a black dinner-jacket and a
panama hat. The fashion was not followed. I read
Marius the Epicurean, and *A Rebours*, which sent me
on to silver Latin and " *faisandé* " prose. I studied
the philosophy of Aristippus of Cyrene, and smoul-
dered with the " hard gem-like flame ". I believed

in living for " golden moments ", in " anything for a sensation ", and read Baudelaire, Verlaine, Hérédia, Moréas, and Mallarmé at French extra Studies with de Satgé, from whom I borrowed *Limbo* and *Crome Yellow*, which I got into trouble for reading.

I went to the rose-show at Windsor and had an intense experience looking at the whitest of white roses ; after that I always had some Frau Karl Druschki's in my room. Rancid with boredom, I burnt melancholy texts round the wall with a poker. " Let us crown ourselves with roses before they be withered " (*Coronemus nos rosis antequam marcescant*) from the *Wisdom of Solomon*, " *Finis venit venit finis, evigilavit adversum te et ecce venit* " from Ezekiel, and from Mallarmé " *La chair est triste, hélas, et j'ai lu tous les livres* ".

I now admired the twelve Cæsars, with their enigmatic deathbed sayings charged with power and satiety, and the last kings of France—" mettons-nous à la fenêtre et ennuyons nous," exclaimed Louis XIII, " Nous ne sommes pas heureux à notre âge " added Louis XIV. Louis XV left no wisdom, but I learnt that on receiving the news of each defeat in the Seven Years War " Il ouvre ses grands yeux tristes, et tout est dit."

A favourite and succulent character was Audubon, in Lowes Dickinson's *Modern Symposium*.

> " And just there is the final demonstration of the malignity of the scheme of things. Time itself works against us. The moments that are evil it eternalises ; the moments that might be good it hurries to annihilation. All that is most precious is most precarious. Vainly do we cry to the moment, " Verweile doch, du bist so schön ! " Only

the heavy hours are heavy-footed. The winged Psyche, even at the moment of birth, is sick with the pangs of dissolution."

Walter Le Strange corroborated.

June 25th. Seven months since I have seen you, sweet book! Cyril has had you—thank God they were no profane hands that touched you, or unholy eyes that read my heart. When I last confided to you I had sunk to depths of æsthetic affectation deeper than I realised at the time. Now I am (I flatter myself) more level-headed. Cyril has once more consented to know me, after some months of estrangement. His conversation is as butter and honey after bread and dripping. Unfortunately, instead of what was, for me at least, friendship, there is now worship. For then we were outwardly (I flatter myself again) equal, now I am (to the world, not mentally, I hope) unchanged, while he has Success. Niké disdains me. I let Cyril influence me more than I mean to. I know all influence (especially an enervating one like his) is bad. But Cyril is so pleasant I cannot resist him even if I wished to try. (O Hypocrite that I am, this is written for his eyes.)

July 12th. Life should be lived, wildly and feverishly within, outwardly with absolute calm and composure. Nor ought one's true opinions to be given to anyone. Everything should bow to expediency and efficiency. How weak I am ! In the evening I make huge resolves, in the morning I remember them and disregard them.

July 15th. Since last I wrote the whole world seems to have been spread before me. I have seen incense burnt on the altar of Dionysus and heard the Antigone acted in the original tongue of Sophocles. I have dined with the Headmaster and talked of Italian Art. Cyril has shown me the most beautiful flowers in the world. I have knelt on the floor looking at a mediæval map beside a Prince Palatine. I have had my 18th birthday. I have four ambitions of which only the third is likely to come true.

(1) To get a scholarship at Kings In December.
(2) To get my College Wall.
(3) To see Florence and Venice.

316

(4) *To be in Pop next summer half.*
To myself I appear a Messiah.
To my friends an ineffectual angel with a touch of the idiot.
To my enemies a negligible knave.
Coronemus nos rosis antequam marcescant. *But I only*
do it because it is the thing to do.
Vain attempts to attract Maud.
The Beggar's Opera *and* Dear Brutus *both tend to show*
" *the utter futility of doing anything under any circumstances.*"

Le Strange at least kept his diary, but my own attempts to write were doomed to failure. I didn't see how one could write in English, and my Greek and Latin were not yet good enough. I took to writing jingles in which a Greek verse was brought in to rhyme with the English; it was not till a year or two later that I was able to discard English, and express myself in Greek epigrams, for to compose in a dead language was the creative activity toward which my education was aiming. Meanwhile there was French.

Roses blanches
Qui se penchent
En songes
Elles m'ont chanté
Des enchantés
Mensonges.

Que la vie est brêve
Rêve d'un rêve, etc. etc.

This was the summer's only inspiration.

Meanwhile a strange pink album had appeared called the *Eton Candle*. It contained poems, and some precious stories, contributions from Max Beerbohm, and those suspect old Etonians, Aldous Huxley, Osbert and Sacheverell Sitwell. One day Teddy

Jessel introduced me to the editor, a boy in his house with a distinguished impertinent face, a sensual mouth, and dark eyes with long lashes. He wrote to ask me to tea. I accepted, on Pop postcard, and went round one summer afternoon to find *foie gras* sandwiches, strawberries and cream, and my postcard of acceptance displayed on the mantelpiece. Seeing it up there for the world to know that Brian Howard had had a Pop to tea with him, I was miserable. I felt that once again I had let the Eton Society down. It was all right for Teddy Jessel to know Brian, who was in the same house. The question was, *Who else did*? I swallowed down my tea like a lady who is offered a swig by a madman in a railway tunnel, and bolted.

Afterwards when I saw Brian alone I would talk to him; when I was with Pops I avoided him, as in the Dark Ages Wilfrid had avoided me. I need not have worried, for he soon became the most fashionable boy in the school, but, as it was, though I grew to know him better, his politeness overwhelmed me. He belonged to a set of boys who were literary and artistic, but too lazy to gargle quotations and become inoculated with the virus of good taste latent in Eton teaching, and too disorderly and bad at games to be overburdened with responsibility, and who gained much from Eton because of the little they gave. There was Harold Acton, a prince of courtesy, his brother William, Robert Byron, who was aggressive, and played jokes on the Corps, the two Messels; Antony Powell, the author of *Afternoon Men*, and Henry Green, who described them in his novel,

Blindness. They were the most vigorous group at Eton, for they lived within their strength, yet my moral cowardice and academic outlook debarred me from making friends with them.

College politics were now less exciting, for we were not in opposition, but in office. Denis was Captain of the School; beatings stopped, fagging was light, the election system languished. College Pop had extended the privileges of reading room to the Upper Half of College, and to belong no longer brought that increase of privacy which, at Eton, formed the substance of promotion. Being in Liberty and in Pop, but not in Sixth Form, I was in an irresponsible position, a school, but not a house prefect. I looked on myself as a kind of Charles James Fox or Wilkes, a Whig to the left of the Whig position although I was more of an anarchist than a Liberal, for I disbelieved in power and authority, and thought them evil, and believed that the goodness of human reason must triumph without them.

The deadly sin, since I was in Pop, was " Worldliness ", and I preached against it when I could. As with many anarchists, there was vanity in my make-up. I did not want to co-operate or be co-operated with, and began to take umbrage with Denis, Roger, Robert Longden, the Caucus who governed College.

Thus after the reform of College Pop into a debating society, I resigned, as a protest against compulsory debates, although the motion, ' that death was preferable to life ', was very close to me. I called everybody in College by their Christian name, and at Liberty Supper I would hold " wantings ", which were parodies

of the dread affairs of my youth, and, on occasion, a
mock beating in which the victims kept their gowns
on, and the canes, notched beforehand, broke in half
at the first stroke.   It was a silly way to behave, as
rumours spread which made more difficult the genuine
reforms of the Caucus.   Anybody could play about
with discipline in that way, since, however much one
might rag " wantings " and fagging, there was no
question of boys not turning up for the wanting, or
not running to be fagged.

I made friends with many of the fags ; in my jaun-
diced state I enjoyed their simplicity and vitality,
besides, I wanted them to be happier than I had been
myself.   I was sometimes suspected of other motives
by my housemaster, which made me scornful and
defiant.   He had once complained of my " infernal
pride " and I lived up to it.   I hated history by now,
it stank of success, and I buried myself in the classics.
I was bored and unhappy, but there was no equal in
whom I could confide.   I was afraid Denis would fail
to understand, the Caucus might lecture me, my
housemaster was antipathetic, Headlam could have
helped me, but I was frightened of him.   He had
pointed out to me the seats which the Sitwells had
occupied in his class-room, but on the other hand he
had condemned as morbid " Ere blowsy tediousness
of summer days ", the last line of a sonnet I wrote.

Urquhart came down from Balliol and had tea
with me ; he seemed to promise release into an adult
world of intellectual excitement and sensible activity
—but after he had gone the white roses, the green
bananas, the clove carnation soap, and the dismal

mottoes resumed their power, and I engaged a fag to sing Gregorian chants outside my room, like Saul and David.

I was eighteen and a half, I had never had sexual intercourse, I had never masturbated. " Lilies that fester smell far worse than weeds," perhaps even St. Wulfric's, even the Eton authorities had not required a chastity so strict.

The end of term arrived. There was still Camp, which was one long operatic farewell for me, but parting was imminent. I had a leaving tea, to which people came, in pairs, and where I played the *Après Midi d'un Faune* on the gramophone.

> Cyril's leaving tea. A beautiful evening, tea and fair faces and good music [wrote Le Strange]. Then Liberty Supper, the last alas ! How banal Liberty suppers will seem next half—*Cyril est épatant, mais comme toujours à la grande manière*. N. got his 22 to-day. He has gone completely off, as has Maud who used to be so very nice.

There was the last chapel, where for the last time I refused to bow my head in the creed, and read Petronius through the leaving hymn, walking afterwards under the limes with Teddy Jessel. The cant of leaving infuriated him, the sentimental farewells, the warnings against the prostitutes of Jermyn Street, and the stupider Pops worrying about their successors. The gruelling election went on all morning, with partisans of one boy putting in two or three blackballs each against nominees of others, until one understood why the College of Cardinals, on such occasions, was locked in and given no food. My principles still kept me from blackballing anyone, but I enjoyed the excitement. Charles was elected, and the second time round I put up Nigel to realise my day-dream of the year before.

In spite of the reconciliation our friendship was in abeyance, it would seem that in the quarrel I had expended the emotion I was capable of feeling. I remembered how at that time noticing the shape of his ear in chapel had moved me, and now he was only a bouncing fellow who had just missed the Eleven. He was not elected, but his gratitude put me to shame.

In *College Annals* Denis wrote the account of his stewardship.

> *The past year has been conspicuous more for an alteration in the general tone of College than for any remarkable achievements. It has always been the hope of my own Election to destroy the inter-election enmity, as it existed a few years ago, to abolish the scandals of College Pop, to reduce the number of beatings to a minimum, and generally to substitute a more harmonious system of government for the old methods of repressions and spite.*
>
> *The actual changes that have occurred may be summed up thus :—When I was a fag it was considered a poor night for the " senior " if no one was beaten, and " wantings " occurred every night, whereas this last half it does not happen to have been necessary to use corporal punishment at all, scarcely a dozen to twenty " wantings " the whole half. As regards College Pop, instead of being a miniature Eton society with exclusive right to Reading Room, it has been reformed with the intention of making it a debating society proper, and I have hopes that the new rules will not allow it again to degenerate into a selfish body of College " chaps ", like School Pop. . . . It is early yet to judge of the success of these experiments, and the universal prediction of the " old men " may be verified, but I can at least honestly record that College has been in every way happier this year than at any time in the last six years.*

The verdict of subsequent Captains of the School

on our experiment can be found in Mr. Eric Parker's *College at Eton* (Macmillan, 1933.) *College Annals* also included a short autobiography of every colleger, usually a list of his athletic distinctions, but, under our decadent administration, more general in tone. Thus Farlow added " *cui bono* " to his list of triumphs, Charles included his gesture in resigning from the Corps, and Le Strange ended up " other minor scholastic achievements there were too, which it would be tedious to enumerate." I added a list of favourite authors, favourite flower, rose (white) and my new motto, " I hate everything public " (σικχαίνω πάντα τὰ δημόσια), concluding " A sentimental cynic, superstitious atheist and Brackenbury scholar of Balliol College Oxford."

Although I affected not to care I dreaded leaving ; one part of me was bored, and looked forward to moving on, the other clung to the past. Once more I had built up a private civilisation of reason and love at a temperature warmer than the world outside ; once again it had to be shattered. " We whose generations are ordained in this setting part of time are providentially taken off from such imaginations " —but I could not repress a dread of the future, of the uglification of life, of Oxford bedrooms and dour undergraduates. Eton is one of the few schools where the standard of comfort is almost in advance of the universities, and unlike most boys, Denis and Robert and I were not looking forward to more liberty than we enjoyed already, to more interesting friendships, or to a room of our own for the first time. Also we were attached to the past, and used to a world of boys, boys with a certain grace, who wore their eighteenth-century clothes with elegance. The world of matey young men, with their pipes and grey bags, the blokeries to which we had been allotted, filled us with despair, we mourned with apprehension, " Not the dead but the ἥβας ἄνθος απολλῦμενον—the flower of youth perishing."

I was now entering the third hot room of English education ; from St. Wulfric's I had got a scholarship to Eton, from Eton to Balliol, and from thence there would, I supposed, be other scholarships awaiting me, I could not imagine a moment when I should not be receiving marks for something, when " poor " or " very fair " or " Beta plus " was not being scrawled across my conduct by the Great Examiner. And yet already I was a defeatist, I remembered Teddy saying to me by the fives courts, in my hour of triumph. " Well, you've got a Balliol scholarship, and you've got into Pop—you know I shouldn't be at all surprised if you never did anything else the rest of your life. After all, what happens to old tugs ? If they're clever they become dons or civil servants, if not they come back here as ushers ; when they're about forty they go to bed with someone, if it's a boy they get sacked, if it's a woman they marry them. The pi ones go into the church and may become bishops. There goes Connolly, K.S., a brilliant fellow, an alpha mind, he got the Rosebery, and the Brackenbury, and all the other berries, and passed top into the Office of Rears ! "

There was much truth in this, in fact were I to deduce anything from my feelings on leaving Eton, it might be called *The Theory of Permanent Adolescence*. It is the theory that the experiences undergone by boys at the great public schools, their glories and disappointments, are so intense as to dominate their lives, and, to arrest their development. From these it results that the greater part of the ruling class remains adolescent, school-minded, self-conscious, cowardly, sentimental, and in the last analysis, homosexual. Early laurels weigh like lead and, of many of the boys whom I knew at Eton, I can say that their lives are over. Those who knew them then knew them at their best and fullest ; now, in their early thirties, they are haunted ruins. When we meet we look at each other, there is a pause of recognition, then a subsequent moment of guilt and fear. " I won't tell on you ", our eyes say, " if you won't tell on me ", and when we do speak, it is to discover peculiar evidence of this obsession. For a nightmare I have often had has been that of finding myself back ; I am still a boy at Eton, still in Pop, still in my old room in Sixth Form Passage, but nobody remembers me, nobody tells me where to go. I am worse than a newboy, I am a new oldboy. I go into Hall and search for a place to eat, I wander in schoolrooms trying to find a class where I am expected. When I first used to have this dream I had only just left Eton, I knew most of the boys and the masters, and the nightmare then took the form of everyone, after my place had been filled, my gap closed over, having to pretend they were glad I had returned. As time went on nobody remembered me, and the dream ended with my ejection. I have found other old Etonians who have had the same experience; some dream they are back in their old rooms, while their wives and children hang about outside to disgrace them.

Once again romanticism, with its deathwish, is to blame, for it lays an emphasis on childhood, on a fall from grace which is not compensated for by any doctrine of future redemption ; we enter the world, trailing clouds of glory, there follow childhood and boyhood, and we are damned. Certainly growing up seems a hurdle which most of us are unable to take, and the lot of the artist is unpleasant in England because he is one of the few who, bending but not breaking, is able to throw off these early experiences, for maturity is the quality that the English dislike most, and the fault of artists is that, like certain foreigners, they are mature.[1] For my own part I was long dominated by impressions of school. The plopping of gas mantles in the class-rooms, the refrain of psalm tunes, the smell of plaster on the stairs, the walk through the fields to the bathing places, or to chapel across the cobbles of School Yard, evoked a vanished Eden of grace and security ; the intimate noises of College, the striking of the clock at night from Agar's plough, the showers running after games of football, the housemaster's squeak, the rattle of tea-things, the poking of fires, as I sat talking with Denis or Charles or Freddie, on some evening when everybody was away at a lecture, were recollected with anguish, and College, after I left, seemed to me like one of those humming fortified paradises in an

---

[1] Even the Jews in England are boyish, like Disraeli, and not the creators of adult philosophies, like Marx or Freud.

Italian primitive, outside which the Master in College stood with his flaming sword.

Procul abest Fridericus, Fridericus capite rubro
Procul abest Nigel, qui solebat mecum ire
Procul absunt pueri qui clamant in cubiculis eorum
Qui sedent super focos pulchri sine arte
Pulchri sunt sed nesciunt, nec decoris eorum habent scientiam—
O Roma, urbs beata, lumen ultra mare.

Since I was unable to write in any living language when I left Eton I was already on the way to becoming a critic. My ambition was to be a poet, but I could not succeed when poetry was immersed in the Georgian or Neo-Tennysonian tradition. I could only have imi...ted Housman, Flecker, Brooke, de la Mare, or Ralph Hodgson. By the time Eliot and Valéry came to save my generation from the romantic dragon, it had already devoured me. I was however well grounded enough to become a critic, and drifted into it through unemployability.

In other respects I had been more deeply scarred. The true religion I had learnt at Eton and St. Wulfric's had not been Christianity, nor even Imperialism but the primitive gospel of the Jealous God, of τo $\phi\theta o\nu\varepsilon\varrho\acute{o}\nu$—a gospel which emerged as much from the old Testament as from Greek tragedy, and was confirmed by experience. Human beings, it taught, are perpetually getting above themselves, and presuming to rise superior to the limitations of their nature; when they reach this state of insolence, or $\H{v}\beta\varrho\iota\varsigma$, they are visited with some catastrophe, the destruction of Sodom or the Sicilian expedition, the fate of Œdipus or Agamemnon, the Fall of Troy or the Tower of Babel. The happiness, to which we aspire, is not well thought of, and is visited with retribution ; though some accounts are allowed to run on longer than others, everything in life has to be paid for.

Even when we say " I am happy " we mean " I was ", for the moment is past, besides, when we are enjoying ourselves most, when we feel secure of our strength, and beloved by our friends, we are intolerable, and our punishment—a beating, for generality, a yellow ticket, a blackball, or a summons from the Headmaster, is in preparation. All we can do is to walk delicately, to live modestly and obscurely, like the Greek chorus, and to pay a careful attention to omens, counting our paces, observing all conventions, taking quotations at random from Homer or the Bible, and acting on them, and doing our best to " keep in favour "—for misfortunes never come alone.

Consider Jacky ; playing fives one afternoon he said " Damn and blast " when he missed a ball. The Headmaster, who was passing, heard him, and told Sixth Form. That night he was beaten. In the excitement of the game he had forgotten to prepare his construe. Others had prepared it, but after the silence before boys are put on to construe, when all diversions have been tried in vain, it was he who was called upon. He was ploughed and given a " ticket " " Failed in Construe " to get signed by his tutor. He had not the courage to show it him, forged his tutor's initials on the bottom, and handed it back. By chance the two masters met, the ticket was mentioned, and the fraud discovered. Within three

328

days of the game of fives the Praepostor came with
the terrible summons. "Is O'Dwyer K.S. in this
division? He is to go to the Headmaster at a quarter
to twelve." The wide doors are open, which means
a birching will take place. The block is put out.
Two boys in Sixth Form are there to see the Headmaster does not raise his arm above the shoulder,
and an old College servant to lower his trousers and
hold him down. "Call no man happy till he's dead.
Next time it may be me."

Morally I was not in advance of this abject religion;
I rejected Christian morals yet was not enough of a
stoic to adopt pagan standards in their place. I was
a *vierge folle* and this gave to my thinking a morbid
tinge.

Politically I was a liberal individualist, but I hated
politics, and wished nothing but to talk to my friends,
go abroad, look at Old Masters and romanesque cathe-
drals, read old books, and devote myself to lost causes
and controversies of the Past.

The cause of the unhappiness I had come across I
put down as Competition. It was Competition that
turned friends into enemies, that exhausted the
scholars in heart-breaking sprints, and rendered the
athletes disappointed and bitter. "Never compete"
was my new commandment, never again to go in for
things, to be put up and blackballed, to score off anyone; only in that way could the sin of Worldliness be
combated, the Splendid Failure be prepared which
was the ultimate "gesture". Otherwise when free
from guilt and fear I was gay, with evening high
spirits hardly distinguishable from drunkenness, and

which rose and rose, until the shutter fell, a glass which cut me off from loving friends, and imagined enemies, and behind which I prepared for that interview with the moment, that sacred breathless confrontation, from which so little always results, and so much is vainly expected. I was also an affected lover of sensations, which I often faked, a satirist in self-defence, a sceptical believer in the Hereclitan flux, an introspective romantic, sensitive, conceited, affectionate, gregarious, and, at the time of leaving Eton, the outstanding moral coward of my generation.

Sometimes I imagine Eton replying to these criticisms, the voice of " Henry's holy shade " answering me with the serenity of a dowager.

" Yes. Very interesting. It was one of my masters, I think, who said, ' Connolly has a vulgar streak '— but we won't discuss that. As I understand, you blame us because our teaching encouraged æstheticism and the vices that are found with it, and then punished them when they occurred. Has it ever occurred to you to blame yourself ? You say winning a scholarship, and getting into Pop, turned your head, and set you back ten years. Well, I'm sorry for you. Other boys achieved this, and more, and were not harmed by it. Look at Robert Longden. The same age as you are, and Headmaster of Wellington, and Lord Dufferin, almost in the Cabinet. You complain that my teaching is cynical, and concentrates on success. Don't forget what Jowett said. ' There are few ways in which a young man can be more harmlessly employed than in making money.' Not that I altogether approve of Pop myself, but since your time its morals have improved, and its powers been restricted. The state of College has improved too, that Bolshy epoch, when some of the post-war unrest reached our little backwater, is a thing of the past.

I think if you had been less vain, less full of the wrong sort of pride, and with a little more stuffing, you would not have been attracted to the ' primrose path '. You would not have let a little success get the better of you. Don't forget we put you in a strong position. The great world is not unlike the Eton Society. Their values are the same. You could have made lasting friendships with people who will govern the country—not flashy people, but those from whose lodges, in a Scotch deer-forest, great decisions are taken. You Bolshies keep on thinking the things we stand for—cricket, shooting, Ascot, Lords, the Guards, the House of Commons, and the Empire are dead. But you all want to put your sons down for Eton. It's twenty years now since you came here. Even then people talked about this world being dead, but what is most alive to-day ? Your Bolshevism, or the English governing class, the Tory Party ?

But let's leave Pop, let's suppose it is no good in after life to a boy—excuse me—with your income. There was always the Balliol scholarship. Why didn't you follow that up ? I see you show a tendency to sneer at the government offices, and the diplomatic service. And yet they rule the country more than ever. If " Pop " leads to the Cabinet, " College " leads to the Permanent Under Secretaryships, the plums of the administration. It was the old

Colleger type, prelate, judge or civil servant who turned out the late king (not an old Etonian) with such absence of friction. They say who's to be given a visa, or permitted to land ; they open the mail, and tap the telephones. I shouldn't sneer at them. You imply our education is no use to you in after life. But no education is. We are not an employment agency ; all we can do is to give you a grounding in the art of mixing with your fellow men, to tell you what to expect from life, and give you an outward manner and inward poise, an old prescription from the eighteenth century, which we call a classical education, an education which confers the infrequent virtues of good sense, and good taste, and the benefit of dual nationality, English and Mediterranean, and which, taking into account the difficulties of modern life, we find the philosophy best able to overcome them.

You complain that Ruskin's cult of beauty and Tennyson's imagery of water and summer still predominate ; but we can't help our buildings being beautiful or our elms stately. If you think boys are happier for a retarded development in unfriendly surroundings, you should have gone to Wellington. You say we are sterile and only encourage composition in dead languages. Shelley and Swinburne and Dr. Bridges wouldn't agree with you. And what matter, if the spirit is alive. Take this :

Quam breve tempus abit quod amando degitur ! Instar Momenti fugiens somnia vix superat.

Exquisite ! It is by Mr. Broadbent. Something you are too bathed in the masochist Celtic twilight to appreciate. You were never a classical scholar. Too lazy. You would not realise that, as one of my masters writes, ' No education is worth having that does not teach the lesson of concentration on a task, however unattractive. These lessons, if not learnt early, will be learnt, if at all, with pain and grief in later life.' Now I expect you have found that out, as you will one day find out about character, too.

About the civilisation of the lilies, Percy Lubbock and Santayana say very different things from you. However, we bear no ill-will. We shall be here when you have gone. Come down and see us some time. I admit we have been disappointed in you. We hoped that you would conquer your faults, but we can't all be Pitt or J. K. Stephen, and, in spite of what you say, we have since turned out a writer who has been able to reconcile being a ' live wire ', with loyalty to the school tradition, even on the Amazon."

I have concluded at this point, for there was now nothing new which could happen to me. Although to the world I appeared a young man going up to Oxford " with the ball at his feet ", I was, in fact, as promising as the Emperor Tiberius retiring to Capri. I knew all about power and popularity, success and failure, beauty and time, I was familiar with the sadness of the lover, and the bleak ultimatums of the beloved. I had formed my ideas, and made my friends, and it was to be years before I could change them. I lived entirely in the past, exhausted by the emotions of adolescence, of understanding, loving, and learning. Denis' fearless intellectual justice, Robert's seven-

teenth-century face, mysterious in it's conventionality, the scorn of Nigel, the gaiety of Freddie, the
languor of Charles, were permanent symbols, like the
old red-brick box, and elmy landscape which contained
them. I was to continue on my useless assignment,
falling in love, going to Spain, and being promising
indefinitely.

Somewhere, in the facts I have recorded, lurks the
cause of that sloth by which I have been disabled,
somewhere lies the sin whose guilt is at my door,
increasing by compound interest faster than promise
(for promise is guilt—promise is the capacity for letting
people down) ; and through them run those romantic
ideas and fallacies, those errors of judgment, against
which the validity of my criticism must be measured.

For the critic's role was implicit in this Georgian
boyhood.

> Beneath the hot incurious sun
> Past stronger beasts and fairer,
> He picks his way, a living gun
> With gun and lens and bible
> A militant enquirer ;
> The friend, the rash, the enemy,
> The essayist, the able,
> Able at times to cry.

It is too early to tell if he has been misled by the
instinct for survival. It may be, that having laid
the ghost of his past, he will be able to declare himself, and come out in the open—or it may be that,
having discarded the alibi of promise, it will only
be to end up in the trenches or the concentration camp.

> Determined on time's honest shield
> The lamb must face the Tigress,

and the Tigress may win, for, in spite of the slow conversion of progressive ideas into the fact of history, the Dark Ages have a way of coming back. Civilisation—the world of affection and reason, and freedom and justice—is a luxury which must be fought for, as dangerous to possess as an oil-field or an unlucky diamond.

Or so now I think ; whom ill-famed Coventry bore, a mother of bicycles, whom England enlightened and Ireland deluded, round-faced, irritable, sun-loving, a man as old as his Redeemer, searching, at this time of year when wars break out, inglorious under the plane.

July 1937—Aug. 1938
" *Post fanum putre Vacunae.*"

INDEX

337